HAVEN'T YOU HEARD?

HAVEN'T YOU HEARD?

GOSSIP, POWER, AND HOW POLITICS REALLY WORKS

MARIE LE CONTE

Published by 535
The Plaza,
535 Kings Road,
Chelsea Harbour,
London, SW10 0SZ

twitter.com/535Books

Hardback – 978-1-788701-77-8
eBook – 978-1-788701-78-5

A CIP catalogue of this book is available from the British Library.

Designed and set by seagulls.net
Printed and bound in Great Britain by Clays Ltd, Elcograf S.p.A

1 3 5 7 9 10 8 6 4 2

535 is an imprint of Bonnier Books UK
www.bonnierbooks.co.uk

To ▮▮▮▮▮▮▮▮▮, *who* ▮▮▮▮▮▮▮
with ▮▮▮▮▮▮▮▮ *and without*
whom I ▮▮▮▮▮▮

CONTENTS

'The foregoing remarks are not intended to imply that politicians are better than other men, but simply that they are like other men. What other men do in their affairs, politicians do in politics. But so high is the standard of behavior expected of the politician that we refuse him the benefit of any doubt until after he is dead. Then, if he is sufficiently eminent and not too odious, we exalt him as a statesman and erect a monument to his memory.'

– Political philosopher Chester C. Maxey, 1954

'When people portray politics for the rest of the population, they leave out the most important thing, which is that it's unbelievably enjoyable and everyone's having a really great time. Why else would we do it?'

– Former political adviser Miranda Green, 2018

ACKNOWLEDGEMENTS

There are a number of people without whom this book couldn't have existed.

Labour MP Tom Watson isn't one of them; when approached for this book, he refused to be interviewed as gossip 'isn't really [his] thing'. This will be news to a number of people. Moving on …

Most of this book was written from The Café, which I originally decided to name then changed my mind as I selfishly want to keep it all to myself. The staff and the regulars are lovely, the music choices charming if occasionally puzzling, and not an eyebrow was raised when I came in five days a week and only ever ordered two drinks a day. A special thanks must be given to Milo as well, the cheeriest and fluffiest dog south London has ever seen.

It also seems fair to say that I wouldn't have come up with the idea for *Haven't You Heard?* if it hadn't been for Daragh, Agnes, Alex and GH, who are and have always been up for a last-minute pint and a gossip in Westminster. You're wonderful people and I doubt I would have lasted long in SW1 without you.

On that note, I certainly wouldn't be where I am today without Joy Lo Dico, who was a brilliant boss, showed me there was a living to be made from clever gossip, and lent me her cottage in the woods when I called her in a panic, convinced that I was never going to hand in my book on time. Few things cannot be solved by escaping to the forest for a few days with an overly enthusiastic Vizsla, it turns out.

This section would be incomplete without Imogen, who agreed to meet me for a coffee after I sent her the vaguest of messages about maybe, potentially, having an idea for a book, then helped me turn that sort of, not-quite plan into a genuine proposal. Joel was an absolute pleasure to work with too, patiently nodding at my madder ideas and letting me realise by myself a few weeks later that they were bad, unfeasible or both. The whole process was surprisingly smooth, especially given that I had no idea what I was doing, and that is entirely down to the two of them, as well as the whole team at 535.

Finally, a hearty thank you to my wonderful, weird and intense friends, everyone who agreed to be interviewed for this book, usually at very short notice, the people who sent me their gossip over the course of 2018, and everyone who follows me on Twitter and was subjected to the daily tedious minutiae of book writing for nearly a year. Oh, and my family whom I adore and now know far more about British politics than any foreigner ever should.

THE PERSONAL AND
THE POLITICAL

When asked if they wanted to be interviewed for a book about political gossip, a lot of people seemed a bit worried. They anxiously wanted to know what the tone of *Haven't You Heard?* was going to be, what its central thesis would end up looking like, and what view it would take on gossip in politics. Is it a good thing? A bad thing? Somewhere uncomfortably in-between?

The first two points will be answered in due course, but the third one is quite straightforward: this book does not make any judgement on gossip in Westminster. Some of it is unquestionably good, some of it is unquestionably bad, the vast majority of it operates in shades of grey, and in any case, a study that takes a moral view on its topic is only of limited interest. Besides, right and wrong are largely subjective values, both in politics and the wider world. An action can be repellent to you but a necessary evil to someone else, and something might be frowned upon in some situations but welcomed in others.

In short, gossip is messy. It is messy because politics is messy, and politics is messy because it is made up of people, and anything with people in it is a mess. Accepting this is a good start-off point. As Maxey's quote sets out, what follows isn't a defence of the political bubble per se; simply an acknowledgement that people who work in SW1 are just that: people. People do stupid things, they get drunk, they're selfish, make mistakes, love each other, hate each other, and let all of the above influence their work in ways it shouldn't. Of course, said work in this case just so happens to dictate what happens to the country at large, which only goes to add another layer of mess to the situation.

On top of all of this, Westminster is an odd place that makes people take odd decisions, which naturally influences the way they talk and act with one another. Rules are often unclear or unspoken, and so little gets written down or taught through the usual channels that the informal matters to an absurd extent. Thousands of words are written about politics every day, but most of them only ever scratch the surface of why things really happen, and how they really work. This can be alienating and perhaps a reason why so many see politics as dry and dull, when it is often anything but.

It isn't the fault of reporters; having to explain exactly why and how every single thing came to happen would make the entire news industry unsustainable. There aren't enough hours in the day for journalists, or enough pages in newspapers. Still, like dark matter hiding in the universe in a form we do not quite understand, this mass of informal conventions, relationships and conversations shapes everything that happens. Take Brexit, for example; as Tim Shipman explains later in this book, much of what has happened in Westminster in the past few years came from friendships, feuds and clashes of personalities. Take them out of the equation and you will find yourself baffled.

There is also something revealing about the way in which parliamentarians never quite took the EU's intransigence seriously. It is, after all, a bureaucratic institution that needs everything to be clear, agreed on and preferably printed and ratified. This realisation seemingly was a culture shock for people here; if British politics can be ruled by nebulous and convenient fudge, then why can't Brexit be too? Similarly, this crisis which has taken over our political discourse is particularly maddening because so little was ever set in stone.

There were stories about sources saying that maybe No 10 would do this while other sources hinted at the fact that a government department would perhaps not agree to it, for reasons that were never clear. MPs you'd never heard of became prominent seemingly out of nowhere for what felt like 17 seconds then disappeared again, but not before unnamed wags let it be known that the MP was a real kingmaker/the true brain behind their faction/a troublemaker with some scores to settle/an idiot put up to it by enemies he thought were his friends/delete as appropriate. Nothing ever happened yet everything constantly did, and missing a few days of coverage either meant coming back to 12 new protagonists and seven new plots or to everything being exactly the same as before.

This is partly because the press didn't quite know how to cover Brexit in a way that was accurate, clear and served their readers, though this isn't what *Haven't You Heard?* is about so we can set it aside. What is relevant here is the fact that those months of confusing reporting on things that may happen or maybe won't and factions being created, disbanded and split in two, more or less at the same time, weren't really special. Well, the reporting of all of this was, as what usually wouldn't be a story turned into one given the wider context, but it largely is how Westminster usually functions.

It may well be the case that politics soon goes back to normal and most of what goes on behind closed doors doesn't bubble up to the surface, but it certainly doesn't look like it at the time of writing. If we can no longer rely on the ways in which politics is supposed to work, we need to understand what other forces make politicians say what they say and do what they do.

There is only so much you can explain without physically bringing people into the heart of Westminster, but it is at least worth trying to show how it all works. Which relationships matter? Who really has power? How does information travel? Who gets caught with their pants down and who doesn't? What deserves to be news? What do people talk about? What *don't* they talk about?

Trying to disentangle all this wasn't easy, and explains why the structure of this book isn't purely thematic; if everything influences everything else, it is hard to decide once and for all how to organise it all. Instead, we will start with a handful of characters, all taking their first steps in Westminster, then follow them as they discover the eccentricities of the Palace and the ways in which its physical spaces influence what happens there. After a quick detour through the Lords, we'll move on to the type of people who choose to join the SW1 beehive, and why their personalities matter. This is where some of the ensemble cast joins us, and we start to look at other corners of the bubble. Once we've established the who and the where, we have to move on to the what – and go through what actually happens in politics – and, of course, the why. Some people and groups will stay with us for the whole journey, while others will pop up occasionally and a handful will make one appearance then leave us to it. Some stories will be true and named, others true but anonymous, some imagined but useful, and one or two almost certainly false but entertaining anyway.

Before we get into this, one quick word of warning: there are few reliable narrators in politics, and I won't pretend to be an exception. I interviewed over 80 people and read over 40 books and academic papers before writing *Haven't You Heard?*, but this does not mean that if someone else were to interview 80 other people and read 40 other books and papers on the topic, they would necessarily come to all the same conclusions. A piece of gossip can be interpreted in many different ways depending on how it is told, so it seems reasonable that a book about gossip would work in the same way.

But anyway, that's enough for now. The Red Lion is getting rammed and the queue for the bar there is hell. Go get us two pints so we can get started; it's your round!

PART 1

PEOPLE

'When people talk about other people's offices and there's a lot of gossip going on in the private sector, they say, "Oh, it's a bit political," don't they? So it's an acknowledgement of the fact that politics involves a lot of gossip.'

– Amber Rudd MP

THE DEEP END

No one who comes into Westminster knows what they're doing. You might argue that this is also the case for most people walking into most jobs, and you might be right, but the learning curve in SW1A is steep.

Take new MPs. They have been elected – finally or by surprise, depending on the circumstances – but what follows is usually unclear. In 1970, Dennis Skinner became the new Member of Parliament for Bolsover, near Sheffield. Unsure what this meant for his immediate future, he stuck to what he knew: 'You never get a letter from an authority saying you're a Member of Parliament,' he once explained to the *New Statesman*, 'so I went back to the pit at Glapwell Colliery on the Monday, and they said, "We voted for you on Thursday, what are you doing here?"'

He did eventually make it to Parliament, but was not the only one with a rough start. In his memoirs, former Conservative MP Jerry Hayes recalls receiving a letter summoning him for a meeting in Parliament after his election in 1983 – a good start. It all fell apart soon enough, however, as police officers refused to believe he really was an MP and would not let him into the Palace of Westminster. Some things have changed since these anecdotes took place, but most have not. When MPs get elected, they are expected to suddenly come barrelling down to London and start doing a job there is no proper guide for. Before even getting into the details of laws and how to make, mend and stop them, there are more concrete issues to deal with. For example, how do you set up an office? Who should you hire? How do you know they are the right person to hire? And so on.

Unless they are one of the lucky few who can be welcomed in by existing MPs they knew outside Parliament, most members hardly know where to start, and have no one to turn to. Still, some kind souls have been known to jump to the rescue. On the first day back after the general election of 2017, at least one veteran Labour researcher spent his evening on the Strangers' terrace (more on that place later) swaying from one new MP to the other, gladly offering to help them set up their office. (It was, of course, out of the kindness of his heart and had nothing to do with the souring relationship between him and his employer).

This particularly entrepreneurial aide might have been slicker than others, but his behaviour isn't in any way unique. No one who comes into Westminster knows what they're doing, and those who are trying to help are generally also trying to help themselves. This isn't to say that Parliament is a pit of snakes where only the most Machiavellian can thrive – simply that there are few innocent bystanders and many interested parties.

But still, back to those parliamentary assistants. If it is hard for MPs to figure out how to do their jobs without much external guidance, think of the people who have to work for them. Usually fresh-faced and recently out of university, aides can be expected, depending on the MP, to be anything from hard-nosed political operators to simple secretaries, or anything in-between. They are hired by the MP themselves, not the Party or Parliament, and there is no formal training for their job either: anecdotally, handover documents for their jobs have ranged from 16-page doorstops to a single Post-it note with relevant passwords.

In any case, their first few weeks will often be a roller coaster. *How to be a Parliamentary Researcher*, a book that does exactly what it says on the tin, explains that on their first day, an aide might be expected to be 'tabling Parliamentary Questions, briefing an MP for a TV interview, writing a letter to a Secretary of State on behalf of a constituent, or trying to talk their employer down from an idea that is likely to result in cold stares from senior colleagues for the foreseeable future'. Easy. That a book on this topic was published in 2015 is a step in the right direction, but most still assume that they can pick it up on the job, that hundreds of pages are unnecessary, and that the advice might not apply to their own MP anyway.

Speaking of people picking things up on the job, now is probably time to throw political journalists into the mix. Journalists don't simply wing stuff as much as they can, they are part of a trade where winging it is a given. There is a reason why most hacks have little time for journalism degrees and Masters, and it is not that their teaching is inadequate (though often it is).

The great journalistic tradition is one of picking things up as you go along, mastering your craft on the field and being able to think on your feet. If you start a job as a reporter, chances are you will be sent out after a story without much advice from the editor. You will then develop a way of working that might be the same as others', but also might not – in an aside during a conversation for this book, a senior hack remarked that though she'd interviewed hundreds of people over the years, she still didn't know if she did it right, as no one had ever taught her.

As a result, starting to report on Westminster can be a daunting task. On top of the journalism itself, you have (at the very least) 650 names and faces to try and memorise, a maze of parliamentary corridors to reckon with, dozens of pages of parliamentary procedures to wrap your head around, and so on. If an old hand offers to help you figure it all out, you can accept the offer, but keep in mind that they might also have some further motives. Back in the newsroom, your editor also won't expect you to take weeks to get acquainted with the place and will eagerly await your first political exclusive. What could possibly go wrong?

SINK OR SWIM

If you have never worked in or around politics, there is one thing you need to know: Westminster is weird. It is a fundamentally weird place which makes people behave in a weird way and where events take a weird turn more often than not. Not everyone who works there is weird – though most are – but spending too much time there will undeniably make you weirder, whether you realise it or not.

For a start, conventions inside the Palace of Westminster are more than a little odd. A famous example is the fact that MPs cannot address each other directly in the chamber, so must make their points to the Speaker of the House of Commons. That is only the tip of the iceberg. In his book on the time he spent as an MP, Gyles Brandreth talks about a particularly puzzling encounter on his first day in 1992. He was welcomed to the Palace by Jeremy Hanley, a long-serving MP, who gave him a tour of the premises. Brandreth attempted to shake his hand, as anyone would, but Hanley declined: MPs, it turns out, do not shake hands with each other.

'The origin of the handshake was physical proof that your hand did not conceal a weapon, that you came in friendship,' he explains. 'As at the House of Commons we are all "Honourable Members", we don't need to prove our good intentions towards one another so between one another we don't shake hands.'

Then there are the votes. Whenever MPs are required to go and vote on a bill or an amendment, the division bell will start ringing across the estate (and in nearby pubs and buildings), meaning that MPs have exactly eight minutes to get into the voting lobbies if they want to be counted. What this means in practice is that on days of important votes, parts of the Palace suddenly get invaded by parliamentarians sharply walking together and having seemingly come out of nowhere, flooding corridors like a stampede of buffaloes finally reaching a body of water.

As it is usually not known precisely when votes will happen, the dreaded bell gives Westminster life a peculiar rhythm, where meetings and drinks can be abandoned at a moment's notice, and idle chats in corners of the building are interrupted by a cabinet minister sprinting past. The building itself also has an important part to play. In what feels like the clunkiest of metaphors, the Palace of Westminster is magnificent, intimidating and confusing, and taking a closer look at it means realising that it is falling apart. Working in Parliament involves being surrounded by grand statues and paintings, and spending most of your time in rooms of plush patterned carpets and matching opulent wallpapers. However, it also means barely noticing the mice any more, occasionally getting rained on indoors and being left with a handle in your fist when all you wanted was to open a door.*

On the other hand, staff working around the Palace look like they could have been plucked out of a historical novel, with their long-tailed coats, slick black tights, polished brogues and heavy jewellery hanging around their waists. Still, one of the first things you realise as you enter Westminster is that, for all its pompous formality, it is mostly a place where people talk. MPs constantly talk to each other and to journalists, who also talk to each other and to other people who work in politics, who in turn talk to each other and to MPs. There might be debates, set meetings,

---

* As one former aide now in the public sector coolly remarked: 'All of the companies I interviewed with went big on salary, personal development, team building, value and interest of work; as if I wouldn't be sold on flushing toilets and no rats…'

rigid events and official written correspondence, but most of what happens and matters is centred around quick coffees, swift pints and brief chats in corridors.

'The thing about these little personal conversations is that there is so much formal stuff, you are absolutely assailed with formal information,' says James Cleverly, a Conservative MP. 'So formal invites, dear colleague letters, pamphlets, articles, op-eds, library briefings, there's so much stuff that comes at you, it's just not possible to absorb it all. And so you do gravitate towards stuff that comes with the endorsement of colleagues.'

Similarly, political journalists could technically fill a paper every day by reading every single press release that reaches their inbox, but the sheer number of them would mean that teams would need to be considerably bigger, and that these armies of hacks would do nothing but hit refresh on their keyboard every other second. Instead, much of the reporting on Westminster happens in person, and the job largely involves walking around, bumping into people and talking to them to try and figure out what the news of the day and week might be.

The issue with so much happening away from formal structures is, of course, that it is hard for someone new to grasp the nuances of these interactions, decide how to go about them and how to use them effectively. Regardless of which part of politics you are getting into, those crucial first few weeks often feel like standing in front of a spinning carousel, wondering when and how to jump in. It is not an unreasonable anxiety. Leap at the right moment and you will find yourself suddenly becoming one of the postcode's rising stars, with all the social and professional privileges that come with it; miss your moment and you will fade into irrelevance before even having had your chance to shine.

Oh, and on top of it all, you will have to do this while managing an absurdly heavy workload. Or, in the words of 2017 intake MP Paul Masterton: 'I basically spent the first few months running around screaming, "Aaaah! So busy!" and barely had the time to go to the toilet.'

NEW FRIENDS; NEW FOES

If Westminster is ruled by the informal, the logical conclusion is that few things matter more than who you know and what relationship you have with them. After all, (nearly) everyone there works endless hours, has a confusing and demanding job, and will need all the help they can get in order to get things done. And because it is a place largely populated by neurotic people too concerned with where they stand on the chessboard, who you hate and why you hate them is just as important. With everyone spending their formative weeks and months desperately trying to dig in their heels, feuds and alliances can happen very quickly, and crystallise even quicker – so who do you pick?

Setting a small ultra-partisan minority aside, most people in Westminster will have a terrible realisation sooner rather than later: people are people. That is, an MP whose views you find abhorrent – or journalist whose work you detest – actually is a genuinely, sincerely, lovely and helpful human being. Or, on the other hand: that one politician whose work and persona you have always been impressed by (publicly or personally, depend-ing on your job) turns out to be boring, a bastard or – worst of all – a boring bastard. This tension between personality and politics is one of the crucial axes of life in the bubble – and a theme that will keep cropping up in other chapters – because it leads to inner conflict in everyone there. Even if political people are odd (and they are) it is only human for someone feeling overwhelmed and lost to turn to people they get along with, as opposed to people they ideologically agree with.

Finding people who fulfil both criteria can happen, but the rest is shades of grey, especially as friendships will often be born out of chance or necessity, not sheer affinity. For Tory MP Bim Afolami, 'It's all a bit like a boarding school. At university people are at least pretending to be grown-up. Here, no one even pretends. It's really childish. People fall out but make up.

'You have to rub along with a bunch of people, most of whom outside of this place would never be your friend. But here, they can often be quite good friends. School people end up spending huge amounts of time with people who in their natural state they wouldn't necessarily be best friends with. Westminster's a bit akin to that.'

On the subject of school – where you went, who your contemporaries were and where you went to university after that – will usually determine what happens next. To misuse a line from TV series *Desperate Housewives*, insiders and outsiders are in such different leagues that they barely play the same sport. If you didn't go to a famous private school then Oxford or Cambridge (or at least spent years in those social circles), chances are that you will feel wildly out of your depth when you arrive. It isn't a question of intellect, simply that you probably won't really know anyone, will be utterly baffled by some of the conventions and generally feel completely out of place. Networks will need to be built from the ground up, and learning done through trial and error, even if you already have some experience in politics.

Kirsty Blackman, now an SNP MP, had been a council-lor for eight years in Aberdeenshire before getting elected, but that experience wasn't much help. 'The council's processes were much more transparent, there was much more clarity about what was going to happen next, and the processes that would be followed,' she explains. 'Here, this place basically runs on gossip – I think part of it is because of the lack of structures and the lack of transparency, and because of the lack of influence the usual channels can have.'

Basically, networks matter because nothing gets done without them. Even if your outsider status pleases you and you would rather stay out of the mess of it all, your career as an MP cannot be built on talent alone.

'There's a limit to how much you can opt out,' says Chi Onwurah, who was elected in 2010. A black engineer from a working-class family in Newcastle, she doesn't have much time for the personal psychodrama of Westminster. Still, she says, 'One of the first things that MPs say to you is that you need to have your networks, you need to have your support, the people who will support you, whether you're being trolled on social media, or when you're standing for select committee, or whether you've got a bill or amendment you want to get through.'

If, however, you're part of the privileged few (of whom there are a lot), the game will be a different one. You won't necessarily feel intimidated by the amount of unspoken knowledge people assume you have, as you will almost certainly have it. Your networks will need to be expanded, but from a pre-existing base, and those who arrived in the bubble before you will be on hand to impart their wisdom. Chances are too that you will have the entitlement that usually comes with an expensive education, so impostor syndrome won't be much of an issue. The flip side, of course, is that with pre-existing friends come pre-existing foes, and rivalries can run deep when everyone has known each other since before puberty. David Cameron and Boris Johnson are an obvious example: both went to Eton, where Boris shone and David did not, then to Oxford, where David got a first and Boris a mere 2:1. For most normal humans, the academic comparisons would have ended there; in this case, some would argue that they resulted in the Brexit vote.

While the background of journalists also plays a part in how well they do once they get dropped into SW1, their relationships often get messier from the outset. The line about journalism being printing things that someone somewhere doesn't want printed might be trite but it is fundamentally correct, at least most of the time. The problems start when it becomes apparent that someone somewhere is also the one who holds the information in need of printing.

'That's the tension at the heart of journalism,' says John Rentoul, a veteran political hack. 'You have to be able to charm people, convince them that you're worth talking to, and then they'll tell you stuff that they don't necessarily want to see in print. The whole process is antagonistic in the sense that you're bound to be publishing stuff that people don't want you to publish, and then they get cross with you. But on the other hand they're not going to tell you stuff in the first place unless there's some kind of relationship with trust.'

In a nutshell, your job is to befriend people who you will almost certainly betray at some point, but until you do, your relationship must be built on trust. Those people know that you will almost certainly betray them at some point, but some will accept your offer of friendship anyway, and probably try to shaft you before you shaft them. This isn't as devious as it sounds: at the end of the day, journalists have to report on what MPs do and MPs want what they do to be reported on.

That friction happens along the way is both understood and expected by most.

Some politicians have made their peace with the nature of that arrangement. In a guide to political journalism, former *Guardian* political editor Michael White recalled one instance of a particularly good-natured MP: 'Gordon [Greig, then political editor of the *Daily Mail*] once forced a Tory minister's resignation (unfairly, I thought), but the ex-minister was seen buying him a drink that evening. He liked him; nothing personal.'

This isn't to say that everything is reversible: sometimes, as a journalist, you will have to write things that mean putting an end to a professional relationship. Then, it becomes a numbers game. This is how Jim Pickard, the *Financial Times*' chief political correspondent, thinks about it:

'You've got 650 MPs, nearly a thousand Lords, you've got aides for them, you've got all the departments, all the NGOs ... you should be able to have a balance where you'll talk to 500 people, but that leaves 3,000 that you can potentially burn without even feeling bad. And you can burn some of the 500 quite happily as well – if you need to, and if they deserve it.'

One issue, of course, is that those 500 people should be burnt across the span of your career – betray one person too many in your first few years as a reporter and you won't find yourself with many sources left. Words travel, and if a journalist starts being seen as untrustworthy, most will think twice before speaking to them. In any case, those contacts do need to be made sharpish: most MPs will only develop a close working relationship with a few journalists, and only a few MPs are truly worth having a close working relationship with. It is a bit like a game of musical chairs: once everyone sits down, you do not want to end up with the politician who everyone knows is out of the loop.

Speaking of which ...

WHITE NOISE /
ON TOP OF THE WORLD

... What makes people get along? Friendships and working relationships can be started for all sorts of reasons, but any social bond cannot be maintained on intent alone, and even the nerdiest of political anoraks cannot talk about policy and nothing else. This is where gossip comes in.

Well, you can call it gossip, rumours or hearsay: a less snappy way to describe it would be 'informal conversations about things which may be true (or might not), and which at least one of the parties involved in the conversation probably shouldn't know about at that point in time'. Or, you know, tittle-tattle.

These conversations can idly happen as a warm-up before serious discussions, as a way to relax after having had those discussions, around a pint or a lunch, or as you bump into someone down a corridor. There are many reasons why they occur and why they are so important, and we will get to them in due course, but you are still in the shoes of someone who has just arrived in Westminster, so let's pace ourselves.

One of the most striking things about entering the bubble is the sheer amount of information that reaches you nearly immediately. You thought you knew how politics worked? You didn't. Being physically around and knowing a handful of people will gain you access to an avalanche of titbits and anecdotes.

Those stories won't necessarily be juicy, or fascinating – most will be inconsequential, but won't feel like that at the time. There's a piece of information that will never make it to the public – about a row between MPs, a cock-up at the launch of a project, a politician having had one too many – but *you* know about it. The curtain has been raised, you're in the thick of it.*

Beyond the sheer volume of information lies another shift: it isn't simply about what you hear, but how that information relates to you. While Westminster gossip will be fun to anyone with an interest in politics, it will only ever feel distant if you aren't a part of that particular circus. Like reading about Rihanna's alleged new boyfriend, album or both, it mostly is an amusing story to passively read about.

Once you join SW1, this changes: in an environment that is incestuous and closed off from the real world, stories take on a new significance. One former Conservative aide puts it well:

'If I went home to Manchester and I told someone who wasn't very interested in politics but who knew who Michael Gove was a story about [Gove], to them I would be talking about a personality. I mean, I've never met him, but I would consider him to be no more than one or two steps removed from me – it's basically social gossip of this weird bubble-sphere. It would be the same if I landed in some Welsh village and everyone knew what someone had done the night before. And I'd think, that's really weird, how does everyone know? But it's just that everyone knows each other.'

One peer agrees: 'When you're outside politics you're thinking everybody are like gods – thinking, *Oh, they're famous people*. And then when you're inside politics, you know that it's not like that at

---

* Well, you aren't – as one former Labour special adviser puts it: 'You get 5% of the gossip and you think, "I'm in, this is it," then you get 20% of the gossip and you're thinking, "Okay, I'm really in it now," then once you get all of it, you realise that most of it is completely irrelevant,' – but that does not stop it from being an enjoyable experience.

all, and that anybody can join any of the political parties and pretty much meet anybody within that party. Quite frankly, pay your £25 a year to the Conservative Party and you'd meet everyone.'

As a staffer, this can feel overwhelming: most have barely reached their mid-twenties when they come in, and suddenly they get the keys to a world where having a mischievous chat with an MP isn't out of the ordinary. There might be a reasonably well-defined hierarchy in Westminster, but information doesn't always respect those boundaries.

As former Labour aide Theo Bertram points out, just because you're the most junior person in the room doesn't mean that you do not get to hear what is said in that room. Having a low-level job can also have its upsides, as you'll get access to intel no one else gets.

'An example would be the person responsible for booking hotel rooms and assigning hotel rooms to cabinet ministers and special advisers at a party conference,' he explains. 'That person is a relatively junior staffer, but the information that they have access to, that we might have an extra because these two people it turns out don't need separate rooms, or so-and-so is insisting that this room should be next to their room, that is quite interesting.

'One of the buzzes about Westminster is that sense of being inside that club of gossip that everyone can belong to. There are the stories that you read in the newspapers or on Twitter, and then there's another level of stories inside the club of what people are willing to tell you when they're pissed.'

This tends to be a happy realisation for journalists as well, but with it comes a hefty caveat: not everything you hear is true, and even if it is, you probably won't be able to prove that it is. It's one thing to pass on a piece of gossip to an acquaintance, but revealing it to the public is a whole other kettle of fish.

For a start, most of what you hear is bollocks. It might be complete bollocks, half-bollocks, or have a kernel of truth hidden inside a big pile of bollocks, but in any case, it is not something you should run to your political editor about.

It is rarely the case that a story was fully made up by someone, though it does occasionally happen – most of the time, someone's bad memory and (conscious or subconscious) need to make an anecdote more interesting will be the culprit, even from those who should know better:

'Journalists are absolutely the worst sources, because they can't help but improve stories,' says Adam Macqueen of *Private Eye*. 'A lot of the time someone phones in or emails in with something that sounds amazing, and all you have to do is ask one question of them and say, "Did you see this first hand, or has this gone round the office a few times?" "Oh no, I heard it from someone who definitely was in the room when someone else…" And actually, it's just things have been massively, massively improved along the way, because journalists can't resist doing that.'*

Though it isn't exactly surprising, politicians also don't tend to make the best of sources. They are party-political, factional, constantly assailed with random bits of information, generally stressed and knackered and above all, have their own ambitions. Every new political journalist has punched the air, thinking they got a stonking exclusive from an MP, and every one of them was eventually proved wrong.

Over time, they will learn how to make sure they won't embarrass themselves in front of their news desk again – all in their own different ways.

---

* In that same conversation, Adam passed on a piece of information to the author that he was certain was true but turned out to be massively exaggerated. That is all.

DIG YOUR HEELS IN

No one who comes into Westminster really knows what they're doing because no one really tells you how to do it, and because there is not one way to do it anyway. MPs come in and no one really tells them anything; they get elected then get on with it. There are 650 of them in Parliament and no two offices are the same: some might have one dedicated aide, others a small army of part-timers; some will make debates in the chamber their life, and others will only rise to speak if they really feel the need to.

You can become an MP because you were a local champion, or because you have worked for the Party since you were a teenager; there might be one area of policy you want to change for the better, or an ideological stance you think deserves to have a shot at changing the country. You can be a campaigning MP or a quiet one; a loyal foot soldier or a rebel with a conscience. Maybe what you want more than anything is to be a cabinet minister, or even in Downing Street – maybe you want to represent your constituency to the best of your abilities.

Reaching out to more experienced colleagues for advice can't hurt, but at the end of the day, you will only be the kind of MP you want to be, and no one can make that decision for you.

Aides are largely the same: depending on your wishes and ambitions, you can focus on policy, the press or both; be out every night in SW1 or have a life outside the bubble; create your own networks within Parliament or stand by your MP no matter what.

The choices are even more numerous for journalists. From the choice of publication (tabloid? broadsheet? online?) and style (news? analysis? comment? features?) to the way of getting stories (lunches? piss-ups? freedom of information requests? reading parliamentary reports? watching what happens in the chamber? data journalism?), the ·possibilities are endless. Your editor will usually be on hand if you have any specific queries, but won't be of much help when it comes to the direction in which you want to take your career.

As we've discussed, there is also the slight issue of Westminster being a fundamentally peculiar place: sometimes, a story that's obviously a story will fall in your lap. Most of the time, it won't even be clear if something is newsworthy or not.

A light example of this took place at the Labour party conference in 2015, not long after the surprising election of Jeremy Corbyn as leader. On the last night, the Party's young people danced until the early hours at the Labour Students' disco, as is customary, and ended the night by heartily singing along to 'Things Can Only Get Better', the New Labour anthem. One delighted young hack, for whom the conference was a first, thought they'd stumbled upon a cracking bit of news.

It wasn't exactly Watergate, but still: Corbyn was supposed to be popular with the youths yet here, in the place where he should have been adored, people showed their defiance by singing an ode to Tony Blair, yadda, yadda. The story was proudly brought into the newsroom then swiftly laughed out of it: it is a tradition for Labour students to sing along to 'Things Can Only Get Better', every year, regardless of people's factional preferences or the leader who happens to be at the helm at the time. You just have to know about it.

In more serious cases, an MP's internal party standing, beliefs and ambitions can have a lot of influence on the newsworthiness of their comments. To take a contemporary example: if Sarah Wollaston, one of the most senior backbenchers in Parliament, criticises the leadership of then Prime Minister Theresa May, it feels like a bigger story than if, say, slightly random former minister Mike Penning does.

It isn't. Anyone with proper knowledge of Parliament will know that Wollaston has always been independent-minded and, more dangerously, has no ambition to ever join the Cabinet.* She can do and say as she pleases, and has been known to do so frequently. Penning, on the other hand, was a minister under Theresa May at the Home Office, and one of her closest allies afterwards. As a result, him calling May's Brexit plan 'dead as a dodo' carried more weight than anything she could have said, even if her profile is considerably higher than his.

These calculations permeate every layer of Westminster, so need to be taken into account by everyone involved. The only issue is – predictably – that not all that information has been formally published, and no one could possibly have the time to read enough to find it all out anyway.

This is where gossip first makes itself indispensable: in order to fully understand how everything works, and how to go about your job, the informal must be taken into account – even academics who study politics say so.

'I think there's a slight snobbery about gossip, because otherwise, what is there to separate academics from journalists?' says Tim Bale, who teaches politics at Queen Mary University and has written countless books about Westminster. 'So we shouldn't really be interested in tittle-tattle and all the sort of stuff that

* This was, as you might have guessed, written before she left the Conservatives for Change UK – The Independent Group**. The analysis still works, though, and given the current political climate, any attempt to find an example that stands the test of time seems doomed anyway.
** Which she left between the first and second edit of this book. By the time this is published, we can only assume she will be an independent MP, somehow Prime Minister or running to be the mayor of Toronto.

people leak to journalists. But actually that's bullshit, because you can't really understand how parties tick, you can't get under a party's skin, unless you have a sense of what people are talking about on a day-to-day level and the way that they're doing it.'

In Westminster as in life, those day-to-day conversations can be about the professional, but a healthy chunk of those will be about the personal. Some of it will involve the swapping of anecdotes purely for entertainment purposes, but, to be blunt, finding out who's shagging whom from the outset can be useful.

Take Conservative MP Philip Davies and (at the time of writing, heaven knows where she will be by the time this is published) Secretary of State for Work and Pensions Esther McVey.* The pair have been an on-again, off-again couple for a few years – the relationship was never announced properly, but did make a few appearances in political gossip columns. Besides the fact that finding out that two MPs got together, there is a point in being aware of that relationship.

In May 2018, it was reported that McVey had strongly objected to government plans to reduce the maximum stake for fixed odds betting terminals (FOBTs) from £100 to £2. So far, so dry. However, sharp political observers remarked that the Secretary of State had gone to Cheltenham races only two months earlier, all for free, courtesy of William Hill. Now, no one is inferring that her interests might have been in any way swayed by the generous freebie, but people should certainly be informed of the sequence of events, then left to make up their minds.

The issue, though, is that the kind gift was never declared by McVey, and she wasn't even at fault. To find the declaration of hospitality, you had to look under the name of ... well, you

---

* This is also out-of-date. Honestly, these people!

can guess. Davies had received the freebie, and invited his girl-friend along. Obviously. Still, to put the pieces of the puzzle together, an awareness of what could easily be described as tittle-tattle was needed.

Looking at this story through the other side of the lens is also useful: this became news and deservedly so, and Esther McVey probably should have known better. If you work in a place where people talk and talk, it seems obvious that someone was going to put two and two together eventually.

It didn't damage her career because she is already in the Cabinet, but becoming the source of gossip early on in your West-minster career can be damaging. Just ask John Hemming. The Lib Dem MP was in Parliament for a whole decade, but if you ask anyone about him, only a few stories will come to mind. The second one was widely covered in the papers – search for 'MP cat mistress' – but it is worth going through the first one now.

Our story begins on the day after the election of 2005 and was recounted by several journalists working for *Private Eye*. Ian Hislop, the editor of the magazine, comes in and says: 'There's this new MP John Hemming. I saw him on election night on the telly and I thought, good God, that's that bloke who used to live along the corridor from me at Oxford.'

Amused to see his contemporary become an elected repre-sentative, Hislop decides to invite him to the *Eye* lunch, which brings together a rolling group of MPs, journalists and all-round interesting people every two weeks. This particular lunch was to take place less than a month after the general election.

The day comes, other guests arrive, Hemming is nowhere to be seen, everyone else sits down. About half an hour later, he stumbles into the room, blind drunk. 'Oh God, oh God, I'm such a mess,' he slurs. The room is silent. He continues, 'I'm such a mess, I was such a mess. The papers are going to be on to me. So, I might as well say it. I've just … I've just discovered that I got my mistress pregnant.'

Another pause.

'… It's all going to come out now. All going to come out. They'll find out … about … the other 24 mistresses.'

Poor John. What had been intended as a nice gesture from an old university friend had clearly been interpreted as a sign that the press were onto him, his questionable behaviour was about to be shared with the whole country, and that he had no choice but to get in front of the news, with some Dutch courage to help him along the way.

That being said, he wasn't wrong: some hacks genuinely had scented blood and news of his affairs were splashed across the tabloids not long after. He even got on the shortlist for the *News of the World*'s 'Love Rat of the Year' award, and phoned in to vote for himself.

Now, you might be thinking that these examples are a tad extreme, and that as a new MP, aide or journalist, you have no immediate intention of influencing Cabinet discussions on anything, or having 25 affairs. This would be fair, but missing the point: at the end of the day, McVey and Davies didn't break any rules by being together and going to the races for free, and neither did Hemming by cheating on his wife (who, by the way, still took him back after all this).

Their actions were still frowned upon and discussed at length, both in and out of the bubble, as they were deemed outside the realm of acceptable behaviour in Westminster. Conveniently, this is something that has been studied before: among other things, gossip is useful to a community as it can help define what is socially permitted and what isn't.

In a paper called 'Reporting Tittle-Tattle', South African academic Nicola Jones discusses the fact that 'gossip is a means of testing or rehearsing community values by exposing conduct the community would seem to proscribe – by doing so, these values [...] may be reaffirmed. Gossip also exposes the wrong-doer to public shame or ridicule and consequently functions as a deterrent to such wrongdoing.'

Now, Westminster isn't most places so that last part isn't always true (see: our friend John Hemming), but the rest still stands. In order to find out what the boundaries are, it is useful to keep an ear out to see what people natter about and adjust your behaviour in consequence. An old way to explain what constitutes news to cub reporters is that 'Dog Bites Man' isn't a story, but 'Man Bites Dog' is. Rumours work similarly: people will only talk behind your back about something you have done if it is something they think you shouldn't have been doing.

Sadly, this system doesn't always work, as different people with different sets of beliefs will have their own ideas of how one ought to behave. There is also a tendency to see the worst in everyone and turn mere sightings into confirmation of bigger things at work. Perhaps unsurprisingly, one group of people tends to feel this more than others.

'If you're a young woman in Westminster, people are always focusing on the fact that you hanging out with a male MP is always going to be a thing,' says one aide. 'I don't want to be linked to someone who hangs out [in the bars] with older men – it does very easily become, "Oh, blah blah was seen talking to blah blah". I think you have to be really careful whom you're seen with, where you're seen and what time of day you're seen doing it.'*

---

* She really does have a point: while interviewing people for this book, the author – a young woman herself – found out that it was apparently common knowledge that she had had an affair with a former MP, which was very much news to her.

That a workplace is tinged with sexism and particularly unkind to young women is hardly headline news, but in an environment where the informal matters so much, having to constantly self-police when interacting with others will be a hindrance to your career.

It might seem like an obvious thing to point out, but it is still a shock to a lot of people starting out in politics: Westminster really is not a level playing field, and anyone pretending that it is has conveniently outed themselves as someone who has been playing the game in easy mode all along.

But anyway, more on this later – our base has now been set. These past few pages have hopefully given you a decent introduction to our main characters, but before we go on, there are a few other people worth mentioning.

INTRODUCING: EVERYONE ELSE

We often talk about the 'Westminster village', but numbers-wise, it is closer to a town. It is impossible to know exactly how many people work in the bubble, as that would require agreeing on what counts as working in politics, but for the purpose of this book, let's say that when we mention SW1A, we mean the 10,000 to 20,000 people who are, to different extents, in the thick of it.

There are many tribes in this town: MPs (650 of them), parliamentary aides (3,150 as of 2015) and journalists (around 400) have already been mentioned. Other obvious groups are peers in the House of Lords (around 800), their aides (560 as of 2015) and government special advisers (87 as of December 2017).

Then, it gets complicated. Civil servants are definitely part of the bubble, but there is no data on how many work specifically in Whitehall; besides, it would be hard to decide whether the bubble dweller status should be linked to the physical location of the office they work in, the nature of the job they do, both, neither, or some other measure entirely. As a result, we will settle on 'a lot' as a general number: there are a lot of civil servants, and that is that.

Defining parliamentary staff is equally hard: their data shows that around 3,200 people are employed by the House of Commons and House of Lords, but they make it clear that there are also a number of contractors on the estate, the number of which has not been made public. It is also unclear, again, whether physically working in the Palace of Westminster means that you automatically become part of that world. For example, there are always a number of builders working onsite, but most probably have no particular enthusiasm for political intrigue. There are also doorkeepers, attendants, housekeepers, chefs, catering and retail staff, who might well hear and see things but not necessarily want to get involved in the whole shebang.

There is also the Serjeant at Arms, who is responsible for keeping order within the House of Commons, and Black Rod, who does the same for the Lords: they are definitely senior enough to be privy to all sorts of information, but their roles may not revolve around gossip as much as others.

Then there are the clerks, who pretty much run the Houses. They can be found working for select committees, the library, and basically everywhere else: they rarely get mentioned in press coverage of Westminster, but it doesn't mean that their influence is to be discounted. Clerks tend to be very well informed, and all talk to one another: they might work in the relative shadows, but as we will see in a bit, the information they gather and the way they use that information is a crucial part of the political machine.

We should now move on to the places but before that, a good conclusion to this introduction comes from former Conservative adviser Will Tanner. 'Politics fundamentally is about two things. It's about people's character, whether or not you believe what they're saying, and then, people's intentions about what they're trying to achieve, where they're trying to get to. Those are the two things that people are really interested in in politics. Who is this person and what are they trying to get, basically. And that's true of the media, it's true of politicians themselves, it's true of the civil service, that's basically the way people think. It's fundamentally judgemental and suspicious. In that respect, gossip is really, really important, because gossip basically is the verifier of whether or not someone's character is right, and whether their intentions are pure or not.'

PART 2

PLACES

'I think it's quite important to be able to distinguish between the chamber persona and people's real personas, though some people are as awful in the chamber as out of it'

– Paul Masterton MP

THE LABYRINTH

A famous line about *Sex and the City* is that it did not have four main characters but five – Carrie, Miranda, Charlotte and Samantha might have been the focus of the show, but the city of New York was equally important. Westminster is similar: there is no point in talking about what people do there if we do not take into account the influence played by the architecture of the place. Winston Churchill knew this: during a debate about the reconstruction of the chamber after it was bombed by the Luftwaffe, he reminded his fellow parliamentarians that 'we shape our buildings and then our buildings shape us'.

This was remarked by Rhodri Walters and Robert Rogers too, in their book *How Parliament Works*: 'From the start, the club-like rooms and common spaces of [Charles] Barry's palace have encouraged members of both Houses to congregate and meet informally,' they write. 'Power Behind the Scenes', an academic paper published in 2018, makes a similar point: 'The use of space for members meeting informally is an intrinsic part of parliamentary life, important to members for learning the rules and practices of the institution, for sharing information with colleagues, especially party colleagues, for gaining support for one's causes and for one's own political advancement.'

What this means in practice is that Parliament feels like Hogwarts, both in its intimidating grandeur and large number of social spaces. There are of course the many bars and tea rooms, but socialisation is even deeply ingrained into the way politics works.

Take voting, for example: when the division bell rings, MPs have to rush to the voting lobbies, either from the chamber or elsewhere on the estate. They walk in with the Ayes or the Noes and are counted by tellers, then the doors lock behind them; the whole process lasts around 15 minutes.

There are many ways in which lawmakers can vote, and this really is not the quickest one, or even the most straightforward. Still, efforts to reform it never really get anywhere, because of how the lobbies are really used (hint: the clue is in the name).

'There's a lot of colleagues who will linger in the division lobbies, sit and wait for their favourite people to come by,' explains Chris Leslie MP. 'You can't really explain it to people who have not been in there, but there are little gaggles within the division lobbies who will sit down and chat, and this place is pretty deliberately set up for it.'

On top of being a good way to bump into colleagues and have a chat, division lobbies can be used to talk to those with more power than you; no matter your status in the House of Commons, you must go into the room with everyone else when the bell rings.

'As a backbencher, I used to love the fact that you'd vote in person going through the voting lobby because it was your opportunity to find out what's going on, talk to other people, most importantly to lobby a minister about something,' says Amber Rudd MP. However, this changed when she started climbing up the ladder, eventually reaching one of the four great offices of state.

'As a minister, you can hardly get through a lobby. There are people, particularly as Home Secretary, coming up and asking you about a problem with their particular immigration issue from one of their constituents. But that sort of access I think is fundamental to checks and balances for our constitution. And the verbal exchange is an effective way of delivering it.'*

---

* Or, as another MP bluntly put it: 'Once the doors are locked, even the Prime Minister can't do anything about it. You can take them by the shoulder or by the throat. They can't get away.'

The division lobbies are also important because only MPs can be in them, so they can chat safely in the knowledge that a pesky journalist won't be casually listening in on their conversations. Another sanctuary for MPs is, of course, the chamber of the House of Commons. Though it would be ill-advised (and discourteous) to launch into endless group discussions while someone is addressing the room, keeping an eye on who sits where can be useful.

The dynamics of it aren't exactly opaque: much like in a classroom, those who sit closer to the front bench tend to be the eager teacher's pets, while those at the very back are the mischief-makers. So far so obvious, but given that chamber proceedings are televised, it is nice to be able to spot someone going from the second row to the back as a visual manifestation of them becoming less keen on their leadership. This is especially true of recently sacked or willingly departed ministers: where will they go once they have to leave the front row? If they end up at the very back with the rebels, it can tell you a lot about how they plan to act now they are no longer subject to the stringent rules of the front bench.

The other places MP have to themselves are the Smoking Room (sadly non-smoking) and the tea room (which does provide tea). These two are, in many ways, where power truly is gained and lost, and where legislation gains traction or starts heading for oblivion.

According to one MP quoted by Lord Norton, academic and constitutional issues expert, the tea room is 'the archetypal venue for the hatching of plots; the starting post for those famous "murmurings of backbench discontent". MPs feel safe here. Away from staff, journos and members of the public, they can gripe away happily to their heart's content, in the sure knowledge that they can be as indiscreet as they like.'

Regardless of your current status or positioning, these are spaces you need to occupy as an MP. If you're a party leader or prime minister, you need to be seen there. As former MP Jerry Hayes puts it – 'The first advice I gave to David Cameron when he became prime minister was basically, you've got to go round the tea rooms, you've got to go round the bars. You've got to, once a week, go into the members' dining room and sit down and talk to these ghastly people, listen to their mad views. Because everyone wants to say to their friends, and anyone who'll bloody listen, "Oh, the Prime Minister was only saying to me the other day ..."'

If you're a cabinet minister, you might lead your department towards an iceberg by not realising that the policies you're pursuing aren't popular with your party. A junior minister? Make sure you're around and have chats with your colleagues, as popularity is a good thing to have during a reshuffle, and you will be appreciated if you can provide a link between the parliamentary party and your boss.

If you have ministerial ambitions, it is good to create a base for yourself and get a good sense of what your fellow MPs like, dislike and generally bitch about. A backbencher with no interest in the greasy pole should still take the time to chatter away, as they will eventually have a policy they deeply care about and will need all the support they can get, especially from people who know that helping them won't even be useful to their careers. Long-term rebels should also haunt these quarters if they want to identify other malcontents and convince waverers to join the resistance.

Another interesting feature of these rooms is how they are laid out, and what it tells us about different Houses. In the members' tea room, Conservatives, Liberal Democrats and Labour MPs all have different areas they sit in. Naturally, the seats aren't marked in any way, and as members go there for the first time, they must either magically guess where to sit, be told, or find out the hard way. This will naturally reinforce the tribalism of the Commons – if most of your socialising is done along party lines, it will be harder for you to develop good personal relationships with members from the other sides, rightly or wrongly. It also compartmentalises information, and can ensure that, say, a piece of gossip or a rumour widely shared within Labour circles takes a long time to reach the Conservative benches, and vice versa.

The House of Lords is different. In their dining room, where most of the mingling is done, the rules are more lax and the 'long table' is what matters. 'You walk in there and you sit down next to the last person who sat down, so you have no choice about where you sit,' explains one baroness. 'You have a choice in that you can sit on the left or the right, but apart from that you're going to the next free seat. If you choose the long table you could be sitting next to a cross-bencher, Lib Dem, Conservative, you don't know. So at that point people are always interesting – they will often just plant themselves down next to you and start chatting.'

According to fellow peer Lord Norton, 'That can make a difference to what you pick up on and then what builds support in the chamber,' which is noticeable: the House of Lords is a place where consensus-building tends to be the way to go and where partisanship is softer.

THE ANTHILL

There is one place in the Palace of Westminster where everyone is free to mingle and chat with everyone else, but it wasn't meant to be used that way. Portcullis House was commissioned in 1992 then opened in 2001, and was built to provide the estate with more office space for MPs and rooms for select committees. The building's atrium was to be used as a meeting place for MPs' staff but overall, PCH was simply seen as an answer to space constraints, and nothing more – then it opened.

With its glass roof, large open space, dozens of tables and multiple cafés and canteens, it quickly became the beating heart of Parliament and changed the working (and socialising) habits of most inhabitants of the bubble.

'It was never meant to become the centre of everyone's life; the centre was supposed to be central lobby, but it's shifted the entire centre of the Palace,' says Philip Cowley, a political scientist and academic. 'When I first used to come to Westminster in the late eighties, early nineties, you walked into central lobby, you could sit on one of those green benches in the central bit and everybody would go by. We'd be able to play that game of "Oh, I thought he was dead!" and you'd see the Prime Minister and you'd see the ministers.

'You only had to be there for half an hour and you'd have got your fame ticked off for the day. It's like fucking tumbleweed in there now sometimes, although there are tourists going in and out. Instead, everything's shifted over to this modern, very open place, almost designed for people to mingle and chat and gossip. I can wander around there and bump into people and chat to people in a way that was harder before.'

In the olden days of the 20th century, there were few places where one could simply sit down and wait for life to come to them, especially if they weren't an MP, and they didn't fancy an alcoholic drink. The tea rooms tend to feature a number of tables to which it might be hard to invite oneself without a specific reason; lobbies aren't really made for long-term lingering and corridors are just that: stand in one for too long and you will look a little odd.

Portcullis is open to everyone and has its own guest entrance, making it the ideal place for just about every type of meeting, free from the constraints of space-based hierarchy. Contrary to the rest of the estate, it also looks modern and airy, and close to the atmosphere of a normal workplace cafeteria.

'Anyone can be there, so you get interaction between members, between peers and MPs. You've got staff, you've got the journalists of course who hang around, and then others coming in,' explains Lord Norton. 'So it's just fascinating watching journalists interacting or just sitting there. You've got everybody in Portcullis, so it is now the social space of Westminster, because there's nothing equivalent to it. It's one of those things that once it's there you think, how did we manage before?'

There is, however, an issue with everyone now meeting in the same place, and it is that everyone can see who is meeting everyone else. If, for example, you see a *Daily Mirror* hack having a coffee with a Labour rebel MP at 1:00pm, you may raise your eyebrow if the next day's *Daily Mirror* features a brutal attack on the Labour leader by an anonymous MP. If this happens you might even, unprompted or if someone asks, mention in passing that you'd seen the reporter and MP having a chat the day before, which of course could mean nothing, or mean everything. That person might then be asked about it by someone else and repeat what they were told and before long, that MP being the source of that story will have become received wisdom, rightly or not.

This happens all the time and is hard to then deny. The *Financial Times'* Jim Pickard gives one example of it: 'A few months ago, I got up from talking to [Labour comms chief] Seumas Milne, and then three minutes later, I tweeted something about a Labour person criticising a centrist Labour MP. It was an entirely different person, but almost immediately someone on Twitter said, "He was sitting talking to Seumas Milne in PCH!" I mean the source of my tweet definitely was not him. It was 100% not him.'

Still, what do you do then? The only solution would have been for him to tweet back 'It wasn't Seumas Milne, it was [name],' which would mean betraying his source, thus breaking what may be the single most important rule of journalism. In these cases, the only option is to blithely deny it, hope it doesn't catch on and move on.

In any case, PCH remains a form of heaven for the hacks: most of their job involves talking to people, and most of the people they could possibly want to talk to will now appear in the same place at one point or another during the day. In order to be as efficient as possible, they all develop different techniques. The more senior ones can afford to sit somewhere and wait for people to come and talk to them – the bit by the escalator on the west side of the atrium is a particularly sought-after spot – while others may wander around, circling like sharks and waiting for a poor innocent fish to swim by alone.

MPs aren't always happy about it. In the words of Paul Masterton, 'It's like something out of a safari. You just have journalists swarming around and you know you'll be sitting down during your lunch, trying to have ten minutes on your own eating, and then you'll just look up and a journalist will be helping themselves to the seat next to you saying, "So how are you, Paul?" I'm eating my jerk chicken, leave me alone!'

Still, the MP/journalist relationship doesn't only go one way, and though they might not always admit it, politicians enjoy knowing that they can casually bump into reporters if they need to. They might also take advantage of the fact that everyone can spy on everyone else. The day after he left the Cabinet over

Brexit disagreements, David Davis strolled into PCH and happily plumped himself down for a solo lunch, grinning contentedly at passers-by. His bet was probably that hard Brexiteers would stop by to congratulate him on his move, and it is exactly what happened: in the space of roughly 30 minutes, he had about a dozen pleasant-looking chats with passing MPs, making him look both relaxed about his decision and popular with his own benches.

It wasn't reported as such, it hardly was breaking news, but anyone who witnessed the scene would have made a mental note of it. Leaving government rarely is a happy occasion, but this showed that he at least seemed to have made the right call. Another classic trick is the public display of reconciliation: if two MPs were either spotted having a massive row or rumoured to have had one, they could do worse than have a very public coffee or lunch in Portcullis House to show everyone just how well they actually get along – nothing to see here!

In a similar vein, rumours can be purposely started with public displays of plotting. 'I saw [Labour pro-Remain MP] Chuka Umunna and [Conservative pro-Remain MP] Anna Soubry having a coffee together in Portcullis House a few months ago,' one peer said. 'Now they must have done that on purpose, because they knew they were going to be seen by everyone else, rather than it being private, they're not stupid.'*

Let's run with that general example. If, say, you wanted to organise a proper cross-party rebellion against Brexit that would need to take people by surprise to work, you would meet in some-one's office or away from Westminster. If, on the other hand, you wanted people to *think* that you're organising a dangerous-looking rebellion against Brexit, having a conspiratorial meeting

---

* This was of course written before Umunna and Soubry decided to jump ship together, but at least now we can guess what the meeting must have been about.

of Remain-supporting Conservative and Labour MPs in PCH would be a good idea.

The substance of the conversation doesn't necessarily matter: what is important is that people will start talking about a Remainer plot, from the journalists to their parliamentary colleagues. What happens next is that some of your colleagues might approach you to say that they want in, which can give you a better idea of what numbers you might get if you really were to prepare a rebellion. Another is that the powers-that-be, either in government or opposition, might start caring about you. It is hard to make yourself heard if you're only a small group meeting in private, but the last thing party leaders and their whips want is something that might undermine their authority, and open plotting can definitely do that.

Of course, this might all backfire: if you're seen publicly fraternising with the (Labour or Conservative) enemy, your actions might be seen as a betrayal and your concerns ignored as a result. Your internal opponents (in this case the hard Brexiteers) might also see it as a call to war, and an excuse to strengthen their own ranks and work on a counter-plot of their own. If you did all this because you actually were struggling to come up with a genuine plan, this result would be less-than-ideal. If you were just having a cup of tea and a whinge with colleagues but found yourself accidentally unleashing the fury of everyone else, it's even worse. As with every tool or weapon, Portcullis House must be used wisely.

EAT, DRINK AND BE MERRY

Speaking of tools to be used wisely: let's talk about booze. The history of British politics is drenched in it, and no exploration of any aspect of Westminster would be worth its salt without taking the drinking into account. It can be excessive and catastrophic, or a needed addition to the dreary day-to-day. Not everyone drinks alcohol in politics, but everyone's career has been influenced in one way or the other by beer, wine or something stronger.

For a start, there are plenty of places in which to get sozzled in Parliament: no matter your role, as long as you're a pass-holder there will be a bar in which you will be expected to pop by at least once in a while. The one at the lowest rung of the ladder is the Sports & Social Club*, which is the haunt of parliamentary aides and other assorted staff.

Going to the Sports & Social for the first time is an incredibly underwhelming experience. If it is where you're headed, chances are that you are on the younger and more junior side, as MPs and peers rarely step foot in there. It might be your first week working in Parliament as a staffer, or you might be going there because a staffer wants to bring you in. In any case, you probably have a mental image of what your evening will involve: a fancy bar, high ceilings, beautiful windows, plush seats, posh women sipping on their champagne and posher men drinking their port – and so on.

In fact, going to the Sports & Social first involves realising that its main entrance is just by the bins of the Palace. The second impression comes from the smell as you walk in; the unmistakable stench of spilled alcohol on old carpets. There aren't any proper windows so once you're indoors, you have no idea if it's day or night, summer or winter. There is either no music playing at all or music playing far too loudly, and rarely anything

---

* Renamed 'the Woolsack' in 2018, which this book refuses to recognise as no one calls it that anyway.

in between. It is also impossible to predict which one it will be before turning up.*

Clientele-wise, it is a mixed bag: the majority of drinkers tend to be aides in their early twenties and the outside friends they're hoping to impress and/or bring home, some of the builders hopelessly trying to stop the Palace from crumbling to dust and the occasional older member of staff. An occasional addition to this merry band of randoms used to be Black Rod himself, at least when the role was held by David Leakey. He would come in, presumably to check that everything was in order, and would find himself mobbed by hordes of drunk 20-something nerds asking for selfies. If you think this sounds like an odd combination of people to stick in one bar, you're largely right.

Most MPs seldom make an appearance down that particular corner of the Palace, but it doesn't mean that what happens there doesn't reach them. One Labour MP who is close to their aide explains: 'I stay out of it, but my assistant picks up loads and loads and loads of information in Sports which, you know, sometimes is just your classic "by the water cooler at work" kind of, "Oh right, oh, so that's happening, is it? That's interesting." And it's completely useless but just kind of nosy. Sometimes it's useful when you know what's going on on the other side.'

Journalists tend to avoid the place as well, but will occasionally pop by when in need of a quick pint, or desperate to get a story. After all, staffers might not know as much as some people higher up the food chain, but few have received any media training and most will be keen to try and overstate their importance by blabbing to hacks about anything and everything

---

* One bartender was once asked to turn the music down as punters couldn't hear each other and firmly replied that the music wasn't for them but so the staff didn't have to listen to the rubbish people talk in Sports. Fair enough.

they've heard. Aides tend to get burnt by the media once or twice then learn their lesson, but before it happens, their knowledge will be a free-for-all.

The Sports is also an oddly welcoming place: as it is mostly used by people who are relatively new to the estate, there is a certain atmosphere that makes people unhesitant to chat to each other. Though the keenest of aides will stick with their clique, it is not rare to see groups of Tories, Labourites and Lib Dems drunkenly mingle and whinge about their jobs. After all, MPs can be difficult to work for no matter the party, and the complaints will often be similar.

According to one centre-left Labour aide, it can even be better to have a good old bitching session with a staffer from another party: 'If I'm talking to Labour people about my boss then they'll be more concerned with what faction I'm on, what faction he's on, and if it's one they don't like, they might use that information against us. If I'm talking to a Tory mate, there's this understanding that we're just having a pint and a whinge and none of it will be repeated afterwards.'

Another Labour staffer put it more bluntly: 'I have the researchers' union – once you're a researcher, I don't care whom you work for, we can chat together. Well, unless you're in the Green Party.'

This party political truce was temporarily disturbed in 2015 when the SNP descended on Parliament with far more MPs than expected. Keen to separate themselves from typical Westminster politicians, they decided to set up camp in Sports, which didn't please everyone. For a start, the place isn't that big and a table of a dozen Scottish Nationalists can soon make a room feel crowded. On top of this, MPs aren't exactly welcome at the bar – they have other watering holes on the estate specifically for them, so the least they could do is stay there. The stand-off was relatively short-lived in the end – the SNP slowly moved back to nicer parts of the Palace and a whole bunch of them lost their seats in 2017 anyway.

Though these days it is often quiet, the Sports is mostly known for its raucous nights. One particular institution is the Thursday night karaoke, where packs of leathered youths belt out any song that could be seen as having a vaguely political meaning. Countless fights have also taken place there – some including MPs – and the majority of Westminster denizens in their twenties will have had at least one night there on which the less is said, the better.*

In a somewhat unsurprising turn of events, parliamentary authorities shut down the place for several weeks after one brawl too many in 2018 and attempted to refurbish it to make it less seedy. The results weren't exactly revolutionary but appear to have worked: as of writing, the 'Woolsack' has not been in the news for many months.

If the idea of sticky carpets and dartboards doesn't appeal to you, there are other options. In order to get to them, you must walk away from the bowels of the Palace and towards the river. At first glance, the Lords bar looks nearly as underwhelming as Sports, albeit in a different way. With its hospital lighting, one and a half stools and the fact that it is attached to the Lords canteen, the peers' drinking hole feels like it is trying to convince you to turn around and leave. The terrace looking over the Thames, however, is a highlight, and is open to all as long as the House of Lords isn't sitting, which is often. In a move that probably would have been

---

* Asked to recall their most embarrassing evening there, a number of aides got in touch but one story really outshone the others: 'I got so drunk in Sports one night I decided I needed some fresh air and went up to the roof, thinking it would be peaceful and I could clear my head. When I got up there I threw up over the side and it nearly hit a Lord, who thankfully did not see me.'

frowned upon by Sir Charles Barry, it also started serving onion rings and mozzarella sticks a few years ago.

Though the other side of the terrace doesn't provide any deep-fried goods, it tends to be where the action actually happens. Much like the Lords', the actual room that constitutes Strangers' Bar is far from glamorous, and essentially one big empty rectangle with a bar on one side, a few battered old seats on the other, and a couple of TVs on one of the walls roughly in the middle. Its name comes from what people who do not work on the estate are technically called in Parliament, as Strangers' is the place where MPs can bring in guests.

As a result, only said MPs (and a few other senior passhold-ers) can buy drinks at the bar, and anyone found lingering on the terrace without being obviously in the company of a Member of Parliament will be politely but firmly asked to leave the premises.

This absolutely does not mean that only MPs and their guests go there: in practice, people who have been around for long enough will merrily turn up assuming they'll know at least one MP there, to whom they can vaguely wave at if an eager doorkeeper asks why they are there. Much like teenagers loitering around an off-licence, it is also not unknown for people to stick a tenner in the palm of an understanding MP so they can go buy them a drink.

What this means is that the terrace often ends up being a mix of MPs, mid-tier to senior journalists, aides with their bosses and, depending on the night, a smattering of special advisers, lobbyists and parliamentarians' spouses and friends. If it is the first half of the week and there are late votes, the place can be quite lively; if it is the first or last day of term and the weather is pleasant, it will be a mess.

For a start, the drinks are cheaper than in most places in central London, which always helps, and Westminster is a place where excessive drinking in the workplace isn't exactly frowned upon. As we will see later, the booze habits of the bubble have changed considerably over the last few decades, but this doesn't mean it has gone dry. After all, in what other industries can someone drink five pints, pop into a room to vote on a new law, then pop out again to down another five? This might be a slightly extreme (though real-life) example, but it remains the case that people can be seen sipping on a drink on the terrace while technically working and no one will bat an eyelid.

This predictably encourages the blurring between the professional and the personal. While having one drink with a colleague won't change the nature of your working relationship, getting thoroughly sozzled with them on more than one occasion will put you on different footing. Miranda Green, a former adviser to then Lib Dem leader Paddy Ashdown, puts it that way: 'When I was in politics, there was a lot of alcohol. The bars were open late and people basically lived there, so that informality was extreme. Everybody was drinking together; different parties, different journalists from different papers, us as advisers, all that, so your social life and your work life were absolutely melded together.'

Nights on the terrace exemplify that: on any given evening, you can seamlessly go from pointed conversations about policy to giving someone advice about their love life (or trying to kick-start your own) and back to having a big old gossip about who might harbour ambitions of becoming a party leader. On a psychological level, this means that the personal has to influence the professional: the type of information you get will depend on the people you're naturally drawn to, and your ability to gain access to that information will also rely on how sociable you can be. The flip side of this is that nights on the lash can often lead to blazing rows, especially when everyone involved feels very strongly about the same things. It is fine if it happens with either

friends or strangers you will never see again, but having a screaming drunken argument with someone rarely is the best way to
make a good first impression.

Mix this with the fact that everyone is overworked and has to
make snap judgements about the nature of the dozens of people
they meet every week, and one 20-minute shouting match at
11:00pm can end with you having made an enemy for life. It is
petty but then again, so are people in politics.

Beyond the sort of things you talk about in Strangers', the
mere fact that you are there – or not – can influence where your
career is going, especially for MPs, and the line to tread is a fine
one. If you're a newish MP, it can be wise for you to be seen
on the terrace relatively often; you probably do not know many
journalists and drinking is a good way to remedy that, both so
you can make your point of view on the issue of the day known,
and so you can establish more long-term relationships. Hacks
also love an MP who is friendly and easy to talk to, and are more
likely to warm to you if you're the sort of person they can have a
casual pint with.

That being said, if you're a very new MP, you probably
shouldn't be seen there *too* often: the people of Westminster do
not know a lot about you, and 'pisshead' is not the first epithet
you want people to come up with when they think of you. It
would also be unwise for you to be one of the regulars once your
career has taken off: there comes a point where people will assume
that you are busy and important, and having the time to drink a
pint or four several nights a week will damage that otherwise flattering image. Similarly, haunting the terrace can be crucial if you
want to be as well informed as possible, or be an effective plotter,
but get spotted there a bit too often and you will get a reputation
for being an inveterate gossip or an untrustworthy rebel.

Still, all of this does not mean that it would be impossible for someone to have a career without spending time in Strangers' – it simply is the case that going to the bars can act as a convenient shortcut. Climbing the greasy pole is impossible without at least some hard work, but informal networks can help enormously, which is why it is worrying that one type of people will generally tend to be more comfortable spending time in the bars.

'Strangers' Bar and the terrace are very male-dominated,' says one female MP. 'The staff there are always jumped-up young men who want to be in the know, and trade gossip and information; that's how they push their status up in here.'

That a drinking environment ends up being male-dominated is hardly surprising, but it is a problem. The more men hang out on the terrace, Sports or others, the more likely it is that the atmosphere will discourage women from joining in, and the fewer women there are in those spaces, the more masculine they will feel – and so on. On top of this, women (especially young ones) who still decide to occupy those places do so at their own risk. As the aide mentioned in a previous chapter, getting a reputation as a woman who spends a lot of time around certain men will do you no good, even if nothing romantic or sexual has ever happened. Try as you might to drink and network like everyone else, you will also be confronted with men who either assume that you're looking for a casting couch promotion, or try to convince you that it is something you should at least consider. Oh, and if you do end up falling for one of them, word will soon go around that you slept your way to whichever position you currently occupy, even if it is demonstrably false. Fun, isn't it?

Women aren't the only casualty of this alcohol-focused work culture, of course – Muslims, people who don't drink for whatever reason and those with young families in London might also not wish to spend their evenings in the bars of Parliament. 'People who are from minority backgrounds, whether that's state education or female, y'know, still a minority here, or BME, are probably less likely to be part of those drinking groups,' says Chi Onwurah MP. 'I probably go to Strangers' for an hour once a month, if I've got people visiting me.'

SW 1A

If you're reading this book, it seems fair to assume that you're broadly aware of the concept of 'pubs', so there probably is no need for a greatly detailed section on the drinking establishments of Westminster. Still, they do matter so it seems worth taking a brief look at them:

The first stop on our tour has to be the Red Lion. Located on Whitehall and by the Derby Gate entrance to Parliament, it is the most famous pub in the area. Should you happen to pop in without knowing what to expect, you wouldn't be shocked by anything in it. It is a pub in central London where the drinks are overpriced and the punters are mostly middle-aged white men in badly fitting suits, and most of them drink on the pavement as the inside is generally too cramped and warm. The one (somewhat crucial) difference is that the Red Lion is host to all sorts of Westminster denizens, if you know who to look out for. There are civil servants, journalists, aides, the occasional MP, lobbyists, policy wonks and all the rest, drinking in small groups and occasionally mingling with each other.

Given its location, the Red Lion is a bit similar to bars within the parliamentary estate, as everyone can see who's drinking with whom, and it is a great spot to stand and watch MPs and ministers grumpily or triumphantly going from No 10 back into the Palace, or vice versa. It has also earned its place in political history, not just because it has been standing for centuries, but more recently because of an evening in late 1997.

New Labour was in power, Tony Blair was pretty keen on the UK joining the euro and Gordon Brown was not. Charlie Whelan was the Treasury's press secretary and liked a drink; the Red Lion was his unofficial HQ and he enjoyed briefing journalists there. His boss, Brown, had given an interview to *The Times* due to be published the next day, where the Chancellor would reveal that joining the eurozone before the next election was effectively off the table. White wine spritzer in hand, Whelan called journalists to talk them through the big news. Entirely unsurprisingly, two Lib Dem staffers happened to be standing next to the Labour man and managed to overhear everything. It was then their turn to call up hacks to deliver the big news, and so the scoop was broken.

It was certainly news to the public (and bad news for *The Times* and their big Saturday story) but it was also new information to someone else: Tony Blair. The Prime Minister was in his Chequers residence that night, but got tipped off that there had been a sudden big policy change. He tried calling Brown, who didn't pick up, and his spokesperson Alastair Campbell, who didn't pick up either. Ben Wright recalls what happened next in his book *Order, Order!*: 'Desperate to discover what was being briefed to the newspapers, Blair called Whelan, who answered his mobile phone in the Red Lion pub. I stepped outside, says Whelan, and Blair said, "What's going on about not joining the euro?" He said we had to kill the story. I told him it's too late. It's already gone in.'

And that was that. One of the biggest policy decisions of the New Labour years, something that drastically altered the direction in which Britain was headed, revealed to the Prime Minister because someone told someone else about it in the pub, and some people overheard it.

The other drinking establishments of the area do not have quite the same legacy, but can still make for a good night out. There is the Westminster Arms behind Parliament Square, where people go when they're bored of the Red Lion, and there's the plush Blue Boar by St James's Park Tube, which is mostly populated by those on the Conservative end of things. Then there is the Old Star, the Speaker, St Stephen's Tavern, the Marquis of Granby, Walkers of Whitehall, the Two Chairmen, the Barley Mow and a handful of others, where you will find an ever-changing combination of Westminster people, alongside whichever civil servants happen to have their department close by.

Each clan will tend to have their own territory, but there is no point in trying to definitely match the group with the boozer as it changes with the times. The Westminster Arms was Tory for a while before it became UKIP, then UKIP largely disappeared and the Tories didn't resurface afterwards; it was the Treasury patch for a generation until it wasn't, or is it again? Et cetera.

What is more interesting is the fact that some pubs will be marked as political and others simply will not – the Lord Moon of the Mall is just by Trafalgar Square but no one seemingly ever goes there; The Feathers, on the other side of Parliament, is also not a pub where interesting drinks are ever held, for no apparent reason. Knowledge of the left-behind pubs can be useful: sometimes people do need to have conversations away from prying eyes and want a pint to go with it. In some cases, there is nothing better than to hide in plain sight: when they were chiefs of staff to Theresa May, Nick Timothy and Fiona Hill made the Clarence their HQ. Though it is on Whitehall and a five-minute walk from Parliament, their meetings were undiscovered and uninterrupted.

Others have more creative solutions. Brexiteers Douglas Carswell and Daniel Hannan chose to plot at the Tate Britain a bit further along the Thames – according to Arron Banks' *The Brexit Club*, they chose the venue because they thought that journalists would not be seen in such 'cultured surroundings'.*

According to *Order, Order!*, one such hack was so adamant that he would not be seen with Labour spinner Damian McBride that he insisted they met at a Stringfellows, though the pair looked so uninterested in the women dancing that they were asked to leave the premises. Another way to go about it is to think creatively, like Conservative MP Greg Hands:

'If we wanted to go and have some secret discussion, the best place to go would be the Chelsea Arts Club. There's no MPs with the exception of me – I'm an honorary member. You've got to be a real artist to be a member of the Chelsea Arts Club, and they don't accept you unless you're a real artist, but there is one honorary member: the MP for Chelsea. I know I can go to the Chelsea Arts Club, because I will never meet another MP there.'

If you happen not to be the MP for Chelsea – and there is no shame in that – Hands also suggests the McDonald's on Whitehall as a good place for a quiet chat.

Should you want to eat something a tad healthier, there are a number of other options. Want to have lunch with someone and be seen by absolutely everyone else? Quirinale is probably your best bet: an Italian restaurant as big as a shoe box, it is usually at least half-full of politicos talking and listening in on the other tables. The Cinnamon Club, a posh Indian round the corner, is similar, and so are Shepherd's, Roux and Osteria Dell'Angolo.

---

* It is true that they were never spotted there, though one could argue that it is mostly because journalists have better things to do on weekdays than go have a stroll in a museum.

Kennington Tandoori just south of the river is also a solid bet, though usually for dinner.

If you would rather have a more private meal, you are still relatively spoilt for choice, as there are a number of decent restaurants close to SW1A, but there is no point in listing them here, as this is a book about politics and gossip, not the Yellow Pages.

WHAT THIS ALL MEANS

On top of the day-to-day socialising, life in Westminster involves a number of set pieces; social events that mark different parts of the yearly calendar. There are a number of summer parties in June and July (good luck getting into *The Spectator*'s), Christmas parties in November and December, and plenty of book launches, award ceremonies, nondescript cocktail receptions, ad nauseam.

For the Westminster people who moved to London for the first time to pursue a political career, this has good and bad sides. On the one hand, they will have enough of a social life to make the capital feel a bit homely, and they will be able to meet like-minded people with relative ease. On the other, it does mean that they will often not bother making friends outside the bubble, so their London won't stretch very far beyond SW1. For those already living in London, the consequences are mostly problematic, as they are faced with two less-than-ideal choices: let yourself get swallowed up whole by the bubble and slowly but surely lose touch with your old friends, or fiercely defend your non-political social life and live with the constant fear of missing out, both personally and professionally.*

---

* It has been said that some people have managed to find a healthy balance between the two: if this is you, do feel free to get in touch with the author to share your wisdom.

In any case, it is tremendously easy to find yourself alienated by life outside this small bubble that has become your home. If you work too hard for too many hours and all your friends and contacts can be found in a 15-minute walk radius of your office, it is hard to remember that there is still another world beyond politics. Much like people who were born and bred in a village can find it hard to envisage life in the big bad world outside their own universe, those who spend too much time in what is basically a square mile can forget that life still exists around it.

This is partly how rumours come to occupy such an important place in people's minds: if Westminster becomes not only your place of work but also the place where you meet your friends and partners, the slightest bit of information can take on unwarranted significance.

There is also the slight issue of politics attracting a specific type of individual. It is a world where the pay isn't great, the day-to-day life is intense, there is often little job security, people can be deeply unpleasant to one another and most of the public hates you: it really is not for everyone. As Bim Afolami (bluntly) put it: 'In case it's not obvious, MPs are not normal people.' Luckily for them, neither is anyone else around here.

PART 3

PERSONALITIES

'People think Westminster is like House of Cards *but it's actually more like* Mean Girls *– so many people come in expecting to be Francis Urquhart but they're just Regina George. There's a lot of Regina Georges in Parliament.'*

– Anonymous Conservative MP

THE SOCIAL NETWORK(S)

Information travels fast in Westminster, but not always in the most obvious ways. Stories which some have heard a thousand times will be completely unknown to others, and depending on who heard them first, some anecdotes will make their way from one corner of the bubble to the other in days while others will sink without a trace.

This is due to the complex and nebulous nature of networks around Parliament, from friendships to working relationships and everything in between. Attempts were made to map out such networks and they failed: as a matter of a fact, a shameful number of napkins were harmed in the making of this book. Still, let's take a stab at it and see where it gets us – pay attention, it's about to get confusing.

Let's start with MPs. You're ... well, let's call you Andrew Smith, and say you're the Labour MP for North West Southamptonshire, backbencher but been around since the 2015 election. Who do you know? Your first circle is your intake; the other Labour MPs who got elected in 2015 – it's all a bit like school.

In the words of one Labour MP who was elected in 2010, 'It very much operates in intake groups. Intake groups seem to be very influential in whom people speak to and whom they mix with.' Whether through WhatsApp groups or frequent dinners, MPs will always tend to be close to the people who arrived at the same time as them, as there is camaraderie to be found when you've all had to figure out a tremendous amount of things in a tremendously short amount of time together.

You might not all get along, and you certainly won't all agree on policies, but there will be an element of trust in there. 'So my 2017 intake, there are lots of things known to us that actually nobody else knows, because actually nobody else is that interested, and there's a certain quiet sense that you guys, you can all talk, and there are things that don't leave that group,' says MP Bim Afolami. 'You look at 2005, 2001, '97, they all have little groups and tight relationships of "we've been through the wars together" and "we've been here 20 years". There are things there that will never get out of that group.'

Who else do you have? If you're in a relatively small parliamentary party like the Liberal Democrats, Plaid Cymru or the SNP, you will get to know your fellow MPs soon enough, but given the number of seats usually gained by Labour and the Conservatives at each election, you cannot reasonably be expected to know all your colleagues.

This is where your politics come into play. As one of Gordon Brown's former advisers points out, 'A lot of the factional thing is historic; there are broad tendencies within the parties, and when you become politically active and join that party, you're probably politically and historically aware enough to understand which strain of that party you identify most with, and that's probably generational. There are pre-existing historical strains running throughout the party, both the parties, and you naturally gravitate towards one of those.'

These factions tend to run along the political spectrum, with centrist, centre-left/right, left/right-wing MPs sticking together, but people also coalesce around the more senior politicians of each political strand. Tony Blair and Gordon Brown are the obvious examples of this: at any given point during the New Labour years, there were Blairite or Brownite cabinet ministers, ministers, backbenchers, advisers and aides. If you're on the senior end of this, it helps to have a clan as you will need to have a base in Parliament to back you when things get tough, and fight some fights on your behalf. On the more junior end, it obviously helps to be able to rely on people in positions of power for influence and advice.

These are relationships not fundamentally based on person-alities, but it doesn't mean they do not stick together. Afolami explains it well: 'So I think there are two levels. You've got first-order relationships, and then second/third-order relation-ships. First-order relationships are entirely whom you get on with. And that crosses intake, it crosses age, crosses committee, it crosses even to some degree party, even though the party thing is more tribal than I think people fully appreciate. That is entirely personal. But those in Westminster terms don't really go very far as to explaining why people are allies with other people.

'The second and third-order relationships between people are really about political factionalism. It's about who's on your team, broadly. So, for example, you have a bunch of people who see themselves as holding up the true Brexit flame. They don't all like each other, more than some people who aren't outside that group they get on with. But they've all bound together around a policy. Normally you will have two or three cabinet ministers who have a bunch of people whom they spend time with, they have drinks with, they give a bit of information to … That group doesn't all hang together because they get on.'

This logic also works for MPs and their aides. Though every office will be different, a good relationship between the two can be mutually beneficial. An ambitious staffer will take it upon themselves to spend time around the bars and with assistants working for other MPs, which means that they will have access to a whole lot of information, both salacious and useful.

A Conservative aide puts it in a slightly unkind way: 'They're really clueless. I can tell MPs that I know, "Oh, did you hear this?" and they say, "Oh my God, no way! Where did you hear that?" "Literally from everybody. Where have you been?"' MPs might be slightly too busy to pick up on everything doing the rounds, but what they do end up hearing tends to be more likely to be true.'*

When it comes to cross-party gossip and relationships, the dynamics aren't exactly straightforward, especially between the main parties. Individuals might get along, but it can be hard to properly get across partisan lines. Two useful set-ups are select committees and all-party parliamentary groups (APPGs) as they involve MPs from all parties having to effectively work together and spend time with each other as a group. While there is also a level of trust involved in these groupings, it does not mean that the information shared within them isn't used for party political purposes.

'If you're on select committees together, or party parliamentary groups, you do form good working relationships that do occasionally lend themselves to "God, it's a terrible nightmare on our side at the moment," or, "Oh, interesting speech by Sajid Javid at the weekend, I didn't think he'd say that," and they say, "Well, that's because he's trying to appease this particular base," or, "That's been leaked because Gavin Williamson tried to do Y,"' says one Labour MP. 'It can be really, really useful to get those snippets and insights, because then you can work out how to divide the government more effectively.'

---

* This is something the staffer quoted above is aware of. She recalls being told in March 2018 that then cabinet minister and leading Brexiteer Andrea Leadsom was about to launch a coup against Theresa May, and that it was due to happen at the Blue Boar the following Monday. Some days passed, Monday arrived and Liz Truss, a different cabinet minister, helped launch a free-market think tank called Freer at the Conrad, the hotel which owns the Blue Boar. If this was an attempted coup, it was a subtle one.

Another angle worth considering is people's identity, both cross-party and within parties. There are too many men in Parliament for them to be considered as a grouping, but until recently, there weren't that many female MPs, so they tended to have a closer relationship than their male counterparts. This doesn't mean that they would go easier on each other, but both main parties have some women-only WhatsApp groups, and women from all across the political spectrum have worked together on issues relating to their gender.

Geography matters too: MPs in neighbouring seats will occasionally have to work together on issues that touch both their constituencies, as well as campaign for each other, and those in areas far from London might travel together to and from the Commons when the House is sitting.*

Age can also help, as those with young families will have an easier time bonding with fellow mothers and fathers than with those with grown-up grandchildren, and though the stigma is mostly gone from the Palace, some LGBT MPs can still have a closer bond with each other than with their straight peers. Ethnicity can be a defining factor too. There is still a shockingly small number of BME MPs, and even if the journeys that took them to the green benches can differ wildly, some of their experiences will be similar. This goes for religion as well.

Given that the country we're talking about is Britain, it feels nearly superfluous to point out that class can help define who hangs out with whom as well. Its influence can be more latent

---

* This was especially fun for Scottish MPs in the days when the House would sit until late on Thursdays. As former MP Lord Foulkes recalls: 'It was fairly regular for the Scots to rush to the sleeper train for 11:50 and then go up to Glasgow and Edinburgh. I'll tell you, there was an awful lot of gossip in the sleeper, because there was a lounge car where you could have a drink with your colleagues and share the gossip of the week.'

within the Labour Party, but it's on the Tory side that it really makes itself felt.

'Class generally in the Conservative Party is one thing that I think people don't really talk very much about,' says Tim Bale of Queen Mary University, 'but actually when you talk to people, you get a sense that it still does matter quite a lot in terms of their personal relationships. There are people who move in circles that don't include other people, and that's partly because of class and there are resentments that are built up. I was talking recently to someone, a friend of John Major's, about John. He was very clear there that [working-class] Major never really got over that "not quite one of us" thing and felt it very strongly.'

Major's resentment wasn't necessarily paranoid: there might be solidarity among working-class MPs, but it is mostly among the upper classes that alliances are formed. A telling example came from Boris Johnson and David Cameron. Though the former PM was incandescent at Johnson and Gove for backing Leave in the Brexit referendum, he eventually made up with his old school chum, but still doesn't talk to Gove. It might be an overinterpretation, but some who know the lot have suggested that class had something to do with it, as poor old Michael was only ever middle class.

This conveniently brings us to the next axis: personal connections. To dreadfully misquote Simone de Beauvoir, you're not born an MP – you become one. Though sometimes people get elected by surprise or mistake, the process to even get selected is a complicated one, and those who go for it will have been involved in politics for a while.

'These people, they've all known each other for fucking years,' says academic Phil Cowley. 'Most of them anyway. Most of them were involved in Conservative students, or Labour students, where they knew some of them. They worked then as an adviser for someone, and they met someone else who was working as an aide for an MP. So they have these friendships that don't go back since they were elected, they go back ten, 15, 20 years.'

This last kind of connection is the trickiest one, as it is virtually impossible to guess whether two people were friends, lovers or enemies a decade before either reached Parliament unless one of them tells you. They can also be the most random: if you saw a Conservative minister and a Labour special adviser heartily hug when bumping into each other, you'd be forgiven for raising an eyebrow, at least until finding out that they were close friends during their undergraduate years.

Yet another angle to consider is, somewhat obviously, common interests. Sports is probably the most important one, with a number of MPs, special advisers, journalists and others happening to support the same obscure football team, or be seen at the cricket even in the most appalling of weathers. The most formal end of this remains parliamentary football and rugby teams, who meet regularly and can be cross-party and cross-jobs. Beyond the general links created through those events, these links can be very directly useful for people who, for whatever reason, do not have access to formal information channels.

Stephen Kinnock is one of them: a Labour MP elected in 2015, he always was one of Jeremy Corbyn's fiercest critics. As a result, he and his centrist colleagues have little to no contact with the leadership team, which can be problematic as they do still need to vaguely know what their party is up to. Luckily, Kinnock has a secret weapon: football.

'I play five-a-side on Tuesday mornings and a few of the guys who play are on the front bench,' he explains. 'I sometimes find that the post-match banter in the changing room can give a pretty useful sense of what's going on.'*

On top of all of this – don't worry, we're nearly done – there are the connections best stored under 'miscellaneous'. These can be, in no particular order:

- Peers, especially for MPs who have been around for a long time
- NGOs and charities, generally for campaigning MPs
- Think tanks, for MPs focused on policy and/or with leadership ambitions
- The parties' HQs, if the MPs were party apparatchiks before being elected
- Unions, for Labour MPs
- Lobbyists, clerks, whips and journalists, whom we're currently ignoring for a reason.

(Do you understand now why all those napkins died?)

So, to sum up: as a backbench MP, you can have connections with your colleagues elected at the same time as you, colleagues with similar politics to you, colleagues from a similar background to you, cross-party MPs you're on committees or APPGs with, MPs you knew before joining Parliament, your staff and then some. You will get gossip from all those people and are likely to share this gossip with anyone else from those circles, who might then share it with their circles, as while some circles overlap, everyone will be part of slightly different groupings.

---

* As we will keep seeing throughout the next chapters, this is a constant: question the efficiency of the informal all you want, but it normally only comes into play when the formal has become too ineffective or redundant.

If you had a hard time visualising all these overlapping connections, buckle up: we're about to add in several extra layers.

THE HELPERS

We have now talked a lot about MPs but avoided the elephant in the room, which is the fact that most MPs either become ministers at some point or at the very least are trying damn hard to. So, what is it like to be a minister, to be working in government, to be so close to the top job that you can smell it?

Well, for a start, you're completely out of the loop. Chris Leslie, who was a junior minister for several years under New Labour, puts it this way: 'There are inverted rules – you assume that ministers are going be so busy and to interrupt them would be such a faux pas, but the further it goes up, the fewer people speak to them or ring them or meet them. If you're stuck in a formal ivory tower somewhere, you're kind of "Ooh, nobody's told me that, I didn't hear that!"'

Being much busier than a backbencher and having to spend most of your time on Whitehall as opposed to Parliament means that you invariably miss out on a lot. As was made obvious in the last chapter, a lot of information flows through Westminster because people bump into each other, grab a quick unplanned coffee with each other and broadly see and talk to other people all day long. Losing that geographical advantage means that you probably will not know what the latest chat is, hear about the more salacious stuff, or even know what your own party is grumbling about.

This is an issue because even the most powerful cabinet minister can fall on their sword if they do not have the support of their MPs on a certain policy agenda. If something really is outrageously controversial, they might receive some formal letters, but often rebellions start with a long grumble that you cannot pick up on unless you're actively listening. This is where Parliamentary Private Secretaries come in.

To borrow a French phrase, PPSs have their arses stuck between two chairs: they work for a cabinet minister (or a ministerial team) but are not technically part of the government, even though they are expected to vote like they are. Their job involves supporting the minister in any way they can, usually by providing a conduit between the backbenchers and their boss, making sure that MPs support their boss in the chamber during key votes and debates, and generally keeping their boss in touch with what happens in Parliament.

The task can often be thankless but if you want to go anywhere as an MP, you need to suck it up and do it: being a good PPS means that you're exponentially more likely to eventually be promoted to a ministerial role, and it is virtually unheard of for someone to miss that stage and join the front bench straight away. It can also be a useful learning experience, depending on how you go about it.

'Ministers' PPSs hang about because they want to pick up on the gossip,' explains Lord Norton. 'They spend a lot of time just sitting, listening, getting the mood, just getting a feel for it. That's part of the PPS's task, to be the eyes and ears of the minister, just to listen to what's going on. It's very important because if you're not aware of it, you can't explain all the outcomes, because what happens in formal space might be a consequence of what happens in informal space; the gossip, joking, picking up on things. So you can not only explain what is in the House, but what isn't. Because there might be a case of "Oh dear, we're getting bad vibes. We'd better not proceed with this, either at the moment or not at all." So, deciding to not do something.'

As a PPS, you also end up in a privileged position, as some MPs might want to pass on some intriguing rumours or relevant tittle-tattle to the minister but know they can't do it directly, so they will tell you instead. Another advantage is that you get to rub shoulders with a group of people known for always having their ears to the ground: special advisers.

Annoyingly nicknamed 'SpAds' (there's frankly no need for that unsightly capital letter), special advisers are temporary civil servants appointed by cabinet ministers, whose roles tend to focus on one or several areas or policies or communications and contact with the press. They're an interesting bunch.

The most recent data comes from the snappily titled 'Special Advisers: Who they are, what they do and why they matter', and tells us that in the coalition years, the median age of government spads was 31 and that a quarter of them were under 30. Overall, spads are also far more likely to be men than women, and around 80% of them went to Russell Group universities.

What this means in practice is that they are younger than ministers, and a more homogenous group of people altogether. Crucially, they also tend to form a tighter social circle. 'Special advisers know much more about what's going on because they talk to each other,' Amber Rudd says of her time as Home Secretary.

Another former cabinet minister agrees, and explains: 'If I wanted something to happen as Secretary of State, and my department would say to me, "Oh no, the xyz secretary won't agree to that," and I'm not sure that's true, I might say to my special adviser, can you call up a SpAd and find out. They have their whole additional network, which is very effective for the Secretary of State to find out what's going on.'

Much like backbenchers might find out what is happening with other MPs by talking to their aide who might know the aides of those MPs, special advisers can act as an effective network between departments without things needing to happen at a ministerial level. Though their loyalties lie with their own department and Secretary of State, they can also be less hard-headed and more prone to sensible conversations.

Because they are younger and somewhat less likely to have young families, spads also tend to frequently socialise with one another. Most Thursdays of the year, a combination of them will meet in a Westminster pub to chat, drink, gossip and attempt to ease tensions between their bosses.

'Thursday drinks is an amazing institution for basically keeping government civil,' says Will Tanner, formerly of the Home Office and No 10. He adds: 'The spad network is really important. It is something very informal, which is basically friendships and long-standing relationships that have grown up over a long period of time, and are based not really on the job that you do but basically when you get on with someone, whether or not you are nice to deal with. There are lots and lots of instances of where the spad network basically either keeps the show on the road or creates massive problems.'

There is, predictably, a flip side to this. Despite occasional reports of the contrary, spads are human beings like you and me, and their lives can be just as messy as everyone else's. This means that friendships can be made and ended, inconvenient affairs can take place and hearts can be broken along the way, which would be all fine if the people involved weren't partly in charge of running the country.*

---

* There is a general understanding in the British media that unless they are dramatically newsworthy, personal stories about special advisers are not to be printed, given that they aren't technically public-facing and cannot defend themselves while in post. This book agrees that it is a sensible way of operating, but will add that it really does not mean that the personal lives of spads do not play a role in how they work.

Still, to give you a general idea, this is what a former government special adviser had to say about themselves and their peers: 'We're all assholes and we're going straight to hell. We had to sell our souls on the way in. None of us are good people.' This is probably a tad unkind, but what they broadly meant was that being a spad involves being switched on 24/7, giving up any hope of a fulfilling personal life and spending far too much time in very stressful situations. It is one of the most intense jobs in Westminster and can turn even the calmest and healthiest wonk into a neurotic, petty mess never too far away from a breakdown.

How petty and neurotic, you ask. Let's have a look at this anecdote from Theo Bertram, who used to work for the Labour Party:

'We had a thing at the Labour Party when I was a staffer there; I think I was in the education policy office at the time, and we were the lowest on the ladder. We would all go to meetings with cabinet ministers and we would all spend a long time doing what special advisers wanted us to do, then we all spread gossip among ourselves. We created this thing called the Spad Deck, which was ridiculous, just a silly thing that you do.

'We were rating the special advisers that we worked with, and we had a spreadsheet at one point with categories like: Do they buy a round? Because they're paid more than us, they're paid a lot more than us! Do they respond to your emails, ever? Will they return a call? Have they done the things that would help us? And then we rated them. It was just a jokey thing that happened in an office one afternoon, and then it just kind of spiralled, because some of the special advisers found out about it, and they were saying, "Well, I want to know where I am on the list!" And we replied, "Well, we can't disclose any of that, we're not disclosing that." And then it became this weapon that we used, where they were saying, "Well, what if I told you this about so-and-so?" And they would bad-mouth each other on the list, and then there were constant questions about who was on top of the list. It didn't last very long.'

Anyway, this is getting off-topic. To sum up what we have so far: if you're a Secretary of State or a minister, your information networks are the MPs in your faction and the ones you're personally friends with, your PPS and your special adviser(s). There is one group missing, the one you actually spend a lot of your time with, and who belong to another species altogether: the civil servants.

DOWN ON WHITEHALL

Having looked at the highs and lows of life as a minister, it only seems fair to mention one crucial fact: when you first join the government, no one from your party will formally be there to hold your hand. Getting shipped out to a department might be exciting, but until the civil service steps in, you're on your own. Interviewed for the Institute for Government's Ministers Reflect series, now Cabinet veteran Ken Clarke had this to say about his humble beginnings on Whitehall:

'When I was first appointed, my first parliamentary secretary job, there was no induction or anything. I was just told by the Prime Minister that she wanted me to go and be Parliamentary Secretary for Transport [...]. Apart from anything else, no one in Downing Street could tell me where the department was, let alone give me any other guidance as to what I was supposed to do. Having found it was in Marsham Street Towers I turned up, rather nervously, and said, "I have just been made a minister here," and a guy came up and said he was my private secretary. And I had no idea what a private secretary was.'

Clarke can be forgiven for not having Googled 'private secretary' before joining the DfT given that Google didn't exist at the time, but as with most things in Westminster, this whole process (or lack thereof) hasn't really changed since the days of Thatcher. New ministers are snatched from Parliament and dropped into a department, then expected to work with a group of people they haven't met until that day.*

There are a number of different civil servants working around the ministerial team in a government department: numbers may vary, but walk through the door of any of these buildings and you will find a policy team, a strategy and/or implementation unit and a communication team, all of which do exactly what they sound like they do. Move closer towards the politicians and you will find the private office, who organise their diary and day-to-day communications within the department and the rest of government.

Because the civil service tends to be more formal and organised than the Palace of Westminster, you'd be forgiven for thinking that people walking into these jobs are adequately prepared for what's coming. Mind you, you would still be wrong. In a very entertaining speech from 2010, former private secretary Edward Bowles explains:

'...There is no guidebook on what it is to be a private secretary. That is not, I suspect, what you thought you'd hear. When I was first appointed, I hoped and expected that, for such a role, it would all be written down, worked out, in tablets of stone – after all, this is the civil service that we are talking about. But no, nothing.'

Still, he then goes on to explain that it is mostly because the relationship between a private secretary and their minister

---

* As Hugh Robertson MP puts it: 'The first time I set eyes on the people who were going to be working closely with me and running my life on a day-to-day basis was when I walked through the door.'

depends so heavily on the personality of both the former and the latter that there would be no point in trying to issue one-size-fits-all guidelines. (Sound familiar?)

We will come back to them in a minute, but to finish our quick overview, we also need to mention the permanent secretaries, who are in charge of the departments. The way all these people interact with each other can be confusing, but Lord Annan once summarised it all pretty well, while attempting to explain the idiosyncrasies of British politics to an American audience:

'The mandarins are the permanent secretaries who are at the head of each ministry. The spies are the young civil servants who are the private secretaries of ministers. Every meeting a minister has is attended by his private secretary, who logs it; every conversation he makes on the phone is recorded; every appointment he makes in Whitehall is monitored. If you try to bend a minister's ear, what you say will be round the civil service in 48 hours: the only way is to catch him at dinner in the evening when his attendant nurse from the mental clinic, his private secretary, is no longer observing his patient.'*

What this extract shows as well is that just because civil servants might be seen as more serious and orderly by people on the outside, it does not mean that their world isn't as ruled by rumours and informal information as anywhere else. The difference is that the gossip is used differently and shared around different circles.

'I think civil servants use gossip just as much as politicians do,' says one former permanent secretary. 'The trouble and difficulty sometimes is that their spheres are so different there's very little overlap between the chit-chat on the civil service and

---

* Bowles himself called this 'not altogether unfair – except to nurses at mental clinics'.

chit-chat of politicians. For a start, civil service careers aren't as straightforward as politicians.' While only a very small minority of the latter will ever get to work in several different areas of government, it is a given for most senior civil servants to have worked in several departments.

Naturally, their colleagues will also have worked across a number of departments, so a piece of information can spread across Whitehall like wildfire without necessarily ever reaching Parliament and those who work there.

'Because you move around so much, there's so much information spreading between units and departments,' says one civil servant. 'I did my time at the Home Office, then the Department for Education and the Cabinet Office, and I moved between press office and private office. Whenever I went to another place I would invite whomever from wherever I used to work, and then we all have drinks together. And you know how there are prison rules, where your currency is based on if you square up to a fight or back down? It's the same thing, you get a bunch of civil servants around the table and they show off about a) the crazy amount of hours they work, or b) the most ridiculous gossip that they know.'

That being said, civil servants aren't kept in a hermetic bubble. Though they are impartial in their work, a number of them were involved in party politics when they were younger, or at least have an affinity for one side or the other, which can mean that they end up developing friendships with people in Parliament. They also love a drink, obviously, and there are few better ways of creating connections than social groups merging outside the Two Chairmen between the fourth and fifth pint.

These alliances and whisper networks don't simply exist for entertainment purposes; it might be the case that the civil service is the more professionalised arm of Westminster, but that doesn't mean that what they do isn't influenced by their party-affiliated neighbours. For a start, understanding politics means under-standing politicians, and as has hopefully become apparent by now, understanding politicians means treating them as human beings. In order to do their job properly, civil servants must know about the personal too.

One former permanent secretary gives a good example of a seemingly trivial detail quickly becoming very relevant: 'When New Labour came in in 1997, the civil service wasn't good enough about who the characters around Tony Blair were. There's a famous story, about Charlie Falconer, who was Blair's right-hand person for much of the Blair years, and was his flatmate. It was obvious that Charlie Falconer was going to be a character, and Charlie Falconer was announced as a minister, and we couldn't find his name in the MPs' list, and they couldn't find the name in the peers' list, and they couldn't spell his name, and who was this? A tribe that had taken a bit more trouble to work out who the incoming lot were would have known backwards that Tony Blair had a flatmate who was a really smart guy who was going to be in government, and that didn't happen.'

A logical conclusion to all this should be that it is in the mutual interest of both civil servants and politicians to maintain a good (and gossipy) relationship. After all, most of them on either side come in unsure of what they are meant to do, they will be demonstrably better at their jobs if they are tapped into informal networks, and they have to spend a whole lot of time with each other, so getting along can only help.

It is, of course, not that easy. Though private offices can have a good relationship with their ministers, spads and PPSs, it can be harder for anyone else to gain access to the politicians, partly because the aforementioned can be fiercely protective of their bosses, but also because the civil service can have a smothering addiction to bureaucracy.

In his Ministers Reflect interview, Tim Loughton lamented the stilted nature of his department. 'I have always worked in open-plan offices and so in [my] previous career in the City, if you had a problem that you needed to resolve, you would get in a lift and go and see the person responsible for it,' he told the IfG. 'That doesn't happen in the Department for Education. So if you want to have a quick chat with somebody about a particular issue that has come up, then it has to be diarised, you have to organise a meeting, [and] you have to have private officials present. And this is complete nonsense. So I found myself just wandering around the building and saying, can we just have a chat about such and such. And people [reacted] like it was a state visit and would leap to attention. [...] It was complete nonsense.'

Then there can be the lack of trust. Ministers wanting to get through revolutionary (or at least sweeping) reforms often fear that the civil service is secretly working against them, as they tend to favour the status quo. A lot of them will also be convinced that due to their roles and impartiality, civil servants can never fully understand Parliament. On the other side, civil servants can be exasperated by the party political whims of their ministers, and inability to work through proper policy-making. These hardly are the best foundations for durable and functioning professional relationships, and in the worst scenarios, personal fractures or lack of communication have led to policy disasters, and we will come back to this in the next part of this book.

In the meantime, let's head away from Whitehall.

IN THEIR OWN WORLD

Political staff and lawmakers may come and go, but civil servants are forever, and so are library researchers. Employed by the House, the fine people at the Commons Library provide MPs and their offices with briefings and answers to any questions they may have. Somewhat disappointingly, even the most enthusiastic prodding failed to find any evidence of gossip-swapping in their quarters.

'The first thing is physically you're detached from the Palace,' says one person who works there. 'We work at Tothill Street so there's a slight gap there, you don't bump into people as much. But also because we're seen as politically impartial, if there's something that we hear or get wind of, we've got to keep quiet about it.'

(Boo.)

Still, the geographical element is interesting: while the library has a few people within the Palace, the majority of them are in a building across Parliament Square. The walk from one building to the other is under ten minutes long, but in Westminster terms, they might as well be down in Croydon. It is worth mentioning that they are an exception in SW1, in that their work focuses on the formal: either something happens and they're required to explain why it happened, or something might be about to happen and their role is to explain what would go down if it were to happen.

What this requires is deep knowledge of Parliament and of certain policy areas, and much of it can be gained without needing those amorphous networks and casual chats. Though the nature of their job means that they do sometimes get pieces of information a few days before most, their working culture is apart from the rest of Westminster, and they will keep the titbits to themselves.

One group they do interact with, partly because some of their offices are adjacent, are the clerks, who are an altogether more entertaining bunch. 'For them gossip's more important,' says a library researcher. 'On the committee side the clerk is kind of the manager of this wayward football team, and they've got to know how their members are going to behave – if you go abroad, will they try and arrange dinner with 100 Ukrainians, that sort of stuff.

'Do they have a bit of a drink problem? What are their proclivities? You're responsible for them, and you're taking them abroad, like a teacher taking a load of kids abroad; it's a nightmare. And that sort of stuff can't really be written down, so understanding from colleagues where the problems are going to be is very, very important.'

The clerks are an interesting tribe: they aren't as withdrawn as their library colleagues, but they function more as a closed circle than most other groupings in Parliament. Though their work makes them a part of most areas of the House's day-to-day business, the ones who work on select committees tend to be the ones who rely on informal information the most. After all, running a select committee effectively involves managing the opinions, interests, personalities and egos of around a dozen MPs from all parties, which is not an easy feat. There is, as ever, no one way to do it, so new clerks have to rely on their elders for much-needed advice.

'Because our institution is so small as clerks, there is a culture of knowledge-sharing between us,' says one. 'There's a really good culture of knowledge-sharing. I think also because one of our main roles is to work with MPs, we spend a lot of time, both designated in terms of training how to deal with MPs, but also with impromptu chats about how to deal with a difficult situation.'

Another was a bit less diplomatic: 'There's a kind of survival mechanism element to gossip. We have to be very discreet and confidential about members – there's stuff I would tell my partner and probably just about no one else outside. But there is a kind of golden circle within clerks that if I tell them X about Y member of my committee, gossip that I've heard, I absolutely know that that won't go any further. I don't even have to say it, it's just part of the culture, and that's actually quite a release valve. Because you know, members can be pretty demanding sometimes, and bastards to deal with, sometimes.

'Not all the time, by a long way, but sometimes. And actually, to be able to say to your friends, "Oh you know what that sod X did today?" It's a way of not going completely bonkers. It's also directly useful for our job: if you find out someone's a pisshead on a visit, you calibrate your expectations. If you know that you have a meeting after lunch, and X is not going to be coming up with the best questions ever, then maybe you try to get the meeting before lunch, or you try to make sure with the chair that X doesn't get the key questions.'

The relationship between clerks and MPs can also become a close one: the chair of one committee is known for occasionally hosting parties at their house to which his committee's clerks are invited, and if both sides have been in Parliament for many years, close friendships can easily develop.

Because clerks have to be impartial on everything they do, those links are more likely to be based on personalities than politics. This doesn't mean that clerks won't have their personal opinion, of course, but as discussed in the first chapter, the nicest people often aren't the ones you'd expect. In the words of a senior clerk: 'It's a bit weird here, isn't it? You sometimes get people whose views you find absolutely abhorrent, but who are lovely to deal with, and the opposite – people whose voting record, you know, if I was an MP would probably match 100%, who are complete arseholes. There's just no correlation. We all respond to humans, don't we?'

Still, it is part of their job to help anyone who comes to them, and they have to juggle many different agendas, especially as they climb through the ranks. Contrary to most party political people, clerks can end up working for either House for decades and decades, and once they reach the top, their networks will cut across every layer of British politics.

Sir David Beamish was one of those; he retired in 2017, after joining the Lords in 1974. In over 40 years there, he went from a common garden clerk to Clerk of the Parliaments, the chief clerk in the House of Lords, in 2011.*

'At a senior level at least we have quite a good network, really,' he explains, then listing 'senior staff in a range of categories in both houses', some civil servants, MPs, 'key office holders' (whips, party leaders, special advisers), peers ('the party leaders in the House of Lords and the cross-benchers have a convener'), journalists ('I was more useful to them than them to me, but it was always interesting to talk to them'), and other clerks.

Still, a fundamental difference between, say, Beamish and most of the people listed above is that senior clerks are trusted to keep secrets. While it is a given that civil servants', MPs' and journalists' networks can (and often will be) porous, the world of clerks is one that is closed-off, and that is just the way it is.

As one of them puts it, 'The institution of clerks has existed for the last 700 years or something ridiculous. And

* It frankly seems odd that the House of Lords' chief clerk would be called the Clerk of the Parliaments and the House of Commons' equivalent the Under Clerk of the Parliaments, but that's beside the point.

there's been a long learning process throughout that, and so we've kind of reached the zenith of that for our generation at least, which is this is how you should act, this is the way you should go about it.'

There is one last group that feels worth mentioning, and is similar to the clerks in the sense that while they see and hear a lot, they are considerably more likely to only spread information between themselves: politicians' protection officers. Because they are such a closed circle, it is basically impossible to get them to talk (though if you are part of it and up for a chat, there's always the second edition).

Still, *Private Eye* deputy editor and veteran hack Francis Wheen had one good anecdote on the topic, and it would be a shame to let it go to waste:

'They have a Christmas party every year, for the Special Branch protection people, and they invite along the people they protect. Salman Rushdie went along one year and took his friend Matthew [former Labour politician Lord Evans], who was a publisher and used to run Faber. And Matthew was quite interested in the selection of people you get at this event; there's Enoch Powell and very elderly politicians, forgotten people who were Defence Secretary in the late seventies, Roy Mason and various other forgotten figures of yesteryear, and Tom King, who was a minister under Mrs Thatcher, and I think John Major possibly, from down in the West Country. He was Northern Ireland Secretary, among other things, which was why he had this lifelong protection.

'[Former Conservative cabinet minister] Tom King was talking to Matthew and to one of these Special Branch people, the guy who had been running his Special Branch protection for the previous few years. He was about to retire and Tom King said, "So, you're about to retire. Perhaps it would be interesting to know all the different people that you've protected over the years, what you make of it all." He said, "Well, I know who the worst person was, that was you." Tom had a farm down in the West Country, and he used these police protection people as sort of unpaid farm hands.

'When it was the harvesting season, when the pigs were giving birth, they would all get raked in to do basically farm labouring jobs, and it turned out that he was by far the most unpopular person they'd ever protected. They all compared notes among themselves, and he said, "I have spoken to my colleagues about this, we have taken a vote, and you are definitely the most unpleasant person we've all guarded over the years." This is very revealing, that only the protection officers would have realised quite how awful Tom King was.'

GOD'S WAITING ROOM

Since we're now in the business of asides, let's go back to the House of Lords; we've talked about the place already, but we should probably mention the people too. To be clear, there isn't a tremendous amount to say; a number of peers were interviewed for this book, all of different ages, experiences and parties, but they agreed on one thing: gossip plays an altogether less important role in their corner of Westminster.

According to one young Labour peer, 'It's much less gossipy here because it's much less sociable; it's quite solitary. It doesn't have the camaraderie of the Commons. I think one of the things that defines the Commons is intake groups, the election you came in; those people tend to form quite close friendships, but we don't have that. Obviously the nature of gossip is to be up to date with what's going on, and you wouldn't describe the House of Lords ever as being particularly up to date. Also, gossip really matters in politics because of power, and there's no real power in the Lords; there's also much less ambition in the Lords. People obviously in the Commons are deeply ambitious, want to get on. Most people in the Lords are at the end of their careers. There's nothing to compete for or to be ambitious about. So once you take away that competitive edge, it's almost like, why bother? Life's too short. Why bother being nasty? It's a much nicer place. When someone new comes to the Commons people immediately think they could be a threat, they could get the job I want etc., whereas in the Lords, if someone new arrives, you're thinking, *Oh, that's nice! Someone new to sit with.* There's no "What are you competing for?"'

A former leader of the House of Lords agreed, and had this to say on her chamber: 'For most people who are peers, it's not their main place of occupation or their main focus in life, it's part of something else, so therefore their engagement with issues is much less consistent than if you are an MP. There are some people within the House of Lords for whom the political aspect of it is what they enjoy and what motivates them, but it's not the same for most peers. So therefore that currency that exists in the Commons is not quite the same in the House of Lords.

'As far as the relationship between the Commons and the Lords and their view of the way in which they interact with us, partly because in the Commons, they've got enough on their plate worrying about their own challenges and their own ebb and flow of stuff, they would not pay as much attention as they might, but also we only really became of interest when we were a problem. They're quite happy to ignore us until they have to.'

Finally, one former Lords staffer remarked that peers were altogether less spicy: 'You know, they've all had their affairs and they're all pretty settled now. So affairs and stuff rarely happen, and when they do, it's always a bit like, "Woo! They're a bit of a goer! Who knew they still had it in them?"'

So, in conclusion: not much goes on in the House of Lords that is of relevance to the topic of this book. Still, this lack of relevance is interesting, and says something about the Lords' green-benched counterparts. An argument that keeps cropping up in these quotes is that there is little power in the Lords, so there is less need for whispers and rumours. What we get from this is that there are a lot of whispers and rumours in the Commons *because* there is so much power to be had there, and we will come back to that in a few chapters. In fact, our lordships will be popping up once in a while to remind us that they exist, as they do in the real world, but we can leave them to it for now.

FRIENDS WITH BENEFITS

Where to even start on the relationship between politicians and the media, and the role it plays in Westminster? Maybe this anecdote from an MP will do:

'I went to some drinks in Parliament a few months ago, and between walking in and getting to the bar at the other end, no fewer than four journalists stopped me and said, "So what's all this about, a new centrist party I hear you're involved with?" And I said, "Well, I'm not involved, but what have *you* heard because no one's telling me anything?" And I was so concerned that by the time I'd got to the end of the room four different people had mentioned it, that I thought, *God, is there something about to launch that I haven't heard?* So I spent the rest of the evening going round the room saying, "What have you heard about this new centrist party?"*

Most MPs and hacks have jobs that will be made more efficient if they manage to relentlessly stay in the loop, and personalities that mean that they probably would do so even if they didn't have to. The trick, of course, is that the latter is employed to hold the former to account, but wouldn't be able to do it without fraternising with them.

This is an ethical dilemma faced by most reporters: in order to cover a beat, you need to properly know the people involved, be able to use them as sources and retain a level of access to the industry or area of society. To do all this, you have to develop good professional relationships with those people, as well as a level of mutual trust. However, getting too close can be an issue. If you are close to the people you're meant to scrutinise, it might influence your work, both consciously if, say, you're tempted not to write a hit job on someone you really like, or subconsciously as you can be less likely to think something is a story if you happen to be friends with the person it's about.

Though these are concerns every journalist has to be conscious of, lines tend to be even blurrier for political hacks. For a start, they live in a professional environment that is deeply informal: while going for a number of pints with an MP every other week feels perfectly normal, this would be the exception rather than the rule for other newsroom desks. There is also the bubble effect, of course, which means both that everyone will physically see everyone else all the time, and that over the years, it becomes easier to identify more with your fellow Westminster denizens than with the world at large.

---

* The author would like to thank the MPs who decided to launch a new centrist party mere months after this book was written. No, really, it was brilliant timing. Thanks.

Then there is the small matter of politics being something no one would willingly start reporting on unless they were truly obsessed with it. While one can be a business reporter without being a City fanatic, it would seem near impossible for someone to develop a career as a lobby reporter without living and breathing the stuff. Oh, and politics itself is different to other beats, in that no one could produce frequent scoops without having those close relationships, as most of what happens is firmly behind closed doors. Freedom of Information requests and forensic studies of MPs' expenses can bring in some stories, but most Westminster reporting has to come from people telling you what they saw or heard, and they will not do it to someone they do not know.

Politico's Jack Blanchard has this to say on the topic: 'There's definitely an issue; as a journalist to get the stories you have to get close to the MPs, otherwise they won't tell you, and the public will never know about them. But then there comes a point where this person becomes quite a close contact, might even become a friend; do you want to start writing antagonistic stories about them? There isn't a simple answer as to whether you do or not, but I am certain that there are stories that don't see the light of day because the journalist that knows about them either likes the MP too much, or feels that they need the trust of the MP too much to write them.'

For some, this is certain proof of sinister conspiracies and an elite class more concerned with protecting one another than serving the public. The truth is altogether more mundane: try as hard as you might – and most lobby journalists really do try – there's no escaping from basic human nature.

Still, it can have an unquestionably problematic effect on the nature of political coverage. An example that was mentioned (unprompted) multiple times during interviews for this book was the non-resignation of then-Labour minister Tessa Jowell.

In 2006, Jowell's husband David Mills was investigated for money laundering and alleged fraud in Italy, from the time he worked as a lawyer for the former prime minister of Italy Silvio Berlusconi. Jowell, meanwhile, was Culture Secretary at the time and was investigated on whether she knew about the £344,000 'gift' her husband had received from one of his clients. She was cleared, the couple announced that they had separated, and Jowell kept her job.

Jason Beattie, who is now the head of politics at the *Daily Mirror*, says of the case: 'I think Tessa Jowell's a really interesting example, a politician who should have resigned because of her business affairs, and the reason she survived is she's extraordinarily good with journalists. Journalists loved her. And she always answered their calls, she was always polite. And I always got the feeling that just before we actually dipped the ink in acid we all held back and just went, no, we like Tessa. And it may explain why she survived and Blunkett didn't and Mandelson didn't. Because actually, she was very decent to us.'*

While this might seem shocking, it merely comes back to the point made by the clerk a few pages ago: once you become a part of Westminster, the sort of person you are can matter far more than the nature of your policies or, in this case, your actions. It is, after all, hard to overstate how much of the relationship between MPs and journalists is based on social interactions. Stilted meetings organised to discuss a specific area can and do happen, but most business is conducted in the Portcullis House atrium, restaurants and pubs.

This closeness is also needed for journalists to be effective, even if it can occasionally have adverse effects on reporting.

---

* Another political correspondent who mentioned the story said that the lobby jolly well thought that Mills and Jowell's separation was largely done for show, but did not do anything about that either.

Interestingly, Conservative MP James Cleverly is the person who explains it best:

'Having a personal relationship with journalists is quite important. If all political journalists populated their columns with formal press releases, then arguably you can say, "Well, how are you adding value?" Because we can just get the press release, come to the news desk, we can rewrite it, fact-check it, critique it, print it and save ourselves a whole lot of money without having all these political correspondents and editors.

'I think there is a legitimate argument to say that those journalists are adding value by also being able to inject into those news pieces what the thinking behind it is, what the mood music is like, whether this is playing badly.

'If someone is not saying anything, is that because they haven't seen that policy announcement? They don't care about that policy announcement? That they are positive about it but think it might be unpopular with their constituents? If they're negative about it, do they think it might go down badly with the whips? Even the reason why people aren't talking about something is important, and if they are talking about it, then why they choose this particular topic rather than some other topic.

'Those are the kind of valuable insights you can't get just by a dispassionate see-it-report-it type of relationship. And this business has a lot of spin. There are facts, and then there's the desire to make sure these facts are interpreted in a particular way. And if journalists are hearing something on the grapevine, they'll want to know how credible that source is. And the credibility of source is something you build over time.'

This last part is something every political journalist has experienced: you're quite junior, you get an MP to start talking to you, you take them out for lunch, then suddenly they start sending you morsels of information and you think, this is it! You've made it! But you quickly realise that there is a reason why this MP took the trouble to befriend you, a junior journalist, and it is that senior journalists do not give them the time of the day because their intelligence is so unreliable, because they are known for blabbing away to journalists so no one tells them anything any more.

Back to square one it is, but over time, you will develop better links with better MPs, and learn that the information flow has to go both ways for the relationship to work. This is perhaps one of the oddest discoveries when becoming a political hack. While you probably assumed that your job would mostly involve getting people to gossip to you about things they have seen and heard, there is in fact nearly as much information going the other way.

'It's very transactional,' says Jason Beattie. 'So you will give information in return for information. In government, for example, the ministers get siloed in their departments, so they're actually quite out of touch. They're looking for information, what's going on, because they just don't know, and they find it frustrating.'

The ministers can certainly turn to their spads/PPS/private secretary/circle/et cetera where appropriate, but these people will only ever have their own networks to rely on, and probably won't be able to get the full picture on most things. Journalists, on the other hand (and in theory), have to go out of their way to remain in touch with people from all parties at all levels and if they want to do their job properly and get as many stories as possible.

In practice, some hacks will always be closer to some factions than others and have their favourite sources, but the point still stands: if you work in politics and want to know what the chatter is about, ask the media. There are, however, two issues with this way of working. The first brings yet another ethical dilemma to journalists, as sharing gossip is one thing but becoming part of the political process is another entirely, and the line between the two can be thin.

Let's take the example of the potential new centrist party* again. Say you're the political editor of a television channel and you start hearing rumours that a group of Labour and Conservative MPs are about to leave their respective parties and launch a new movement together. This could well be the scoop of the year, but rumours are what they are, and cannot be printed as such. So, what do you do? Identifying the MPs would be a good start; asking them out for a quick coffee and prodding them on their immediate future would be the obvious second step.

So you're sitting there with Adrian Hullingsworth, a centrist MP openly unhappy with the leadership of the Conservative Party and who might well lose the marginal seat of South Shropshire North West and The Milling at the next election anyway. You tell him what you've heard, and ask him if it's true. Now, there is a chance that he actually is plotting, but let's say he is not – let's even go further and assume that Adrian, having been too busy with the all-party parliamentary group for Tanzanian zebras, had not even been aware that plotting was taking place. You, a journalist, have just informed him of it and whatever he does next, be it warn the leadership in an uncharacteristic show of loyalty (and/or desperate move to finally get on the front bench), or tell his colleagues that there's a new show in town and convince them to join it, will be on you.

Now Adrian's move might not change anything in the long run, but it might also turn into the centrist party actually coming into existence, or the two party leaders realising what's

___
* Seriously. This felt like a good hypothetical example to choose at the time.

happening and removing the whip from the MPs involved. You will then be expected to report on this massive story, knowing that it wouldn't have happened if you hadn't tried to corroborate a piece of gossip days earlier.

This is of course an extreme scenario – and would have been less ethically fraught had it turned out that our friend Hullingsworth really was plotting – but journalists can still play an unwilling role in how something plays out in smaller ways. As that drinks reception at the beginning of the chapter showed, the importance of gossip is not just based on the content of a conversation between two or more people, it can also be about the fact that the conversation happened at all. In fairness, this also happens in other areas of life: if you're told by one colleague that Linda from HR and James from Accounts are having an affair, you might brush it off as a vague rumour. If several people mention to you at lunch that swear to God they've been told that James and Linda are having it off with each other, you will become more inclined to believe it is true. There is no rational reason for it to be the case; after all, maybe all your colleagues heard it from the same person. Still, the fact that it has become the talk of the town will make it feel like it is more likely to be true.

When asked about her view on all this, Labour MP Lisa Nandy said: 'It's all very cosy, and I thought it might be, but even more so than I realised, particularly the relationship between politicians and journalists [...] I definitely think it's a two-way street – well, it's more like a sort of circle which becomes very circular and very self-reinforcing. One of the big problems with the way that this place works and politics generally works is groupthink, and you do often get received wisdom that becomes received wisdom because maybe you heard it from a Tory MP, and you've repeated it to me, and then I repeat it to Jo Swinson when I bump into her, then she repeats it to Chuka [Umunna]. And you can suddenly find that everybody shares a set of beliefs that actually, out there in the country, don't hold true at all. And the extent to which journalists are integrated into that, I think, is quite problematic.'

Nandy is absolutely right, but solving this would be easier said than done: if journalists had to stop chatting away with MPs, there are a lot of stories they could not cover. Their lives would become considerably more tedious as well; if your job were to only involve talking to serious people about serious things, up to 13 hours a day, there wouldn't be much competition to join the lobby. There is also the fact that relationships cannot be built on mutual interest alone, and MPs are fickle things with fragile egos: though deep down they must know that what journalists are after is information, a number of them would rather pretend it is a chummy relationship that just so happens to include the occasional useful bit of gossip.

In order to develop such a chummy relationship, talking like normal people and about things normal people would talk about is a necessity. This normally involves an amusing and slightly awkward wide-ranging discussion, where both parties try to find some mutual interests and/or common ground.

'I've been really barrel-scraping. I once brought up that I was Catholic to a senior politician,' says one reporter. 'That's part of the point of the drinking stuff – to think about it formally. You're trying to create the idea in their heads that you don't just use them, that there's something else there, and that you'd talk to them if they lost their job.'

Jim Pickard from the *Financial Times*, has another way of looking at it: 'If journalists are meeting politicians and they're sitting down for two hours at some white tablecloth restaurant, you can't expect to only talk about the policy of the department that they happen to be working in or shadowing. So part of it's just the kind of normal social easing of conversation which would otherwise be incredibly dull, but it also plays a role just in terms of people's assessment of politics. There's not always any reason or logic to who rises to the top, right? There are loads of talented people on the backbenches and loads of duds on the front benches. So how do we take the view that one person is talented enough to be in the Cabinet? How do we decide that another person isn't?'

Getting to properly know them and talk to them about things beyond their brief is a good start. More broadly, another thing to take into account is that the relationship between the two sides is perhaps more equal than it would seem from the outside. While it is journalists' jobs to chase stories and people, what happens in the political press has a tremendous amount of influence on how politics actually plays out, which creates an interesting dynamic. While junior hacks know not to even try and befriend senior cabinet ministers, for example, junior MPs are just as star-struck by senior journalists.

'There's sort of a pecking order of journalists, as there is a pecking order for MPs,' explains former minister Greg Hands. 'And being seen to be matey with whomever is perceived to be the top of the pecking order, someone like Laura Kuenssberg, for example, or Tim Shipman can be useful.'*

There are also MPs who like to be chased and ones who are more than happy to do the chasing themselves. Politicians, after all, enjoy feeling important and being seen to inform the press as someone who is in the thick of it can please the ego. Only elected in 2017, Paul Masterton remains baffled by 'some MPs who are

---

* This was proved during one of the interviews for this book, when the face of a young Tory MP lit up as Shipman got mentioned in passing, and he wistfully said, 'Oh, I've never met Tim before, but hopefully one day I'll get to talk to him!'

absolute desperate rent-a-quotes, who are actively seeking out journalists to give their two pence to, whether the journalist wants it or not'.

A former Labour special adviser, on the other hand, was always amused by MPs' keenness to interact with hacks: 'Politicians love – absolutely love – seeing their anonymised quotes,' he said. 'I used to get texts and emails saying, "See that anonymous quote today, page four of the *Guardian*? That was me!" They love it, they want to be Oscar Wilde, they love the fact that they're going to have the damning rhetoric.'

Though journalists interact with MPs a lot, they also regularly chat with special advisers, political advisers (the charmingly nicknamed 'PAds' who work for the opposition front bench), civil servants and the occasional clerk and parliamentary aide. The dynamics there are different, because they are less straightforward: MPs are public-facing figures, thus fair game, and it is the job of journalists to write about all the good and bad things they do.

Everyone else in Westminster, however, usually remains unnamed and behind the scenes, and there is a whole spectrum on how much they are expected to interact with the press. While some spads are essentially hired to chat to hacks and nothing else, most clerks and junior civil servants are taught from the cradle onwards to avoid the media like the plague. That doesn't always stop them, of course, but for them, making contact with journalists has to be more of a conscious choice, with potential consequences.

Just like MPs, they can also let their ego get the better of them, which is something journalists have been known to exploit. 'Officials go out with journalists and are absolutely determined to show that they're in the know about things, so they will give the journalist a bit of an inside story because that shows that they're an important person who knows about things,' explains Jill Rutter.

'One of my big things when I was the Treasury press secretary was just trying to find out who'd told what to which journalist. Because when all the papers got on to it that all the Treasury officials were middle-aged or older men, they hired quite a lot of youngish women as their correspondents. And these guys would go out to lunch with them and it'd be, you know, Caroline to Terry, "So tell me what's in the forecast, Terry?" And Terry would just spiel around about what was in the forecast. And I used to say, "Look, just because she's a 20- to 30-something woman with lovely hair, does not mean she's not a competent journalist. So please do not just try and impress these people. Please do not go out for lunch with them if you can't shut up."'

Still, this exchange of confidential information is the bedrock of the relationship; you simply need to figure out what you can and can't babble about.

'No one gives you any training on these things [but] I just had a rule,' says one former Conservative spad. 'You've got to feed the fish. It's about having enough information on people who don't matter to you – you've always got to have some things to pepper your conversation with so you don't have to talk about anything that matters to you, which is where the gossip is keeping the train going. I would know to go in prepped, and always have enough to talk about.'*

This conveniently brings us to something you probably knew was coming. If you take a group of neurotic and ambitious people, lock them all in a bubble 12 hours a day, expect them to go drinking together or at least spend a lot of time around each other, what can you possibly get …?

---

* Said special adviser was widely liked by the lobby and has had a great career since leaving government, so if you are reading this to plan your future political career, this is advice you should keep in mind.

THIS TIME IT'S PERSONAL

An amusing story did the rounds in the papers in April 2015; it involved Ed Miliband, the then Labour leader, and Stephanie Flanders, the former BBC economics editor. It was revealed that shock!, horror!, the pair had been an item at some point in 2004. Coy journalists called it a relationship, though the fact that Flanders phrased it as her and Miliband having 'dated' (her quotation marks) fleetingly probably means that the fling was more carnal than emotional.

This was hardly Watergate, and it did disappear after a few days, but it was quite a telling tale. When they were seeing each other, Miliband was working at the Treasury and Flanders was *Newsnight*'s economics correspondent; though it surely must have been a decent piece of gossip to get at the time, a political adviser and a journalist having a fling would not have raised many an eyebrow. Still, both their careers skyrocketed, and suddenly it became something worth telling the public about. This is revealing in two ways, but we'll keep the second one for later.

First, let's look at the obvious. We've already discussed the closeness of people and blurring of professional and personal boundaries in Westminster at length, but there is something missing: the fact that a lot of people who come into politics will be there for years, if not decades. While some MPs and peers do only join their respective benches in their forties or later, and after having lived a real life in the real world, most denizens of SW1 got into the bubble in their twenties, early thirties at most, and intend to stay there for as long as they can. They are also fundamentally odd people who are more likely than most to be reasonably alienated from the rest of the country. The results are, well, predictable.

'Everyone was at it, because people in politics are mad, and they spend all their time in politics, and they socialise with people in politics. And so if they're going to have sex with anyone it's going to be people in politics,' says one former Labour adviser. 'It's a bit like when people said Brangelina enhanced both of their statuses – in political relationships, your networks become their networks if you're a political couple. I've got a lot of friends who are in political relationships, and I definitely think it adds value to that end.'

Someone who once found themselves in that situation confirmed this view, adding: 'At the point at which I was going out with another special adviser, I knew way more stuff! I knew all the stuff I knew, and all the stuff the other special adviser knew, at least when we had time to talk about it. And so suddenly you become incredibly powerful with the knowledge of what's going on, because you've got the knowledge of two special advisers.'

If you do end up dating someone you have no conflict of interest with and you fall in love and it lasts and you get married and you have children then it's all great; a cottage and 2.4 children has never titillated anyone, so your peers won't be talking behind your back and there won't be any repercussions in either of your jobs.

If you end up breaking up with them, or worse, having an affair, or breaking up with someone and dating someone else in the bubble straight afterwards, there will be trouble ahead. For a start, a lot of people you know will be dying to get every detail of your fling, and pass them along to other people.*

'That happened during the last election quite a lot,' says one political wag. 'People were saying, "Oh, blah blah's sleeping with

* They might even do that if they *think* you are having a fling which, one could argue, means that you might as well have a fling anyway.

blah blah." But if they're all sleeping with all these people they a) wouldn't get any work done and b) they'd probably have an STI by now. So how about we just rein it in a little bit and just gossip about things that we know are true? Because I have no qualms about doing that.' (How charitable.)

In fairness to this staffer and the people like her, it can be genuinely useful to know who is sleeping with whom in order to do your job properly, or at least not step your foot in it. Esther McVey and Philip Davies' relationship is a good example of that, and Yvette Cooper and Ed Balls is another famous one.

'I remember when I was Treasury press secretary [in the mid-90s], Yvette Cooper who was economics correspondent with the *Independent* came to see me and Gus O'Donnell for a briefing on the government preparations for the euro,' says Jill Rutter. And she said, "What do you think Labour thinks of it?" We looked at her and said, "Well, we actually think you're better placed to answer that."'

Ed Balls was, of course, working in the Shadow Treasury team at the time. While this should have been a pretty clear-cut case of blatant conflict of interest, they remained together and eventually both became Labour MPs, which made matters easier.

It is also impossible to overstate just how common these relationships can be. In 2017, Politico tried to compile a list of Westminster's power couples. Among others, they listed: MP Bernard Jenkin and peer Baroness Jenkin, leader of the House of Lords Baroness Evans and special adviser James Wild, the *Guardian*'s Patrick Wintour and *The Times*' Rachel Sylvester, special advisers Lizzie Loudon and Will Tanner, the *Telegraph*'s Peter Dominiczak and special adviser Lottie Dexter, the *Sunday Times*' Tim Shipman and No 10's Charlotte Todman, *The Spectator*'s Isabel Hardman and MP John Woodcock, MP Ben Bradshaw and the BBC's Neal Dalgleish, MP Jo Johnson and the *Guardian*'s Amelia Gentleman and many (many, many) more.

The list was far from exhaustive, as it only mentioned ongoing and public long-term relationships between relatively well-known people; naming everyone who has dated in Westminster in the past ten years would probably take a whole other book altogether.

Oh, and it didn't take affairs and drunken one-night stands into account – which is fair enough – but it does not mean that they do not happen with a degree of frequency. There is the famous story of the special adviser and the journalist shagging against a window in a hotel room at a party conference, oblivious to the fact that a gaggle of press photographers were waiting for politicians to come out of the hotel, and instead killed time by looking up and enjoying the show. To their credit, the story has done the rounds many times but never with names attached to it, though it might be that they did not know who the pair actually were.

There is also the story of the junior minister who started sleeping with a senior No 10 adviser then found themselves appearing on television more than ever before; the prominent Leave campaigner and Remain campaigner who would argue on television then make up at home; the senior party staffer who secretly broke the heart of a political journalist; the two special advisers who stopped talking after breaking up, which meant that communication broke down between their two departments; the several love triangles in No 10; and so on.*

These stories were worth mentioning because they have some colour to them, but for each of them there must be about

---

* All of these people could be named but will not; firstly, because none of those liaisons are ongoing or newsworthy, and secondly, because the author does not wish to make more enemies than she already has.

a dozen dull ones no one really finds out about or cares about; the MPs who sleep with their aides, the spads who sleep with their bosses, the journalists who sleep together, and more.

The obvious question here is: Why do they do it? There are different ways to look at it. The first one is that the people of Westminster are just people, and it's not infrequent for colleagues to have a snog at the Christmas party or a fling that lasts for a few months then trails off. In quite a revealing move regarding the social class of political people, several of this book's interviewees compared the promiscuousness of SW1 to the worlds of medicine and law. According to them, there is just as much if not more shagging and drama happening in hospitals and chambers, it's just that no one outside those industries cares about it. That is a reasonable point, though one might argue that the potential for conflicts of interest when, say, a barrister and a clerk go at it are less of a pressing issue.

The other hypothesis comes from Isabel Hardman's *Why We Get The Wrong Politicians*. In it, she explains: 'In his book *The Winner Effect*, neuroscientist Ian Robertson describes how the brains of people in power change as they experience more of it. Power – and sex – causes a surge in testosterone, he writes, adding that "high testosterone levels further increase the appetite for power and sex, in a politico-erotic vicious circle".'

This chimes in with the assessment of former MP Jerry Hayes, which does somewhat feel like wishful thinking: 'For some reason, some young men and young women find the power of an MP attractive. God knows why. I remember I was having a drink with a very attractive girl years ago, and she said to me, "I really want to fuck John Major." I said, "Really? Why?" And she said, "Well, he's the Prime Minister! Doesn't everyone want to fuck the Prime Minister?" I said, "I don't really know.""*

Before moving on, it should be pointed out that despite what this chapter might have made it sound like, Westminster is not a place where people don't do much besides fucking like rabbits. The majority of people do manage to keep it in their pants, and some are even said to be in stable, long-term, loving relationships. This does not mean that they do not have to wrestle with the complex nature of blurry lines between acceptable friendships and problematic closeness. But let's quickly go back to where we left off at the end of the first part.

BEST OF FRENEMIES

So you're a journalist and you're roughly three months into your life as a political hack. You've got a few sources at your disposal and you're starting to understand the place. Fast forward about a year; you've now got a decent amount of sources, with whom you keep in touch by going for either lunch, coffee or drinks every other week. Some of them are just that; sources you occasionally see, talk about work, maybe sprinkle in the occasional bit of gossip, but nothing more than that. Others have already started slipping into friendship territory; you started out with a light 'Oh, did you hear that…?', it was followed by a 'By the way, has anyone told you…?' and long story short, it is now someone you see socially as well as professionally.

---

* Another hypothesis, not backed by any academic or scientific evidence as far as the author knows, is that a lot of people who work in politics are weird nerds who did not get to sleep around at school and university and are so baffled to find themselves suddenly popular that they are desperately making up for lost time.

Beyond the obvious use of functional information networks in politics, there is a reason why friendships happen when people start gossiping with each other – even academics say so. In the sexily named study 'The co-evolution of gossip and friendship in workplace social networks', Lea Ellwardt, Christian Steglich and Rafael Wittek conclude: 'Gossip favors the creation of friendship relations, rather than vice versa; gossip is often shared between employees who are not friends (yet). [...] A key finding of our study is that talking about absent colleagues can strengthen informal relationships between employees.'

Now, let's fast forward some more; it is a good few years into your career, you're a senior political correspondent at a national newspaper, and that special adviser/parliamentary assistant/newly elected MP has become an influential figure in government or opposition. How do you deal with it?

'Michael White's rule was never in your house and never in theirs,' says one long-term hack. 'But you do make friends with people – there was one MP at my fortieth birthday dinner. But he was somebody I knew before he was an MP, and he's actually now sort of rising somewhat. My bosses know that he is my mate, and I've said, "Look, I'm the wrong person to write an interview or profile of this guy because he's my mate, and I feel that that would be dishonest."'

Tim Shipman puts it slightly differently: 'For a long time, my social life was totally separate from my Westminster life, but if you're doing the job properly that becomes untenable because you spend so much time here. I ended up marrying someone who at the time was working in No 10, and inevitably you develop social friendships that are helpful to your understanding of what's going on and sometimes that means you hear things but most journalists in those situations would be pretty careful about using information that they found in a social situation. [...] I don't think friendships with politicians can ever be the same as friendships with non-politicians because they're grown-ups and they know that one day you might write something unpleasant about them, and I've written a number of unpleasant things about people I get on with very well.'

This feels like a reasonable place at which to draw the line, but the example given is one of the more clear-cut ones. Though journalists certainly like to think that they can remain impartial when it comes to a good scoop, it isn't always that easy. The Tessa Jowell story was a good example of this; another, broader one can be about implicit bias. If you hear or see something that is definitely in the public interest, it is not hard to decide to publish it. If, however, the story is a bit more gossipy, perhaps a bit more trivial, can you be certain that your friendship or lack thereof with an MP would have no influence on what you do with that piece of intelligence?

We will come back to the general question of newsworthiness in a bit, but it seems absolutely fair to point out now that there are many known things in Westminster which never make it out of the place. While some of them remain open secrets because they are impossible to properly stand up, others are simply shared around the bubble, as people would do in an office or a group of friends, which would be fine if the people mentioned weren't running Britain.

As James Cleverly puts it: 'I think where it's sometimes had a reputation as a bit of an unhealthy relationship is where journalists who have been, either drinking with, or drinking near politicians who have said or done something stupid, and a journalist has said, "Actually you know what? I'm not going to report that because I know they didn't really quite mean it like that, or

I suspect they didn't quite mean it like that." And then at some point in the future when those comments hit the public domain, there's been question marks over … well, hang on? If everybody knew that was happening, why did nobody report it? And I think that does undermine our collective credibility both as politicians and journalists.'

Cleverly certainly has a point, but it is still worth thinking about whether all gossip by definition is in the public interest, and if not, where the line is drawn. After all, there have already been complaints for decades (rightly or wrongly) about how the political press tends to focus on tittle-tattle as opposed to hard news. If journalists were to suddenly publish every titbit they hear on the grapevine, the sheer amount of information coming out of Westminster would be overwhelming to the point of becoming useless. Still, this has often gone too far the other way, as the multiple sexual harassment and bullying scandals of 2017 and 2018 have shown.

BAD BEHAVIOUR /
THE WHISPER NETWORK

When a story comes out about a politician being creepy, gropey or worse, the typical reaction from people in Westminster tends to be, 'Finally! I swear everyone's known about this for ages,' or, at a push, 'So apparently everyone knew about this but me?' This is not a hypothetical statement: when, for example, Defence Secretary Michael Fallon left the Cabinet because of the way he had behaved towards some female journalists, bubble dwellers tripped over themselves to emphasise just how unsurprised they were by the allegations. In fact, the consensus quickly became that he resigned because he knew that there was a lot more about to come out about his behaviour, and so did everyone else.

We will probably never know if this really was the case or not, but it is true that a number of rumours about him had been swirling around the Palace for years, most repeated so wildly that no one can really tell where they originally came from. He is not an exception: if someone has groped or cheated their way through Parliament, a lot of people will know about it. Well, at least a lot of young men and women will, depending on the sexual preferences of the creep in question.

'I remember an MP in the private members' ballot who agreed to take on our bill,' recalls one aide, 'and being warned by every woman that heard, "You want to watch out for that ..." and so it proved.'

There are the MPs who are known as 'handsy' (or for their 'wandering hands'), ones who are 'not safe in taxis', ones to avoid one-on-one when drunk, and ones to avoid altogether. There is the MP who caresses the thigh of whoever is young, male and nearby, the one who gets young women so drunk they wake up with no idea whether he did something to them or not, the one who brings young men to his hotel room at a conference, the one who pounces on young women on trips abroad, and so many more.

These MPs will not remain anonymous because of social reasons, but because doing so could ruin the careers of the people they preyed on. It is deeply unfair and infuriating that having been sexually assaulted and outing the culprit can make you less employable than you used to be, but it's still how it works. There is also no certainty that anything would happen to these men, as women have been known to courageously come out with allegations, only for the accused to keep their career anyway.

Not long ago, campaigner Jasvinder Sanghera accused Lord Lester of having groped her and told her that if she slept with him, he would make her a baroness. The privileges and conduct committee decided to suspend him from the House of Lords for four years, but the move was blocked by a vote in the House of Lords. Asked about the case, Sanghera said that she would not recommend going to parliamentary authorities to anyone in a similar situation to hers, as it clearly is not worth it.

Even if you are believed and the person faces some consequences for their actions, chances are that you will still be defined by the event. Nearly a year after she wrote about then cabinet minister Damian Green's inappropriate behaviour towards her, journalist and commentator Kate Maltby was described in a prominent political morning briefing as 'the writer who accused Damian Green [etc.]'. Oh, and she got her very own tabloid character assassination at the time, obviously.

'The problem is that MPs, even the ones with wandering hands, have loads and loads of friends, and unless that person was actually physically assaulting people in a violent way, the attitude that you would have been greeted with, had you reported somebody like that would have been, you know, "He's harmless, and you are destroying an essentially harmless good man by doing that," and your career would suffer,' says one adviser who worked in politics until the mid-2000s.

'You would make enemies by doing that. And if they were an MP that was supportive to the leadership, or a loyal voting fodder MP, you would do yourself an awful lot of damage. People would consider it unhelpful. And when you're trying to forge your path in a world that isn't particularly welcoming to young women anyway, I think that that's why women don't come forward.'

While she is speaking here about her personal experience around 15 years ago, not much has changed since then. There are more women in Parliament who might be more likely to support victims, and more men living in the 21st century, thus inclined to believe women, but the reality is that women coming forward with accusations about powerful men still do so at their own risk.

This is where gossip comes in: if something unpleasant or awful has happened to you and you do not want it to happen to others, how do you warn them without going public? You let the whisper network do its thing. By telling a few people who will then tell a few others, you can hopefully manage to build a reputation that will stick. As well-intentioned as this is, two problems can arise.

The first one is that malevolent souls can always take advantage of these networks to try and destroy one of their opponents, and that due to the nature of the whole thing, something that started small can quickly go big. An example of this can be the left-wing activist who behaved poorly to a woman after a date; while this was worth sharing as a piece of cautionary information, it had turned into a story about him raping a woman at knifepoint in an alleyway in only a few weeks.

The second is that it means people are left unsure what to do if they come across worrying whispers. 'There was a rumour that I must have heard dozens of times about a minister who had allegedly beaten up his wife, put his wife in hospital,' says one former Labour adviser. 'And to this day I have absolutely no idea whether it was true or not, but the possibility that it isn't true is actually quite shocking given that so many of us had heard about it. I never ever saw any evidence that it was true, but it might have been.'

In that case, what do you do? You can investigate it if you're a journalist or ask a journalist to investigate it if you aren't one, but allegations as serious as this are actually tough to stand up. To start with, the name of the person it may or may not have happened to usually gets lost quickly, either to retain their anonymity or because they tend to not be a well-known figure. Even if you do have the name, it is very likely that the person will not want to talk to you, for reasons discussed above. To top it all off, journalists are mostly over-worked and underpaid and there are a tremendous amount of rumours floating around Westminster, so if they decided to thoroughly look into each one of these stories they would never get anything published.

What you're left with, then, is a story about a male MP groping young female aides when drunk, to pick an example so common the author cannot get sued by one MP in partic-ular. What do you do with it? Realistically, it was told to you third hand, so you cannot exactly go over to the person and ask for more details. Still, you've learnt something that sounds true about someone who is presumably senior to you and can be a potential danger to other young women like you. Do you decide to warn them in case it is true? If so, how do you do it?

This is a conundrum which has been made far more complex by the growing importance of social media, both in Westminster and in society. Telling one or two people some-thing is different from sending it to, say, a WhatsApp group of 20 or so female staffers. Still, it is the way people tend to communicate nowadays (much, much more on that later) and it cannot be avoided.

Just take the spreadsheet that was splashed across the front page of the *Sun* in 2017, detailing a number of unsavoury allegations against a number of Conservative MPs. It is still unclear who originally made it, though reliable fingers pointed towards female staffers, and it listed a number of Conservative MPs, along with a list of bad things they had allegedly done. 'Bad things' in this context is quite wide; indeed, reading the spreadsheet without knowing what to expect might cause a degree of whiplash.

MPs earned their place on the document by allegedly (in order); getting a former researcher pregnant and making her have an abortion, having 'odd sexual penchants' (no further details), being 'perpetually intoxicated and very inappropriate with women', being urinated on by three men, having used sex workers, not being safe in taxis and having had a relationship (not an affair) with another single MP.

The line between fun gossip, concerning behaviour and deeply serious allegations here is so blurry it might as well not exist; what is said to have been a list written up to keep young women in Westminster safe simply turned into a repository for salacious stories. On top of that, several of the stories were completely untrue, some of them had a kernel of truth to them and others were true, but about someone else (awkward).

An interesting detail here was the speed with which the spreadsheet travelled across Westminster; its existence was made public one evening by the *Sun*, though it was not published in full, and within under 48 hours, discussions were started in the bubble with the assumption that every present party had knowledge of all the names.

Crucially, though, the existence (and publication) of the spreadsheet entirely derailed coverage of the #MeToo scandal in Westminster. After a few weeks of focusing on trying to out MPs whose behaviour in Westminster had been unacceptable, the spotlight shifted on to guesswork about who might have created the spreadsheet, which of the lesser (and funnier) allegations were true, and so on. Not for the first time, the political bubble got distracted by lurid gossip and looked away from structural issues.

Parliament eventually launched an inquiry about it all, though at the time of writing, it is impossible to tell if it will change anything or not. The inquiry will not only focus on sexual harassment, but on the culture of bullying, which largely works in similar ways.

There are people in positions of power who abuse it and people in junior positions who are too afraid of what might happen if they speak out publicly; you could call a number of MPs a 'bully' to the well-informed of Westminster and they would not bat an eyelid; it is up to informal networks of people to try and curtail the power of these bullies.

Like creeps, MPs who bully people tend to get away with it, because those who could stop it are rarely aware of it, as the people they bully – parliamentary aides, clerks, junior civil servants – mostly move in different worlds. As a journalist, there is nothing quite as disappointing as getting to know an MP, finding them thoroughly decent and respecting their work, only to later find out that they treat their staff appallingly.

Things are slowly starting to change, but until recently, some very senior MPs managed to leave Parliament with a clear record even after decades of being thoroughly horrid to anyone more junior than them. While some aides managed to not ever work for them as they had been warned off, it is always easy enough for bullies to hire people who are new to politics, so have no way of accessing those informal networks of knowledge.

When it comes to clerks, things are slightly different: as a relatively closed-off part of the Palace, they have a level of inherited knowledge, from the more senior clerks to the newer ones. 'When I first joined we had a lot of discreet advice about dealing with members, but as a block; no individuals were named,' says one clerk. 'But then as you progress through the organisation and you begin to work with more and more MPs there are sometimes situations where people say, you know, be aware of that person, or keep this in mind while working with someone.'

This is not an overreaction; according to a *Newsnight* investigation broadcast in 2018, clerks, as anonymous faces away from the spotlight, can and have been routinely treated appallingly by MPs. Knowing what you're in for if you're about to go to work for a certain select committee can be vital.*

There is, in theory, one place those mistreated staffers and clerks could go to if they wanted something done internally; a few groups of people who deal with bad behaviour and sometimes trade on it. They rely more on gossip than perhaps any other parts of Westminster, and are absolute treasure troves of clandestine information – or are they?

Turn down the lights, fire up the smoke machine, and do not under any circumstances get too close to them – here come the whips.

WHIP IT GOOD

The whips of a political party have a fairly straightforward job: they are the MPs who are tasked with making their colleagues vote the way their party leader wants them to vote, as well as

---

* Rumour has it that the clerks have a list of MPs known for mistreating their kind; it is a true credit to their attachment to secrecy that it has somehow yet to leak.

generally making sure that parties retain a vague appearance of unity. How they go about it is an entirely different matter. Let's take a look at some of the things that have been written about them.

First, there is the story about Gyles Brandreth's first encounter with the whips as a new MP, which he recounted in his book *Breaking the Code*. 'All the government whips sat on the platform in a line and we new boys (plus the four new girls) sat, cowed, below at school desks – yes, school desks with ridges for your pencil and square holes for inkwells,' he explains. The whips gave a short speech to the new crop of parliamentarians, explaining just what was expected of them, including that 'when there is a three-line whip you will be here to vote – unless you can produce a doctor's certificate (pause) showing you are dead.'

Then there is former Conservative MP Jerry Hayes, who recalled in his memoirs very nearly missing an important vote because he was away from the Palace, but being saved at the last minute by then Labour leader Neil Kinnock, who made him jump in his car. 'So there I was in the back of the leader of the opposition's car with the man himself, sweeping through Carriage Gates,' he wrote. 'Heaven knows what people would have thought. Neil read my mind. "Leave it to me, boyo. Look those whip bastards in the eye and tell them you were with me. I'll ring the Chief and explain." To his credit, he did. And my genitalia remained intact. For the time being.'

Finally, there is an anecdote in *Who Goes Home?* by Robert Rogers, about Labour MP Maurice Edelman, who once told Chief Whip Michael Cocks that he might miss a crucial vote as he was hosting a dinner party at his home. 'Cocks exploded. "Snapey, go round to Edelman," he instructed his whip colleague

Peter Snape, "and tell that bastard that if he isn't in the lobby tonight he's dead. Dead!" Snape went round to Edelman's house and delivered the message, then as he drove home, heard on the radio that Edelman had just passed away. In a somewhat nervous state he got home, parked his car and was unlocking his front door when he heard the telephone in the hall. He rushed in. It was the Chief Whip. There was a two-word conversation: "Snapey? Overkill.'"*

Are you spotting a pattern yet? If you're currently picturing a group of shadowy figures inhabiting dark corridors and wearing thick black velvet capes (vampire fangs optional), that is because it's the image whips want to project. They are not to be messed with, and any MP who is foolhardy enough not to take them seriously and vote however they see fit might one day wake up with a horse's head on their pillow. This is all a slight exaggeration, of course, but whips' offices do have a flair for the theatrical; there is a bona fide whip in their office, which looks like it would hurt.

There are a bunch of reasons why they are seen that way. The first one is that in order to do their jobs properly, they must retain an impressive (and up-to-date) cache of personal information about MPs. The story goes that whips usually have a 'Black Book', or 'Dirt Book', kept under lock and key in the Chief Whip's office. It is unclear whether this is true, used to be true or is just something they like people to think is true, but in any case, their meticulous collecting of potentially damaging information isn't as sinister as it seems.

---

* As a bonus, it is said that in the Cameron years, one MP who was planning to rebel on an important vote was summoned to the whips' office. Once there, he was given an envelope. He opened it, looked at its contents and fainted.

After all, their role is to ensure that a party wins the votes it puts through Parliament, and they would be useless at it if they didn't know what really motivated MPs. Politics is about people, and politicians won't always vote for or against something purely based on the merit of the policy.

If whips want to know how people are going to vote, they need to see them as just that – anything else will make them ineffectual. In fact, Jerry Hayes has a good example of this, from his days in the Commons:

'Years and years ago when Thatcher was under threat, Mike Brunson, who used to be ITN political editor, and I sat down a whole load of seriously bright people, psephologists, to work out how the voting was going to go. They kept saying, "Oh well, he's a wet, he's a dry, he's right-wing, he's left-wing," and we said, "No, no. It's not going to work like that." And what Mike and I did is make up this list of: Who's she pissed off? Who's she overlooked? Who hasn't she promoted? And we got it within three votes. That's the reality: people get upset and vote against leaders for a whole range of reasons, and it's not always about policy.'

So, how do the whips gather all that information? They're everywhere in the Palace. The whole team is usually around 15 MPs for the party of government, and slightly fewer for the opposition. The Chief has better things to do than hang around and eavesdrop, but most of the others are expected to loiter and make sure that their MPs aren't misbehaving. In her book *How to be a Government Whip*, Helen Jones explains: 'The tea room, the dining room and the bar are as much your places of work as the office is. Listen to what people tell you and try to assist them if they have a genuine grievance.

[…] All this hanging about is not time wasted but, rather, time invested.'*

Each one will have their stalking grounds and will keep an eye on their colleagues then report back to the Chief if they see anything particularly untoward. Some of them will even get a bit creative, as one former MP explains, 'Toilet whips are really interesting. One thing that guys do is that, when they're having a piss, they talk. Always my advice to new MPs is to push every cubicle door to make sure that there's no one there listening, because there used to be a whip designated to sit for about an hour, listening to the gossip.'

To be fair to them, one of the reasons they aim to physically be around the House as often as possible is also so they can act as makeshift counsellors. If an MP has some personal problems and, for example, life is not rosy at home back up in the constituency, they might need to go and spend more time there, and would need to explain to the whips why it isn't simple laziness on their part. Because everyone knows what it does, the whips' office can also be used by MPs who have got information they want to pass on, either because it will make a person they loathe look bad, a person they like look good, or because they think being useful to the whips might be a good move for them.

'I worked for four years in the government whips' office and it either willingly or unwillingly becomes a lot of the collecting point of parliamentary gossip,' says Conservative MP Greg Hands. 'Sometimes willingly, as the whips' office wants to find out what's going on, particularly if it's something that might bring the party or the MP into difficulties. Then sometimes unwillingly because

---

* As a matter of fact, several interviews for this book were conducted in the House of Commons and became noticeably less interesting once the MP realised that their whip had just sat at a table behind them.

sometimes people think that the role of the government whips' office is to investigate parliamentary misbehaviour, for want of a better term. So suddenly you get somebody bursting into the whips' office and saying, "I've just seen MP X do something with MP Y! What are you guys going to do about it?" And your initial reaction is, "Well, we're a bit busy at the moment."'

Beyond walking around and talking to their colleagues, whips must also develop good networks to try and gather information from all possible sources. One of them can be their staff; aides and MPs will often have a chatty relationship, but it takes on a new level when the MP in question is in the whips' office. Being seen in a good light by the whips can do wonders for someone, so ambitious staffers will be keen to be the foot soldiers of their bosses. The Chief Whip of the party in power also has a special adviser, which means that they can easily report back on what happens in that corner of Westminster.

On top of all this, whips must rely on their personal contacts and their wit to collect other pieces of intelligence. In her book, Jones gives a nice example of this: 'One group of disaffected ministers in the last government met for regular suppers outside Parliament. Stupidly, they had this regular engagement put into their ministerial diaries and the whips always knew when this was happening through a contact with one of their diary secretaries. [...] Being nice to people on the lower rungs of the Whitehall ladder pays off in the long term, often in unexpected ways.'

The obvious follow-up question to this is: why do whips need all that information? Getting a broad sense of who your MPs are is one thing, but being aware of their peccadilloes, affairs and drinking habits is another. The received wisdom is that whips then use those secrets to twist the arm of their colleagues if they are threatening not to vote with the whip on something. The problem with this, however, is that the only way to do this would be to tell the MP in question that the night they once had on the terrace and would rather forget about might be making its way to the front page of a newspaper.

There are definitely stories about this happening. One amusing one is about a woman standing to be a Labour MP in the election of 1997. In her first meeting with the whips, she and other new parliamentarians were told that they needed to fess up to anything embarrassing and potentially newsworthy they might have done in their past; if the whips knew about it, they could help you with it and make sure it didn't get out.

As everyone went on to tell them about their sexual and/or drunken shame, the woman realised to her horror that she had never done anything bad enough to be a story, and had mostly had what some might call a dull life. The social awkwardness took over, as she didn't want the whips to think that she was hiding something from them, so she made something up; in her university years, she went through a shameful period of being a white witch. The whips thanked her and moved on.

Years passed and the woman enjoyed her time as a reasonably docile Labour MP, until one day when she found herself profoundly disagreeing with a bill her party had put forward. Word reached the whips that she was planning to vote against the government and she was brought in for a meeting. 'So, we've heard that you're planning to rebel on this,' they told her. 'It would be a shame if your years as a white witch were to become a story, wouldn't it?' She then had to gladly tell the whips that she'd unwittingly outsmarted them and went on to merrily vote the way she wanted to.

It is a lovely anecdote but there is one issue with it: all of those who tell it are unable to name the MP or even the bill.

It is possible that the first few people who spread it around thought it was too good not to share but did not want to betray their friend, but it does seem likely that it was made up. To use a certain newsroom saying: if it sounds too good to be true, it probably is.

Talking to whips and former whips directly was a more underwhelming experience. When asked about whether they would ever leak a story about an MP on their own side, they all denied it, even when speaking off the record. It might well be that it is not in their interest to admit to such things, but there is also another possibility, which is that they know that regardless of how unhelpful an MP is being, making their own party look bad in the press is probably never worth it.

This is what one of them had to say on the topic: 'I was in the whips' office for a number of years, and the role of gossip in the more benign sense is your job as a whip is to understand what's going on in people's lives, and whether that shapes their ability to do their job, so you've got to know a lot about people's personal lives, but in the context of trying to help and understand where possible if someone has a family crisis or ill health.

'In my time in the whips' office I don't remember there ever being a conscious plan to leak something about an MP. The whips' office have got a serious job going running the business of the government in Parliament and keeping over 300 MPs onside and reasonably happy. Doing extra-curricular stuff is probably beyond what 17 people have really got the resources to do,' was Greg Hands' straightforward answer.

So, again: why do whips collect all that information? The right answer might simply be that they want others to think that they have all that information. Academic Phil Cowley has done a lot of work on whips, which apparently pleased them:

'Years ago, a senior Labour MP said, "The whips love your work because it makes it sound like they're really important. That they're doing lots of stuff." And he said they're not really; they're never as omnipotent as they claim to be. It's in their interest to claim to be omnipotent. And it's somewhat even in the interest of MPs to claim they're omnipotent, because then why did this rebellion fail? Well, you know, the whips got to us. As opposed to there just weren't enough of us, and we're shit. We were undone by the whips' office and their terribly Machiavellian ways, as opposed to not being able to organise a piss-up in a brewery.'

Being able to look like you know absolutely everything clearly has its advantages, and you don't even need to actually know everything to do so. As Cowley pointed out too, it is convenient for everyone that whips are portrayed in such a dramatic fashion. In order for this to work, they must be as opaque as possible about what they actually do know; revealing secrets to others might also accidentally reveal that you do not know the whole story.*

Another reason why the whips might want to appear threatening is that there is actually not much they can do to keep the party in shape. They can say no when an MP wants to miss a day in Parliament for whatever reason, and they are in charge of office allocation, so can give MPs a shoebox in a mouldy corner of the estate if needed. At a push, they can also help you climb the ministerial ladder if that is what you wish and you have been a good boy or girl, but they can equally use that as a carrot without doing much to show for it afterwards. That's it.

---

* They can, however, keep their party leader informed of what their MPs are actually up to, even if it displeases them. One of the few wryly funny lines to come out of Westminster's #MeToo scandal was the revelation that whenever Chief Whip Gavin Williamson would have his weekly mischief-makers meeting with Theresa May, she would respond with a weary, 'Why can't they just do their jobs?'

The realisation that they are not in fact some all-powerful 'Eye of Sauron' outfit always comes to MPs at some point. Gyles Brandreth entertainingly explains this in his memoir; he was about to vote against the government on an amendment, and this is what happened next:

'You know this will be noticed in the whips' office, so think carefully before you do this.'

'That's not a threat, is it?'

'No, but it does mean, well, we'll look at you differently in the future.'

'How?'

'Well, it means …'

Pause.

'…We will look at you in a funny way in future!'

'And that's the moment it dawned on me. I was once told the whips are all-powerful. Yet the reality is the whips are only as powerful as you choose to make them.'

Isn't this a far cry from the US remake of *House of Cards*? In a nutshell, whips are only a danger to those who are not of many talents but are dying to become ministers so must do so via patronage; those who really do behave appallingly, and who shouldn't be in the Commons in the first place, and that's it.

In Cowley's words: 'The brighter ones have already worked out, there's a line about the Spanish Inquisition, which is that most confessions came as soon as they saw the torture instruments. You didn't actually need to deploy any of those things, because you'd look at it and go, "Oh, fair enough! Fair enough!" Insofar as the whips have weapons, which they don't really have weapons, you know what they are.'

It is all even more sedate in the House of Lords. One former adviser to the whips there explains: 'Very rarely would people do the thumbscrews: "Here's a bit of information I know about you." That is properly rare. The main thing is actually knowing why someone's going about something, or knowing the inter-relationships of people, thus knowing the networks. So you would make sure your whips' office is comprised of all the different cliques. And you just needed one person in it, they didn't need to be the leader; you needed to have the gossipy ladies, the smokers, the old hereditaries and all that. Having someone from each different gang meant that you were getting the information and the flow and who was feeling restless, because they were all connecting with each other externally as well, and catching up and seeing how they felt.'

The other thing worth considering is that (most) MPs aren't stupid: they know which personal problems to go to the whips with and which ones to hide from them. If what they need is advice from someone who isn't just one of their friends, at least one party has a place to go: the 1922 Committee.

The group was created in 1923 (don't ask) and represents the backbenches of the Conservative Party. Funnily enough, its chairman at the time of writing is Sir Graham Brady, a former whip. 'Most whips would think that they have a kind of a function in looking out for the welfare of colleagues as well as just making sure they vote the right way, but there is also an inherent conflict,' he explains. 'The whips' office is there explicitly to serve the government, or the shadow administration if we're in opposition. So if the interests of a colleague and the interests of the government are in conflict, or potentially in conflict, then the whips are always going to go with the government. So one could imagine a situation where a colleague has done or said something silly, something embarrassing … Do they go to the whips and risk the possibility that they'll say, "Come on, we can't stand behind you on this, or the government might look bad if we defended your conduct?" People might then come to me or one of the other members of the executive and just ask for a bit of advice and support.'

Because the 1922 Committee is meant as a group representing Conservative backbenchers, its aims are somewhat different than that of the whips; until 2010, ministers weren't even allowed to take part in meetings. Its executive is also formed of a number of MPs meant to represent the breadth of the party, both in terms of cliques and ideologies, and who are elected by their peers. The group of 18 parliamentarians meet once a week and interestingly, what they discuss genuinely is secret.

'The great advantage of it is that if you have a full plenary meeting of the whole of the parliamentary party, then it's very likely that somebody's going to brief somebody on what's been said, either formally or inadvertently,' says one MP who is part of the committee. 'The 22 exec very, very seldom leaks, so normally we can have a proper discussion, mirroring most strands of opinion in the party, and it doesn't get out.'

It could well be that what they discuss simply is too dull to leak, but the fact that we cannot know for sure remains tantalising, and also proof that MPs can occasionally keep their mouths shut if needed, which is frankly a bit of a surprise.*

This conveniently brings us to our next part. We know that politicians can behave badly and we know that there are not many ways in which their peers or juniors can seek action; we know that most people in Westminster enjoy a good gossip and we know that a lot of them talk to journalists.

This leaves one question: what gets published and why?

---

* A few stories did come out of the '22 exec when Theresa May was on the verge of leaving, but every rule needs an exception.

HOW IS THIS NEWS?

Asking political journalists what the difference is between gossip and news is an amusing thing to do, provided that you enjoy people searching for words and not quite finishing their confused sentences. That is because answering this means answering a number of questions, namely about what news is, what gossip is, and whether gossip stops being gossip when it becomes news.

In *Gossip: The Untrivial Pursuit*, Joseph Epstein takes a stab at (sort of) answering it. 'A character in *Scoop*, Evelyn Waugh's novel about journalism, says of the news that it is what people want to read, except once it's printed it's no longer news and hence not of much interest,' he writes. 'The less widespread, the less well known, the news, the more potent, by virtue of its exclusivity, and the more interesting it is. Serious gossip ought to be an intimate affair, one person telling another, two or three others at most, something hitherto unknown about an absent person. Too widely broadcast, gossip, like the news once printed, no longer holds much interest.'

In 'Spin Doctors And Political News Management', academic Thomas Quinn tackles the topic from the other side and concludes: 'Political news is problematical. Unlike entertainment stories, which consumers enjoy for their own sake, the utility consumers derive from political coverage is not immediately evident. The minute probability of casting the decisive vote in an election implies that most individuals remain "rationally ignorant" about politics, relying on free information to determine their votes.' Nevertheless, Quinn identifies three reasons why consumers might demand political news: duty, diversion and drama. 'Some people feel a duty to become informed about politics. Others are fascinated by political strategy and facts in the way sports fans are interested in statistics. A third group views politics as a form of entertainment and enjoys the drama and human-interest elements.'

Coming back to Westminster, one of the people who did manage to deftly answer the impossible question was Jim Waterson of the *Guardian*: 'Gossip is anything of interest that's not been published yet, or it's the particularly interesting stuff which is too salacious but you could never get over the line. I mean, who's shagging who – there's no real public interest most of the time, but my God, we all want to know. And then there's the sweet spot where gossip can be transferred into actual news by virtue of evidence.'

Another good one came from the editor of a newspaper, who argued: 'There's no hard and fast rule where you draw the line. If gossip or personality stories are revealing of the character of a politician then they definitely cross the line and they get into print. So when, to give you a random example, it emerged that Samantha Cameron and Mrs Gove (columnist Sarah Vine) had had a stand-up row in public; that was gossip, but it was definitely a political story in the sense that it reflected the division between David Cameron and Michael Gove, and the fact that there was a rift between them that had not healed and is unlikely to heal even though I think they're godparents to one another's children. So that's definitely gossip, but it's definitely a story.'

Let's try to work on a closer definition. For something to be gossip, it needs to be a piece of information not known to many people. There can be exceptions, but in most cases, every new person who hears a piece of information decreases its value. It must be interesting, by which we mean unusual, titillating, or out of character for someone. It is not formal; even if, say, a government press release wasn't read by many, what it says is not gossip. There is also an element of transgression; if the piece of information is something the person it's about definitely wants spread, it also loses its value. Entertainment value is key here: boring gossip is no gossip at all. It can be first hand but doesn't need to be; as a result, something does not need to be definitely true and provable to be a piece of gossip. If anything, unprovable alleged facts often make the best piece of gossip, which is why sex is frequently talked about in such terms; unless you were in the room, it is impossible, really, for someone to definitively say that something happened (or didn't).

Most of these things apply to news stories. A news story must also not be about something that is widely known; if it is, it is no longer news – the clue is in the name. There must also be an element of unusualness for something to turn into news; if something ordinary happens, it is not worth writing about. Similarly, a news story will only really be good if it can show an element of transgression; of something that shouldn't have happened, or went wrong. So far, so similar, but there are also things that set the two apart.

For a start, a news story must be true; it must have reliable sources, as much proof as possible, and the journalist must be able to defend the story and say with absolute certainty that the chain of events described, for example, was the correct one. The second and perhaps biggest difference is that a news story must be in the public interest. If you have all of the above but cannot show why a story needed to be published, you will not go very far. Some journalists have certainly been known to stretch the definition of 'public interest', but they still always know that they may need to make a case for it at some point.

So, to sum up: a piece of gossip can also be a news story if it is definitely (and provably) true, and if publishing it is in the public interest. On the other hand, a news story can be gossip if it is fun on top of being relevant, and has not been published anywhere else before. This leaves journalists an awful lot of space to play with. Still, there are only so many hours in a day and journalists at an organisation, so they cannot just run absolutely everything that stands up and tickles their fancy, but what to pick?

The Samantha Cameron and Sarah Vine example is a very good one, because many stories are built like it. Neither Samantha nor Sarah are politicians, so them no longer getting along should not be a political story. The fact that they had a public row is also not in itself that interesting: friends have rows all the time, and they are, again, not in any positions of power. The reason it is a worthwhile piece of information, and news, is because they are married to two prominent politicians who were very close friends prior to the referendum (as well as being Cabinet colleagues) and they no longer talk. That their political disagreement was so severe that it broke off the friendship of their wives is fundamentally interesting, because it tells us about how personally they both took their position on Brexit. Most politicians, especially those in the same party, and who already were friends before joining Parliament, can go through policy disagreements without losing their closeness. This story shows that Brexit was not only worryingly divisive in the country, but within the highest ranks of the Conservative Party as well.

This is a template that is often used, and with good reason: a story may sound like pointless gossip to hard-nosed cynics, but if it reveals something about the wider character of someone in a position of power, then it is worth telling your readers. Oh, and on that note, if we're talking about what is and isn't a story, it is probably time to bring in the readers. As a matter of fact, what is and isn't a story is decided by everything discussed above but also, and perhaps more importantly, by what will be a story for an organisation's readers (or watchers, or listeners).

The reason why no journalist managed to come up with a definitive, industry-wide answer to the question 'what is news and what is gossip?' is that there is none, and the line will move widely from one outlet to the other.

'It depends entirely on whom you work for,' says Jack Blanchard. 'Where I work now, at [morning briefing on Westminster news] Playbook, what constitutes something I would put in the email is very different to what it would have been in the *Mirror*, and would be very different to somewhere else. The line between gossip and a story changes depending on where you work and what the values are and the editorial judgements are of that place. So at the *Mirror*, I used to hear so much gossip, but only 5% would be of interest to the *Daily Mirror* readers. I used to think all the time, God, that's a good story, but I would never be able to do anything with it, because people who buy the *Daily Mirror* don't care about that Westminster tittle-tattle, 95% of the time. A lot of that stuff just never saw the light of day, because it wasn't my job to report it then. They wanted real stories, that really mattered to people in the real world.

'Now it's completely changed. I work for Playbook and I write for people who live in the bubble and who are the bubble, and I write for those people and about those people. And so suddenly little titbits of gossip about people become something that I am interested in to publish, because I know that my readers are interested in, because it is them. It's their mates, it's their contacts, it's their colleagues and so on. And I think you'll find that at every publication. Something that I would consider gossip at the *Mirror* might be a story at *The Times* as well. And so it's not a fixed thing, it depends on what your publication is interested in, and crucially, who you're writing for.'

Another thing that can wildly vary from publication to publication is the extent to which a story must be demonstrably true before getting published. While snobs might argue that the dividing line is between broadsheets and tabloids, it isn't necessarily the case: the former have been known for publishing the occasional shoddy single-source story and the latter are mostly as scrupulous as their more highbrow neighbours. This is because the level of certainty required before a story definitely becomes one doesn't just vary from outlet to outlet, but editor to editor.

'There's no one paper that's particularly bad for it,' says one political reporter. 'It changes depending on who the news editors are at that time, and who the journalists are at that time, and how someone will say, "I need this triple-sourced before we're even going to look at it!" and others will say, "That's a good line. And it's a good headline, let's run it and see what happens." And that changes with different papers with different staff.'

This 'let's see what happens' is a great journalistic tradition, and one that has more merit than it initially seems. Sometimes, newspapers will publish items that really do look like pointless bits of gossip no one normal could possibly care about. These can be published for a few reasons, none of them related to their readers outside the bubble. The first can be nicknamed the 'let's shake that tree and see what falls down' approach; you have heard rumours about someone doing something, you're pretty sure it's true but you cannot fully stand it up with your own sources, so you publish a smaller, broadly related story about that individual, then sit and wait. If you're lucky, better sources with actual knowledge of the bad thing the person has done will notice the article, realise that it is an area you're keen to explore, then get in touch. If it doesn't work after the first try, no problem: just keep dripping these small stories out until you can stand up the main one.

The second one, 'we know, you know we know, we know you know we know', works fairly similarly, but has a different start-off point. The set-up usually consists of one important person who has done something questionable, one paper who has become aware of it, and some reason why the story cannot be published. It is usually a reason involving lawyers, or the fact that though both parties know the story to be true, it is impossible to gather just quite enough evidence to publish it. In this case, what a newspaper might do is dig around for minor negative stories about the person, and publish them at a frequent rate. Drip, drip, drip. It is not as good as publishing the real thing, but petty enough to do the trick.

There is one other genre of gossipy, not-strictly-important story that can get published, and it is stories that journalists think are funny. There's not a lot more to them: editors just find them entertaining and want to share the joy with their readers. In order to do it, they occasionally have to stretch the definition of 'public interest' to an amusing extent.

A great example of the genre came from the *Sun* in 2016. The headline was 'Sleazy MP Simon Danczuk, 49, had spanking sessions and sex with woman, 22, on desk in his office'. It's all pretty self-explanatory but to recap: Danczuk, then a single man, had consensual sex with an adult woman. That's it. That's the story. Still, the woman talked to the *Sun* so provided a lot of colour, including an unforgettable text exchange where she asked the MP what would happen to Eurovision should the UK leave the EU, to which he replied, 'I'm going to fuck you so hard you won't even think about the fucking Eurovision!!!'

That is undoubtedly fun, but it's unclear why the press should have a duty to report this to the public – or is it? The first line of the *Sun* scoop read: 'MP Simon Danczuk had sex with a 22-year-old woman on a desk in his taxpayer-funded constituency office.' Boom! There we have it – the sex happened in his office, which is paid for by taxpayers, so it is in the public interest to write about it.

Asked about that specific story, someone who worked at the *Sun* at the time said, 'I would admit that's flimsy. There's obviously a certain degree to which all tabloid journalists are massive hypocrites, because they lead lives of varying degrees of debauchery and then act as moral arbiters when politicians get up to similar things.'

Another industry favourite is the 'blackmail risk' angle. Have you discovered that an MP has unusual sexual proclivities? He could be blackmailed if someone were to find out! Does someone in Westminster have peculiar hobbies that could be frowned on even if they are entirely legal? At risk of blackmail! And so on. A stellar example of this came from the *Mirror* in 2018, with their big exclusive that then housing minister Dominic Raab's diary secretary was a sugar baby.*

One might argue that the story falls more into the 'I heard the weirdest and funniest thing, you'll never believe it' pub chat end of the spectrum, but the *Mirror* clearly wanted to publish something about it, which is why the opening lines of the story were:

'A top Tory minister's aide raised security fears after she was caught selling sex to sugar daddies online. Housing chief Dominic Raab's diary secretary joked how she'd "love to get

---

* For the more sheltered among us, a 'sugar baby' is a young woman seeking usually older and wealthier men to develop a dating relationship with, in exchange for a weekly or monthly stipend.

sacked" for romping on her boss's desk as she made herself a blackmail target.'

And there you have it! The story here definitely is not that someone in politics secretly sells sex in the evenings, it is that a minister is at risk of being surveilled by Russian spies (yes, really).

Finally, one last justification hacks may jump to if they want to publish pure, unadulterated gossip with a stern face is hypocrisy. It usually is a reasonable point: it is not just about shameless journalists exposing politicians for doing things they also do every other weekend, but about questioning the public image politicians build of themselves in order to get elected.

Stephen Crabb offers a solid cautionary tale. The married Conservative MP ran for the leadership of his party in 2016 then pulled out, and *The Times* revealed shortly afterwards that he had sent salacious texts to a young woman. There was no suggestion that the pair had got physical, and the most explicit text involved Crabb telling the woman he wanted to kiss her 'everywhere'.

(What is it with MPs and corny sexts?)

Had it been another MP, this probably would not have been a story; it is vaguely interesting, sure, but the details aren't as fun as the Danczuk and the Raab exposés, and the allegations are overall pretty small compared to what other MPs get up to. The crucial difference here is that Stephen Crabb is a devoutly Christian politician with links to an anti-LGBT advocacy group, and who voted for tighter abortion laws and against same-sex marriage. His political platform is that of a proud family man standing for family values. In this context, the people who voted for him and the electorate at large do deserve to know what he gets up to in private.

This was also the thinking behind the story on 'Lord Coke', a peer caught taking drugs with sex workers while wearing an orange bra, a bedazzled leather jacket and not much else. 'I remember when we first looked at what they had on him,' says one former *Sun* journalist. 'Obviously you had the coke and the prostitutes, which is straight up illegal, so that makes it news. Doing anything illegal while sitting in elected office, you're fair game. But the thing that I really liked in that story is that literally about two weeks earlier he'd written a blog on the *Huffington Post* about how members of the House of Lords need to really watch how they behave, and their standards of behaviour, because he was the Lords Commissioner for Standards.

'And it's that hypocrisy – I mean, you see it all the time, the sort of family values people are the ones who are having loads of affairs and all that. That makes it fair game, because you can't try and get elected on one thing, and then basically mislead the people. It's quite high and mighty for the *Sun*, but I think to a certain extent that is what turns it from being just idle gossip into news.'

So there you have it: gossip is gossip, unless you can (seriously or mischievously) explain why it deserves to be spread beyond Westminster, in which case it is news. There is, however, a flip side to this: because there are so many rumours and so much tittle-tattle in politics, stories that are news can sometimes be treated as gossip, thus taken less seriously by the bubble.

There is one huge and obvious example of this in recent memory: the expenses scandal. The story was mentioned unprompted by several MPs in interviews for this book, and discussed in an unexpected tone.

According to Labour MP Chris Bryant, 'the whole expenses scandal was a great big old chunk of gossip dressed up as moral outrage'; for Conservative MP Greg Hands, 'For the first time, MPs' expenses proved that there was money to be made out of parliamentary gossip; the *Telegraph* sales skyrocketed as a result of their investment in the unredacted version of the MPs' expenses. Suddenly you could actually prove there was public interest in what MPs had spent on cushions for their second home.'

Tin-eared stuff, right? Journalists uncovered endemic cheating of the system and preposterous spending of taxpayers' money, and MPs' response to it is flippant at best. One of the editors who worked on the story at the *Telegraph* was unsurprisingly not impressed when those quotes were put to them, and had this to say in response:

'In their world it was gossip, in the sense that everybody knew that everybody else was at it, but when it became apparent to the wider population that this was going on in a very substantial way, it became the most important political story from the crash up to, but not including, Brexit. It has transformed people's impressions of their elected representatives, and I don't see that being reversed any time soon. A good number of people went to jail, and there are quite a substantial number of other MPs who lost their seats, or were forced to stand down and got peerages, given knighthoods, etc., so it cleared house quite substantially.

'And it went on for quite a few years, because it wasn't like we just found evidence of malpractice and put it into the public domain: some of the MPs had been really clever in covering their tracks, and it took months of detective work by a very big *Telegraph* team; it took months of detective work to actually work out, a mortgage here, another claim there, when were they living there? And while MPs might have thought, well, everybody knew everybody else was at it, the fact that it became front-page news for three months would tell you otherwise. That it wasn't gossip or tittle-tattle, but actually a terrible public wrong which needed exposing.'

Given what the two sides put forward there, this feels like it should be a clear-cut case; one of an elite group of people who are so used to treating everything as varying degrees of gossip that they are unable to understand that sometimes, bad behaviour is not simply to be frowned upon, but actually so wrong that exposing it is in the public interest. That being said, it is not the case, or at least not quite: they both have a point.

The *Telegraph* journalist is absolutely right to say that the story shook the very foundations of Westminster, and that it was stellar reporting. Greg Hands is also right in saying that what it proved is at least partly that people wanted to know about MPs' tastes in cushions. Though an incredible number of MPs were exposed for misusing Parliament's expenses system, some of them had to entirely leave their political careers behind over it, while others are still happily sitting on the green benches at the time of writing. This wasn't all to do with the degrees of severity of the infractions; some of the former had made what could be seen as honest mistakes, while a few of the latter were some of the worst offenders.

The differences between them are, if anything, barely related to the gravity of their actions; it all depended on whether their story came out on a busy news day or a quiet one, whether they used their expensable cash in a dull way or on something silly or preposterous, and on whether the leadership and party machines thought highly of them or not.

According to Jim Pickard from the *Financial Times*, 'It is a very good illustration of how some people got completely tarred and feathered for relatively minor things, and some people who did quite major things aren't really remembered at all. Everyone remembers the duck house, and there is a case to be made that the duck house guy just submitted a load of expenses, hoping they would sort out which ones were legitimate or not, and yet he is remembered as the epitome of greed. If you were unlucky enough to be on the front page that day, you're more likely to be remembered.

'David Laws, I'm not taking any moral view on whether what he did was good or bad, but he had a secret boyfriend whom he was renting from and vice versa. What happened was that didn't come out in the original mass bump of expenses, it came out a few months later, and therefore it was the *Telegraph* splash and everyone noticed it. If it had come out amid 500 other stories, Laws would be less well remembered for it. He was particularly unlucky.'

Seen that way, the expenses scandal suddenly does look a bit more like gossip: it was scandalous not just because of the gravity of the actions, but because of the colour and the details; if you stuck in people's memory, you were more likely to not get away with it. The sword didn't fall in a just way, and what was more likely to get people talking inherently became a more serious allegation.

This is because the public, much like people in the bubble, really enjoys gossip and cares about little else. If you live in SW1, it can be hard to wrap your head around just how little normal people follow politics; days and weeks can pass with a scandal a minute and the majority of people will barely notice any of it.

'Lots of people did very boring things about flipping their houses round and claiming this one as first residence and the other one as first residence. Those aren't the ones who got in trouble – the ones who really got in trouble were like the one with the duck house, because he got it and it's noticeable and it's human and people noticed it,' says Anthony Wells, YouGov's director of political polling.

'One other example is Tim Yeo, who got in trouble because he claimed a laptop. Of course a laptop is a perfectly reasonable thing to claim, but it was a pink laptop. And yeah, it's the human things that people notice because no one cares at all about the details of policy. You're not going to stop and read that, but you are going to read the things about the human things that people have done. No one's going to listen to most speeches; no one's going to really understand or care about their reports.'

This is a good reminder that what newspapers publish shouldn't just be in the public interest, they also need to be of interest to the public. It's all well and good for the snobbish among us to complain about the media not taking its political reporting seriously enough, but if journalists were to suddenly only start writing about policy papers, there soon wouldn't be newspapers for them to write for.

'Often the stuff that does reach people is the most salacious stuff, whether it's true or not. That does have cut-through,' says Joe Twyman of political polling firm Deltapoll. 'And so when Brooks Newmark shows his penis to [reporter pretending to be a young female activist to catch creepy MPs] Alex Wickham, people might not remember that it's Brooks Newmark unless they happen to be in his constituency, but they all remember that MP that showed that journalist his penis. And the mundane stuff about, oh, so-and-so attended this many votes, or voted for that … Nobody cares. And the idea that there's people out there carefully downloading each party's manifesto, reading it from cover to cover, and they come into an informed decision about which party they're going to vote for based on that doesn't happen.'

This might sound like a cynical exaggeration but it really isn't; if you are reading this book, you are in the small minority of people who actually do care about politics – and it really is small.

Obama and Cameron's election strategist has always been fond of saying that people only spend four minutes a week thinking about politics. While it is hard to tell if this is a real stat or one that is too good to be true, there are concrete examples we can look at.

Here is what the editor of a national newspaper had to say on this: 'Ed Miliband announced a raft of interesting policies and had the Tories on the back foot – you know, we're going to crack down on the power companies, they were ripping people off, all this quite good populist stuff. When readers were questioned about him, almost the only thing that they could remember about Ed Miliband was that he nicked his brother's job. So those people are not paying attention all the time. In fact, they're not paying attention most of the time.

'Michael Ashcroft is fond of telling a story about some research he did, and it was in the wake of the party conference season, people were polled about "What was the big political event over the past month?" Was it David Cameron's speech? Was it Ed Miliband's speech? Was it this resignation, was it that drama, etc. And an overwhelming majority of people, north of 80%, could remember not one. Nothing. Hours of coverage, acres of space, conference diaries and over 80% of people remembered not a single political event.'

This certainly feels depressing and is something that has been written about again and again, with no one offering a workable solution. In the meantime, journalists must work with the readers they have, not the ones they want, and that means injecting drama and fun personal details into their reporting. It is also worth saying that the personal can absolutely be as relevant as the political; a story does not need to be about a dry parliamentary report to be serious, and the most insightful reporting can often be the one focusing on softer, more personal aspects of Westminster.

'I've always found the personal battles and intrigues as interesting as the policy stuff,' says *Sunday Times* political editor Tim Shipman. 'There's a tendency for some journalists to be rather pompous about being serious journalists who write about policy unlike those of us who write a bunch of posh gossip, but the posh gossip is what has determined where this country's gone over the last two years, rather than the grand sweep of policies. If you look at what's happened with Brexit over the past few years, the decisions of individual people and their relationships with each other are absolutely pivotal. We are living in an age when, yes, there is this broad thrust towards populism and big shifts appear to be going on in the world, but within 500 yards of this building, the interactions of individuals have been hugely important in shaping the path this country has taken over the last couple of years.'

SPINNING AROUND

It would be unfair to start this part without paying tribute to 'The Spin Doctor', a washing machine repairman based in London who managed to get to the third result on Google for 'spin doctor'. Politics could do with more brains like his.

Putting this aside, what reliable sources tell us is that the term 'spin doctor' first started being used in its political sense in the mid-80s, though it only really became a commonly used phrase in the UK during the New Labour years. Alastair Campbell was one, Peter Mandelson was one, and what they did was referred to as 'the dark arts'; like magicians but with disappearing and reappearing stories, as opposed to rabbits. Their job nominally involved talking to journalists and making sure that the Labour Party's aims, actions and policies were always portrayed in the best possible light in the media. This is easier said than done, and in order to work efficiently, they did, said and threatened things that eventually left them with a tarnished reputation, and the questionable legacy of having created a toxic political culture.

They also arrived at a time when technology was being revolutionised, which made the shift drastic in more ways than one. Here is a former civil servant explaining what life was like in the John Major years:

'During the '90s, when I worked in a press office at No 10, well, first of all, we didn't have email and mobile phones were still quite uncommon. And in No 10, the press office was a purely civil service regime. There was a political office, but that was a political office with about four people, and they didn't really do any media press operations. And I think that our press office amounted to, including administrative staff, ten people? It was tiny, and we were all gifted amateurs. Our approach to media and comms back then was much less about how to seek to control the media in that way, it was very much about how we relayed information. So it was quite unsophisticated, really.

'Of course we had lots of scandals back then, but I don't know that we got much by way of pre-warning of them. Back then, there wasn't quite the iron grip from No 10 on the rest of Whitehall in the way there is now – this started during Blair's time. So people were effectively controlling their own information when they published it.

'Really, the most effect you can have is on controlling what news comes out on what dates. And No 10 have now a much stronger grip on that than there ever was in the past. We used to have a Whitehall weekly meeting of press officers, and it was not unusual for half of the Whitehall press officers not to turn up. Now I think about it, it's amazing we got anything done.'

Doesn't this sound quaint? Spinners are now everywhere, and when the government is vaguely functioning, the tentacles of No 10 retain a firm grip on nearly everything that comes out of Whitehall. There are lines to take, ministers sent out to trot out those lines, headline-making news is prepared weeks if not months in advance, and fires are extinguished long before the first spark makes itself known. At their best, they can keep the media docile enough not to be too much of a pain in the arse to their bosses; at their worst, they will throw opponents (internal and external) to the wolves with no chance of survival.

How do they do it? They chat, mostly. To journalists, to each other, to people in their party – they spend a lot of their time talking.

This is how Sean Kemp, a Liberal Democrat comms spad in the coalition years, describes it: 'There were two parts of my job, one was just the internal political stuff; the other part, which is the engaging with journalists bit, that's entirely gossip. Basically, the simple foundation of what you tell people, how you do good media management, is you've got to do a lobby round. So you've got to do it every day, me or James McGrory. Usually James. You'd go and do a lobby round. Even if you've got nothing to pitch, nothing to say, you'd go into every single newspaper office and you'd have a chat for, like, ten or 15 minutes. And some of that is useful, some of that, you're just having chats. All of your press and conduct operations, it's not press releases. There's a bit of that but it's almost entirely basically based upon having loads and loads of chats. It's all you do, spend your time talking and joking with journalists.'

The obvious questions here are: what do they talk about, and why do they talk that much? The former is fairly straightforward – both sides are politically obsessive, professionally and most of the time personally, so it cannot be hard for them to come up

with endless topics, from the dry end of future policy announce-
ments to the more fun titbits about the rumour(s) of the day.

As mentioned earlier as well, good spinners will always try
to have some crumbs up their sleeve, a fun bit of information or
gossip to catch the attention of the news hounds and keep them
off their backs. Bored hacks still have deadlines and might well
start digging in inconvenient places if there is nothing obvious
for them to write about. They are, in that respect, a bit like cats:
if you don't give them toys to play with, they might end up
jumping on the counter and throwing cups on the ground. Well,
they might do that anyway but are slightly less likely to if you
provide them with enough distractions.

This also works when they are very busy, which is pretty
much all the time, as Thomas Quinn explains in 'Spin Doctors
And Political News Management': 'The predominance of deadlines ensures that time is a journalist's most important resource,
and hence time is money for the firms that pay their salaries.
Everything a journalist does incurs an opportunity cost because
of the constant onset of deadlines.'

You are also acting as a conduit between journalists and your
party; the people you work for will often be too busy to always be
in the loop, so being able to give them frequent updates on what
is happening is a vital part of your job.

'There's very little currency more valuable to journalists, if
any, than gossip,' says former Lib Dem spinner James McGrory.
'If your bosses want to know the finer points of some policy
paper, they can ask someone cleverer than me. If journalists want
to know the ins and outs of how a policy's going to work on
pension reform, they can speak to someone cleverer than me. The
only reason I have any currency with either of those two people
is because I can tell them what the other side is thinking. So I

can tell my bosses and the politicians, well, this is what the lobby are saying, and that works both ways. If you think of yourself as a business, you only have two clients. Your bosses, the politicians and senior advisers who are more senior to you, and journalists.'

Another reason why they might want to pop by and have a biscuit and a chat is that it is useful to spot potential problems arising and nip them in the bud. Like ministers with the low grumbling of backbenchers slowly getting louder, comms advisers must keep an eye on what issues journalists are starting to get preoccupied by, which minister they've begun gossiping about, and so on. Big stories rarely come out of nowhere, and whenever possible, it is better to be prepared than get surprised by an embarrassing scoop for your party that you did not see coming.

This cannot always happen, especially as people in your party will rarely come to you if they've done something wrong, as they assume (or at least hope) that it will quietly go away. If it does not, a conversation needs to happen between the spad and the person who's messed up, which according to one of the latter usually goes a bit like this: 'You always have this chat, which is, "Did you say it?" And generally the response is, "Oh, I can't remember." "Is it possible that someone recorded you saying it?" Then you suddenly find that the answer is, "Er ... I don't know." So we can't actively deny it, can we? And that sort of drags out for a while.'

There are ways to go around this. During his time in government, McGrory came up with a technique to anticipate potential stories and, perhaps more importantly, find out where the bodies are buried before they catch the attention of journalists. It goes like this:

'Sometimes you pick up stuff about your own MPs, a bit of information in your life that has the potential to be damaging. And my tactic was that I'd ring them up and I'd say, "This has been put to me by …" And then you just name the publication of the person who told you about it in the pub, and who is not writing it as a story, because they can't stand it up or they're not interested or the desk don't give a shit or whatever. And they would think, *Fuck, they're writing a story about this.* And so I'd be saying, "Look, they don't seem to have very much. I think I can kill this."

'The person at the other end of the line would then almost always give you, if not a properly true version of events, then at the very least their side of the story, and then you say to them, "Listen, I'm pretty sure they've not got enough to run this. I'll speak to them." Of course you don't have to actually speak to them because they've not put anything to you, it's a rumour you heard in the pub last night or two nights ago. So you just end up ringing them back and saying, "It's all sorted, they're not going to run this. If you hear a whisper about any of this again, let me know, and I'll do the same at my end. But I think we're safe for now." Then you've inherited more gossip.'*

Of course, the whole job of a spinner isn't solely to prevent stories from being printed, they also have to try and get positive stories about their parties published, even if said stories aren't always riveting. That can be done by chatting to journalists and explaining that a seemingly dull-as-dishwater policy announcement would actually be life-changing for their readers, though it is easier said than done. The real talent here is to find the one eye-catching angle the hacks were probably too busy to spot themselves.

There isn't always one, sadly, and spinners have been known to try and work it the other way around, by getting a sense of what journalists might want to write about, and building stories around them. It is hardly the best way to go about policy-making,

---

* Apologies to current and future spinners reading this: your secret is out.

but that doesn't mean it doesn't happen. Ben Wright offers a good example of this in *Order, Order!*, with an anecdote that starts off with a piss-up involving reporters and New Labour spad Charlie Whelan, and ends with the Queen crying by the seaside.

'The royal yacht supposedly ruled the waves, but 1997 was a time of cool Britannia, not old Britannia, and the Treasury was keen to cut the £11 million a year cost of keeping the Queen's boat afloat. So when the Chancellor's spin doctor was drinking with a couple of Sunday newspaper journalists soon after the general election, they agreed to splash on *Britannia* being scrapped. "We dreamed up the idea that doing in the royal yacht would be a good idea, a good story. That was dreamed up over a few drinks at the bar," claims Whelan. Like many Sunday newspaper stories it was a kite-flyer, a way of gauging reaction to a policy plan before formally announcing it. And within months the Queen was standing on the dock at Portsmouth naval base watching her beloved ship being decommissioned.'

This story worked because it was a colourful one, and one that meant far more than the Treasury trying to find a way to save a bit of money. It said something about the Britain New Labour wanted to create and the choices they were making to get there; the decommissioning of the royal yacht was symbolic of a country slowly getting ready for the 21st century, and that is why it piqued the interest of those Sunday reporters.

Good advisers know this, obviously – journalists are not stupid, so won't find something interesting purely because you tell them that it is interesting, but there are ways of making dry news sound more exciting, so more likely to get published.

'The truth that journalists won't really want to hear is that a lot of the time the little rumour-type stories that appear in the papers, we're giving them to journalists intentionally with a view to them printing them. Which I think sometimes some people get and some people don't get,' says one former Labour adviser who worked for Ed Miliband.

'When you're briefing a journalist and you want a bit of the story to carry, you want it to go somewhere, you're adding a bit of colour and stuff about it. I remember the time they wanted a phone hacking story to carry about Ed negotiating with the other parties about Leveson. And they just briefed out this part of it that it was all done over pizza, which made it the most interesting part of the story. It became the pizza briefing. And that was totally intentional. That was Stewart Wood, and he didn't accidentally go into the pizza thing. He thought, how can I make this sound interesting?'

This absolutely worked: a glance at the papers from that day in March 2013 shows that the *Guardian*, the *Mirror*, the *Independent* and the *Telegraph*, among others, published a story about the late-night negotiations that mentioned pizza. While hardly a fascinating detail, it unquestionably brought a bit more life to a story that would otherwise have been about the future of press regulation and nothing else.

This wasn't a piece of gossip per se, as it was willingly shared around by people who had taken part in the pizza eating, and because eating pizza hardly is scandalous, but it remains a part of the same ecosystem. Information will travel faster if it is interesting and has a human element to it; organic rumours may be more fun, but manufactured colour is the next best thing.

That being said, all the rules spelled out above only really work if confronted with political journalists whose job is solely to report (relatively) impartially on what goes on in Westminster. For some other hacks, this approach is far too strait-laced and nowhere near entertaining enough. Lobby journalists can certainly create some chaos if they so wish, but it isn't really part of their job description. That role falls to another group: the mischief-makers.

LOOKING FOR TROUBLE

We've established that newspapers will publish gossip if it is indicative of someone's character or, more generally, has a wider meaning. What we haven't discussed so far is political gossip that is just that: an amusing or scandalous piece of information that serves no real purpose besides its entertainment value. It has a fine (if controversial) history in newspapers, and can all be tracked down to one man: James Gordon Bennett Sr.

According to Joel Wiener's *The Americanization of the British Press*, Bennett launched the *New York Herald* in 1835 at a time when political reporters were told to provide 'no insight into what transpired behind the scenes at the national capital', and turned everything on its head. The *Herald* dedicated many of its inches to 'gossip and chat', to the delight of its readers, and jealous competitors soon launched their own 'Washington Letters', as they were called at the time.

The format was a 'frothy concoction of social and political information', and crossed the Atlantic not long afterwards. One of the people responsible for the move was T.P. O'Connor, without whom Westminster may not have been infected by Washington's tittle-tattle obsession. The political journalist was also an MP and wrote in 1889 that 'everything that can be talked about can also be written about [...] No one's life is now private; the private dinner party, the intimate conversation, all are told.'

Though O'Connor's beliefs on privacy rights (or the lack thereof) helped create the environment we have today, circumstances also had their part to play. Until 1881, provincial newspaper journalists weren't allowed to sit in the Press Gallery in Parliament with their London counterparts, meaning that they couldn't do any first-hand reporting of speeches and debates in the House of Commons. Resourceful as always, the hacks decided to instead specialise in 'descriptive' political gossip, while the London papers wrote about parliamentary proceedings. The journalists were eventually allowed to join the Gallery, but the revolution had already started.

It eventually blossomed in 1916 with the creation of the 'Londoner's Diary', a collection of three daily columns written 'by gentlemen for gentlemen' in the *Evening Standard* and described as a 'daily causerie of the world, the flesh and the city'. The rest of the trade sharply followed once more, and according to H Simonis' *The Street of Ink*, it was remarked only a year later that 'the best tribute to the "Londoner's Diary" is the fact that it now has its counterpart in the other penny evening papers in London'. Intended as a repository for gossip, the diaries quickly became one of the most powerful parts of newspapers: more than frivolous entertainment, whispers and rumours could also be used to enhance one's status in society, as well as building people up and knocking them back down.

Press baron and then-owner of the paper Lord Beaverbrook was even said to have regarded the 'Londoner' as 'his own personal fiefdom, an armoury from which he could seize a weapon at will; bludgeon, cudgel and rapier lay at his disposal as he sought to fight his way to ever-greater heights of power and influence in between-the-wars Britain'. Ethical or not, this succeeded: Beaverbrook ended up becoming close to everyone who mattered in Britain at the time, hosting Lloyd George, Winston Churchill and the Duke and Duchess of Windsor at his stately home in Surrey. He also acquired a remarkable reputation for ruthlessness when it came to socialising, inspiring Evelyn Waugh to once quip, 'Of course I believe in the devil. How else could I account for Lord Beaverbrook?'

Some time has passed, and the media and societal landscapes have changed, but diary columns have largely remained the same, which is to say that they can still contain a multitude of widely different stories. As a matter of fact, a diary item can be many things: it might hint at a politician and a journalist having an affair, or keep a tally of the amount of drinks receptions a certain minister with ambitions has been spotted at recently. It can also be drier, and take a close look at some obscure policy announcement, or it can be entirely inconsequential and point to a funny joke in a backbencher's speech.

A diary story is, essentially, something that must get a reaction from the reader. While red tops have the 'Fuck me, Doris!' factor – which is what they imagined a man will say to his wife when reading a particularly jaw-dropping scoop – gossip must make some waves, and get people talking. *Diary at 50*, a book cataloguing some of the best *Times* diary items, offers two good examples of how wide the spectrum can be.

In the first, the humble diary column gets in trouble with the authorities and, with the help of someone on the inside, manages to see the (surprisingly serious) story through to its logical end. 'In 1985, a leak inquiry was launched in the Commons to find who had passed PHS [as the diary column was called then] the details of the draft of a select committee report on the Special Branch,' current editor Patrick Kidd explained. 'Twenty MPs gave evidence that it was not them. [...] The committee of privileges met late at night to discuss the issue. A report of that session was also leaked to PHS.'

The second is considerably lighter but still drew the ire of the highest levels of government, when in 2000 the Belgian

Ambassador told a diarist that his prime minister had offered Tony Blair the use of his Tuscan villa for a holiday.

'Downing Street went ballistic, Alastair Campbell, Blair's spin doctor, demanded that the reporter be sacked (he's now on the *Mail on Sunday*) and the ambassador retracted his story,' the book explains. Man of the people Tony could not, after all, be seen as the type to abscond to the glamorous houses of foreign dignitaries while in office.

While these are as representative as it gets, a diary story can still be many other things. According to Joy Lo Dico, who used to edit the 'Londoner', 'The perfect diary story has got a mixture of something serious and inane in it, or absurd.' During her time at the helm of the column, she would tell her reporters to try and get a serious quote from someone silly, or a silly quote from someone serious; funny anecdotes about the pets of cabinet ministers and stern opinions about Brexit from TV celebrities are always a good bet.

Another classic is to take a story currently being covered everywhere else in a straight-faced fashion, and find one angle that suits the column. A brilliant one of those came during the Damian Green scandal, shortly after journalist Kate Maltby accused the Secretary of State of putting his hand on her thigh as she was asking him for career advice. Green's camp had shot back by saying that she must have been confused and felt the tablecloth on her leg, as he had not touched her. A classic he-said, she-said, surely? Well, not for the 'Londoner':

'The diary story did not engage specifically in the kind of politics around the allegation. Like a lawyer, we went along one particular detail, which is we found out where the bar was, and we were thinking, hang on a second. Damian Green replied, saying it could have been a tablecloth. And lo and behold, my staff knew the bar, and we checked some photos, we found somebody who'd been there very recently, and we called up the bar as well. They said no, no tablecloths – once in a blue moon we have a set dinner, but it certainly wasn't that. And at that point you can undermine Damian Green for just tiny little inaccuracies, which may be human failing, but may also be him trying to pull out a defence via his friends.'

This detail didn't change the course of history, but it was still something worth exploring that other journalists had either not thought of or considered too minor a clarification. A Westminster-wide scandal was taking place and the diary played its part. In some ways, this is diary columns at their best, though their primary role remains to be entertaining, which gives them some leeway to occasionally publish something utterly absurd and pointless that happened to cross their desk.

Take the toenails. 'There was a story about the former Director-General of the BBC John Birt,' explains one journalist who used to work at the 'Londoner'. 'And it was a story that he kept his toenail cuttings in a little box. That was the story. And you know, it was so memorable, that out of all the great Birtean strategic differences he was making at the BBC, they still couldn't get out of their minds what kind of person would keep their toenail cuttings in a box.'

The story does not say what Birt himself made of that story, especially as there is no way for someone to tangibly prove that they do not keep their toenail clippings in a little box. Still, working at the diary means having to deal with peculiar characters who do not take kindly to being mischievously written about. Sarah Sands, a former editor of the 'Londoner', recalls one of her most memorable encounters: 'I remember Bron Waugh, the son of Evelyn Waugh, writing to me to say that he was putting a curse on me after a story he had not liked. He said it gave him no pleasure, but something terrible would befall me.'

Waugh clearly needed to brush up on his occult skills, as Sands then went on to become – among others – the editor of the *Evening Standard* and the *Today* programme after that. She is far from the only senior media figure to have started out by slumming it on a diary desk.

The full list would take too long to type, but to use wide-ranging examples, former *Guardian* editor Alan Rusbridger and former *Telegraph* editor Charles Moore were also once diarists before eventually taking the helm of their paper. There's a number of reasons for this. One is that to be a good diarist, you really have to be a good journalist: while reporters will often get their quotes from, say, a press conference or an arranged interview, diarists have to roam the streets and parties of London in search of stories. Most of their job happens at night, at parties and drinks receptions attended by the great and the good. You might think that it'd be easier to get a line out of someone when they're three champagne flutes down, and you'd be partially correct, but it is harder than it seems to turn up to a party, sometimes uninvited, often not knowing anyone there, and mingle without seeming out of place, and trying to make important people stop talking to their friends to talk to you, a journalist, instead.

If you really were uninvited, chances are that your editor won't take 'Sorry, just couldn't get in' as an excuse – if the desk wants you there, you'll have to find a way in. This can involve pretending to be someone else, climbing over a balcony, finding the fire exit, hiding in a cloakroom, walking around with an empty glass in your bag to be able to pretend that you'd just gone for a cigarette – just get it done. Once inside, you need to know exactly who is there and who is worth talking to, so a large portion of your brain must be effectively turned into one big Rolodex of London society. You must then go and talk to them, either interrupting their conversation or hovering like a shark until they find themselves alone, and convince them to have a pleasant chat with you. Convention differs from one diary to the other, but good etiquette usually means introducing yourself as a diarist, which basically means fessing up to trying to fish a funny or awkward quote out of your new-found friend.

Given that it is a chat and not an interview, you need to charm them and have a proper conversation with them, as opposed to going up to them with a number of questions and asking them. That being said, you do need to have some questions prepared so you can slide them in: you are, after all, out looking for stories. Some diarists can make it up as they go along, but it is not always easy. A solid cautionary tale comes from a former *Times* diarist, who was having so much fun at a bash that he got merrily drunk and forgot to ask anyone anything. The party was about to end and he panicked, as the only person of interest left was famously dry Philip Hammond, then Defence Secretary. The diarist went up to him, introduced himself and shook his hand, then realised to his horror that he'd forgotten to think of a question to ask. Stumped, he followed his hello with, 'So, Minister, what's your favourite gun?' Philip Hammond asked him to leave and the diarist went home empty-handed.

Even if well prepared, this can be an issue: not everyone is interesting, ready to give out a quote freely to some random journalist, or both. A diary column must be entertaining above all, and the page won't fill itself, so diarists will often need to use their inventiveness to liven up the stories.

After all, no one reads that part of the paper while expecting everything to be absolutely true; a good diary column is one that makes good occasional use of poetic licence. While each paper will have a slightly different version of that motto, the broad rule of the desk is: 'Every column you write has got to have a couple of stories that are definitely true, a couple of stories that are probably true but you don't want to check out too much in case there's deniability, and then one or two that are probably not true but you're not going to get sued over it.'

A stellar example of the latter is also (oddly) linked to Philip Hammond, this time during his tenure as Chancellor. One diarist went to talk to someone who worked for him and struggled to find out anything amusing; the only thing they said was that Hammond was known to enjoy a KitKat. Boring? Sure. Has easy room for improvement? Definitely. The diarist remembered that new pound coins had recently come out and proved to be a pain in the arse as they didn't work in most vending machines.

How to link those two facts together? Easy: in the next day's paper, a fun short story could be found about Philip Hammond's obsessive love of KitKats, which led to sightings of desperate aides trying to rub their new pound coins to trick the vending machines into taking them, all so they could keep the Chancellor happy with a constant supply of his favourite chocolate bars.

Is everything in this story strictly speaking correct? No. Would anyone be terribly upset by the aspects of this story that aren't strictly speaking correct? Almost certainly not. Do the not strictly speaking correct details turn what would have otherwise been dull into a fun little story? Absolutely.

Another angle of this is that the diaries have been around for a long time, and mischief is expected of them; they might sometimes be wrong, but there is rarely a point in trying to publicly complain about how they've covered you. By all means talk to the diary editor if you feel you were unfairly done in, but any retribution more serious than that will probably be more amusing to them than useful to you.

'One of my favourite stories was the time I was sued by the Royal Navy over a story involving the Prime Minister, hardcore pornography and submariners,' says Patrick Kidd of *The Times* diary.

'There was an LGBT reception at Downing Street. My diarist Grant had been there, and he'd spoken to two submariners who'd chatted to May, and not unreasonably, he asked them what they talked about. And they said, "Well, she asked what could you do to make life better on board the ship." And they said, "Well, you can improve the Wi-Fi because it's very slow." And then the other one said, "I told her it's hard to download porn, you have to bring it in on hard disk." And I put that in the column and we got a stinking complaint. In fact, I met someone in the Royal Navy press office recently who told me how much hoo-ha it caused. It's terrible when people take diary stories too seriously. But the top brass were very upset, went to the submariners, and they said we never said that. So then we got the legal letter, and of course we got the sniffy, "I understand you didn't run it past Downing Street." I am not going to ring up and ask, did the Prime Minister discuss porn with submariners?

'But also, Grant had got it from them directly, and I trust Grant, you know? And he said that actually he'd heard it, that they'd said it to someone else who then reported it circularly. So what I suspect happened is that they'd wished they'd said that to the Prime Minister. And we've all done that, we've all embellished something, not thinking perhaps it would end up in *The Times*. And yeah, legal letters were exchanged, and in the end there were two other things, that the Navy said that they don't watch pornography, and they also said, and this is where I was wrong, I admitted that one of them was rather refreshed. We always use clichés like that, because I assumed you wouldn't discuss porn with the Prime Minister unless you'd had a drink. And they said these submariners don't drink. And so I said to our lawyer, well, let's print a correction saying that they are members of the Royal Navy who don't watch porn, they don't drink, but I think that's more damaging to their reputation! But nonetheless we backed out of it and just said their version. I did argue with our lawyer that we should go to court though, because I quite like the idea of the Prime Minister taking the stand to discuss porn.'

This is pure, unadulterated mischief, but then that's what the diaries are for, and why they can get away with it: a well-informed and fun diary column is good for the readers, and even better for its editor. The press might have drastically changed since the days of Beaverbrook, but diaries remain one of the most useful parts of the paper for the one at the helm. After all, a journalist's job is to know what's going on, and where better to turn for information than your society columnists? Just like the PPS of a minister must keep them in the loop while they are holed up in their Whitehall department, a good diarist will go out on the town and soak up all the rumours so they can regurgitate them to the people at the top who are too busy for endless cocktail receptions.

An editor who feels they are up-to-date with all the latest gossip is a happy one, and one likely to be kind to the person providing them with all that tittle-tattle, hence the rapid career progression of most sharp diarists. According to Patrick Kidd, 'The editor wants political gossip, and actually even stuff that he doesn't want in the column, he wants political gossip for his own gratification. Editors want to know what's going on and they also want to feel that they know what other people don't know is going on, so it's the best way to titillate them. I didn't have a formal interview for the diary, but when I was asked to go and chat to John in early 2013 about taking on the diary, the first thing I did was to drop in a couple of titbits I knew about MPs and stuff, because I knew people liked to hear it.'

This comes back to the importance of the personal; even someone who religiously reads every newspaper and magazine and watches or listens to every political programme will never be able to fully grasp what goes on, and why it happens. The more personal information you can gather on Westminster, the better you will be at understanding its intricacies and unexpected movements. And while the news pages of a paper are generally aimed at your garden variety readers and no one else, a good diary column will have the bubble in mind as well; some of the stories will be utterly irrelevant to people with no connection to SW1, and that is fine.

'The diary should feel like the sort of stuff you talk about over a dinner party,' says Lo Dico. 'Did you hear this? Did you hear that? Because you are talking, in a sense, to a group of people at a dinner party, with whom you feel you can share confidences. London and Westminster, and the media around Westminster, it's like a very large family. Strangely enough, when you're inside Westminster, it's, "No, no, no, it's huge, we don't all know each other actually". And then every so often you look at this or that party and say, "Well, actually we do sort of all know each other, or we're all about one removed from all the key players."

'By having those little things on the record, like who goes hiking in the mountains with whom, at some later point in time you've understood a social connection. We all have our official jobs, we all have our official titles, and we look like we sit in these little cubicles in our lives doing various things, but actually beneath it all it's wholesale social connections that inform whom you know, how you can get on, how you can get ahead, which are built up incrementally over years. And from that you can look at how people source information, trade information, how business deals are done, how political media deals are done. And they're all done on some level through a personal relationship; it's quite rare to have something that's totally raw.'

This has not only been noticed by diarists: though they might mostly concern themselves with more serious stories and occasionally turn their noses up at the trivial gossip of diary columns, political reporters can and do rely on them to help them join the dots. 'The number of times when looking into people you think who are wrong 'uns, you find that they have an obscure mention in a diary column from ten years ago which gives you a massive pointer to something else,' says Jim Waterson. 'That's the one thing I think a lot of gossip provides, the, "Oh, that's funny that that person's got connections with that businessman". And then years later, you're looking at that business and you go, "Oh yeah! Doesn't that MP speak for him? Oh, let's go through his Hansard, let's see. Oh, he's spoken up on behalf of that businessman. Great, okay. Now this feels like a proper story that might actually be a scandal." And you might have only read that they were tennis partners.'

There is also a degree of hypocrisy at the heart of the relationship between political journalists and diarists; though the former will often look down on the latter, they not only rely on the pieces of information hidden within diary columns for their reporting, but also send information their way if it is something they cannot fully stand up. As it stands, a lot of diary items will come from lobby journalists and political editors who might want something to get out but know that it isn't really a story, or that it is too mischievous to be printed under their byline. After all, diary columns rarely have bylines, and only the name of the editor tends to be fully public, so the diary elves will have fewer qualms about publishing something that might come back to bite them in the arse.

Francis Wheen, who went on to become the deputy editor of *Private Eye*, once edited the *Independent*'s diary column and freely admits that his 'single best source' was the paper's political editor Tony Bevins. In one anecdote from the early 2000s, he explains how ingrained the diary culture is for those in the bubble:

'I remember Charlie Whelan coming to blows with Tom Watson, and having to be pulled apart. They were both off their heads. It was at the Gay Hussar. The drink was flowing, as it tends to, and suddenly Charlie Whelan, who was then still Gordon Brown's spin doctor, spotted Tom Watson, who had only recently been elected an MP, and for some reason he decided that Tom Watson was a Blairite, which he very much wasn't. There was some ancient trade union rivalry as well, I think. Charlie staggered up to Watson, who was there with his wife, saying, "I know who you are. You're a Labour MP, aren't you? And you're a fucking cunt, that's who you are!" And Tom Watson was a bit taken aback, and Charlie said, "Yeah, that's what you are. Do you deny it?" And Tom Watson replied, "Could you please not carry on like that?" Charlie replies, "All right, do you want to come outside then? And we'll carry on …" And the next thing they were fighting on the pavement, being pulled apart. And you think, *Oh God, this'll be in 'Londoner's Diary' tomorrow. Who's going to be the first person to ring 'Londoner's Diary' to make sure it's in?'**

This great tradition of grassing on your friends and enemies to the nearest diarist has sadly nearly died down. An odd beast

---

* Asked about the incident, Tom Watson said that while he does not recall any physical fighting, he does remember that night and that Whelan was wearing a kilt, which he lifted at Mrs Watson. What a clarification.

covering too much ground and preferring the nudge and a wink approach to straightforward scoops, the diary was always going to find it hard to move online with everything else. A good diary also needs a small army of elves despatched to all corners of the city every night, which is something newspapers in financial ill health can do without. Social media has also had its part to play in the diaries' downfall, as why send a tip to a column when you can tweet it instead?

The *Guardian* had a diary column until it hadn't, and so did the *Telegraph* and the *Independent*. The *Mirror* and the *Sun* have one each but both focus on showbiz, which just isn't the same. *The Times* had one then didn't and has one again, and the *Express*, the *Daily Mail* and *Mail on Sunday* still have them, but they aren't as relevant as they once were. This is partly because they now have more competition (and we'll get to that in a minute) but also because, well, they won: diary columns stopped being special because everything became a diary.

'Diaries took over the world,' says Francis Wheen. 'Lots of papers don't have diaries any more for that reason, because the sort of things that used to be diary stories are now on every other page as well. In the eighties, they started spreading to other bits of the paper. [...] Before then, it was regarded as not a proper story if you simply ran a speculative thing saying, "There are rumours ...", and I think it's much more common in political news these days to write that. At the time, political coverage had much more to do with what was officially said at briefings and what was said in the chamber, rather than just vague gossip in the members' lobby. Places like *The Times* and the *Telegraph* used to have a whole page every day of just straight Hansard-type gallery reporting. And then there would be one weekly political column usually, where the political editor or the columnist might be a bit more speculative and say, "Friends of Mr Heseltine have not ruled out the possibility …" but it would all be fairly vague and dressed up so it didn't look too gossipy.'

With a lot of political reporting now more speculative and – dare we say? – mischievous, the humble old diary column has lost its spot in the sunshine, at least for now. It isn't all over for salacious gossip lovers, however: someone else has picked up the mantle already, and is causing trouble in their own way.

FUN, FUN, FUN

Popbitch was launched in the early 2000s. It is a weekly email newsletter that is focused on gossip: serious gossip, silly gossip, salacious gossip, gossip about footballers, gossip about politicians, gossip about TV celebrities. Gossip, gossip, gossip. It didn't really cover Westminster when it started, and still isn't entirely of that world, but every instalment will usually have at least one political item, which generally tends to be true (or at least hard to disprove).

One of its favourite features is the cock spot, which probably doesn't require any further explanation, and relies on men of Westminster glancing around when in urinals then telling their friends about what they saw.*

Rumour has it that legal advice they got means that they only publish stories about the, erm, luckier male MPs among us, but this is only partly true: Popbitch doesn't do items on Westminster's smaller appendages because it would feel too mean-spirited. Still, the ones they publish aren't for the faint-hearted. They once remarked that former Lib Dem MP Lembit Opik had 'a cock

---

* The author can confirm that one of the most eyebrow-raising work emails to ever land in her inbox was a cheerful 'Can you get us some urinal-wanking/cock spots, etc?' from the Popbitch editor on the eve of a party conference.

like a swan's neck; occupied both of his hands'. Jeremy Paxman's, meanwhile, was like 'a bull's heart on a tube of Pringles'. It is also something they take very seriously; they once described Nigel Farage's penis as possessing 'choad-like qualities', but corrected themselves later after someone with first-hand experience of the situation got in touch to say it 'actually more closely resembles a pepper grinder'.

It's not just cock-and-balls stories, however. They also run more innocent politician sightings (from 2014: Vince Cable spotted at Bloomberg 'stuffing his face at the free buffet. He couldn't get it in quick enough'). Meanwhile, other stories can be gossip with a purpose. Take this tale from 2017:

'Members of a northern branch of the Labour Party became increasingly frustrated at the sporadic appearances their constituency MP was making at local party meetings, never letting anyone know if he was planning to be there or not. It was only when they discovered that a "beautiful, plump lass" he was "pals with" kept her Twitter geolocation settings turned on. Every time the Party members saw that she was tweeting from their city – lo and behold! – he would be around to turn up to meetings. And when she was elsewhere, weirdly, so was he. FYI: It's not Danczuk, but the seat isn't a million miles away from Rochdale.'

It's a fun little story, and it is anonymous, but if you are in Labour circles, it can't have been hard to find out who this was about if you didn't already know, and if you did already know, it provided you with an excuse to share it around. On the other hand, our lusty MP will have found out eventually that he'd been outed by Popbitch, and would have perhaps taken it as a cue to start acting a bit more professionally. After all, if you strip the salaciousness away from this story, it remains mostly about an MP neglecting his local party. It never was picked up by a more mainstream outlet, but chances are that the item made life slightly worse for that MP, which he arguably deserved.

Others are more straightforward. In 2016, it published this blind item: 'Which married SNP MP developed an enormous enthusiasm for Iceland – angling to become an ambassador to the country in the wake of independence so he could continue shagging two Icelandic women?'

Again, it wouldn't be hard for people in or close to the SNP to figure out who this was about, including people in charge of deciding which MPs gradually become more senior, and which ones remain exactly where they are. An MP cheating on his wife with two Icelandic women and pushing for a position enabling his shagging is not illegal, but it could turn into a scandal if found out, and is generally indicative of that MP's character.

Oh, and this should go without saying, but even if you are not in a position to influence the career of that MP in any way, it is still a very funny story and makes for a very entertaining read, and you can then pass it on to fellow politically-minded friends down the pub.

In any case, there is (slightly) more to Popbitch than salacious stories any other outlet would stay well away from. The best people to explain the ins and outs of the outlet are probably the people who work for it, so grab a beer, sit down, and enjoy this conversation between founder Camilla Wright and her right-hand man Chris Lochery – and get ready for some colourful language.

Wright: It was really pop that started it; it was stories about people and pop music. That was the very, very first thing. It was a time when pop stars seemed to be more fun, the world was easier to misbehave in; pre-smartphones, pre-social media. But then, well, everybody enjoyed gossip, so very quickly you had journalists, people in PR, getting in touch, and therefore it was probably two or three years in before we did any stories that were politics-based, but by then it felt quite organic. And then you realised that it's the same people gossiping about all those things.

Lochery: People find the sex lives of politicians to be fascinating, and not just the sex lives – we get a lot of stuff about politicians' dicks and balls.

W: MPs are unlikely to want to leak saucy stories to us, but the people who work for them throw it out there. Sometimes their gossip is probably not right for us, it's too specialist, too behind the scenes, it's too much like inside baseball. So we don't often use it, but we find out a lot about that world by listening to it and then work out if there's a filthy story somewhere. [...] We're determinedly non-partisan. You could probably work out roughly our politics from it, but people don't, so there's a sort of defence there; all parties could be covered without us being necessarily partisan.

L: We're more interested in whether each story is unusual, funny or something that you won't read elsewhere, rather than trying to protect anybody's interests, or bring anyone down. The reservations we have with politics is that there are people trying to spread rumours to get one over each other; there's much more of a competition with politicians so you've got to be a lot more wary of the motivation of people leaking, whereas you know when people are leaking about Girls Aloud or whatever, it's no huge issue. I also think there's something in the fact that since Popbitch started, and this isn't anything to do with Popbitch specifically, but the nature of politics appears to have become a bit more pop culture-lite. You know, you have people like Ed Balls on *Strictly Come Dancing*. The people that would have originally given us stories are now coming into contact with politicians a lot more, because they'll come out with Ed Sheeran and talk about whatever. The pool of regular sources have a lot more to do these days with politicians, and now those worlds are bleeding into one another, pop culture and politics.

W: The lines are much blurrier, that's right. People now just think of it all as conversation and gossip, and it doesn't really matter who it's about. Anybody who is in the public eye is fair game. And if it's someone in a suit and tie, and he looks like he should be quite puritan, and you find out that they're doing something ...

L: Like Michael Gove doing the Wham Rap! or something like that. It wouldn't be weird if, you know, Mick Hucknall had done that when he was interviewed in front of some schoolkids. You'd be saying, well yeah, it's Mick Hucknall. But to watch Gove do it – there's something excruciating about it. And to even know that he knows the lyrics to the Wham Rap! ...

W: Yeah, I think that's the idea. It's the weirdness of the blurring of the lines.

[...]

W: I don't think we would sit down and try and construct a public interest defence, except that things that happen in popular culture inform a debate and inform the culture we're in, and therefore I think are in the public interest. I think there should be a much wider definition of public interest than there is. But generally we publish things if we think they're true, they're not massively mean, and they're funny. Quite often, not everything. Or that there's a reason for doing it, there's actually a point to be made.

L: I think it's largely led by whether we find it interesting or funny. I mean, we have to also think of it as true or it's come from a good source. But even if something comes to us that we think is true, it's not always for us. It's not like we have to fill any of the newsletter with politics if we don't want to, so it has to fulfil a secondary brief of being interesting, funny, or within Popbitch's remit, which is sort of salacious.

W: The story for us is not always the story, it's the story behind the story. Why is this coming out? Who's trying to push it? Can we trace a route? Can we tell people how these stories come out? Why it's come out now? So you're trying to illustrate the wheel of the organisations. Why is Damian Green in the firing line? Why is this newspaper after him? Who's been paid to do this? That's the story for us. And I think that sometimes stories come to us because people know we'll set it in a context that people will understand. We'll only do politicians that the wider population has heard of.

W: I guess we've always said that we, Popbitch, exist in the gap between the public image and the private reality. It's not really just about who's having an affair, who's doing what, who's horrible to whom, but where there's a dissonance between what people market themselves as or what you think of them, and what they're really like. And politicians are great for this, because so much is hidden. You want to be elected so you're going to behave like this, but behind the scenes you're all raving shaggers. Therefore, that's why I think we've moved into that space a bit, in that it's just there, and not many people want to cover it in a family newspaper or because it suits them to not publicise that people who share their political views are X or Y. We don't give a fuck.

L: Or I suppose that byline journalists don't want to get a reputation for outing people and being indiscreet.

W: So people who want the stories to come out, but can't because they're beholden to special interests, whether it's politics or film, or anything that breaks the code, that comes to us. And that's why politics is a part of the mix.

L: Information is power in this industry, in a way that, for example, in the film industry it's not quite the same, in the music industry it's not quite the same. There's no real currency to information per se. People who are drawn to it also have a particular cocktail of personality traits that lend themselves to risky behaviours from time to time. Not everybody obviously, but there is a certain type of person that is very ego-driven, very self-centred, to the exclusion of common sense sometimes.

W: So you end up with the sort of stories that we're drawn to because of the peculiar human interest side of it, plus it's important and powerful people doing it, plus it's not really getting anywhere. It's one of those things that is kind of celebrated in the world of rock 'n' roll, this kind of excess, but it happens in politics too, and it's more scandalous in politics because of the nature of the people doing it. That makes it perfect for us, in that sense, because it just has that extra punch when it's somebody who was dressed in a suit and tie and sitting down on *Andrew Marr*.

One interesting aspect of this conversation is their utter lack of shame regarding their pursuit of explicitly salacious stories, which is entirely to their credit as they are the only ones really doing it. As we saw earlier, tabloids do enjoy the occasional sex scandal, but tend to get all high and mighty about them. We know they're publishing it to titillate their readers, they know they're publishing it to titillate their readers, but it is a family newspaper and they will only print shagging stories if they can throw in a layer of judgement and puritanism. This is fair enough, but makes it less fun. Diary columns, on the other hand, tend to avoid sex stories altogether. There is no immediately obvious reasoning behind this, apart from the fact that it seems to be a convention. The 'Londoner's Diary' never covered society shagging, and then editor of the *Sunday Express* John Junor once said that according to his paper's owner Lord Beaverbrook (yes, him again), 'all fucking is private.'

Had they launched earlier, Popbitch would have had one competitor when it came to covering the sex lives of the great and powerful: *Private Eye*.

THE ALL-SEEING EYE

'Well, we don't not do sex stories,' says Adam Macqueen of *Private Eye*, 'but the sex has to be relevant to something. Sex can be quite a big factor in things, sometimes, but just sex for sex's sake is not necessarily very interesting.'

This wasn't always the case – Francis Wheen, the deputy editor of the magazine, explains what happened: 'When Richard Ingrams was editor, he was terrifically keen on the sex scandal stories. A lot of the stories were ... well, some of them were true, and some of them were possibly less true, to say the least. We got into trouble though with some of them, and even when they were true sometimes he managed to get them wrong. There was one about Cecil Parkinson when he was a cabinet minister, who had impregnated his secretary, Sara Keays. Ingrams ran a story saying that Parkinson's secretary was pregnant but saying that she had got pregnant by another Tory MP, Sir Marcus Fox, so he had to apologise to him.

'But anyway, when Ian Hislop took over, he let it be known that he wasn't so keen on "leg-over stories", as he put it. So if you want to get a sex story in, you have to somehow persuade him that it's not purely prurient "Oh, look who's having an affair".

There's got to be somewhat further justification; he tends to recoil from those sorts of things.'

While his predecessor Richard Ingrams was 'once heard to say that he thought all his readers should have access to the gossip available to the upper middle classes', Hislop has a different view on what counts as worthwhile gossip. 'I thought society gossip was outdated,' he once explained to the *Guardian*. 'It was just leg-over constantly. I'd always thought the thing that defined the *Eye* at its best was investigative journalism and jokes, and I suppose what I've put in place of society gossip is professional gossip – people talking about how their industries, businesses, professions work, rather than saying the Duke of Cumberland was seen in White's with someone who wasn't the Duchess of Cumberland.'

This is a sad state of affairs for the lowbrow among us (author included), but it doesn't mean that *Private Eye* doesn't have anything to write about. Between journalists' bad behaviour, MPs' hypocrisy and murky dealings between the two, the *Eye* has been the go-to for gossip for decades, and its influence shows no sign of waning. While most other organisations have had to drastically evolve to get used to the online age, the *Eye* retains a largely useless website, mostly encouraging visitors to subscribe to the print magazine.

If anything, it hasn't really changed since its first issues in 1961, when a lawyer was asked to check one of them to see if any of the stories in it were libellous, and it turned out all of them were. These days, just under a quarter of their turnover is apparently set aside for potential libel settlements, which is as good a statement of intent as any. It might seem excessive, but makes sense when you pick up an issue of the *Eye*; the quote about publishing things someone somewhere doesn't want printed being journalism and everything else being PR might be a tad overused, but it does apply to the magazine.

The *Eye* tends to go where a lot of places won't, and delights in publishing what others have tried and failed to put in the public domain. One brilliant example of this comes from 2016, and involves a Conservative minister, an affair with a dominatrix and several cover-ups:

'The John Whittingdale story was a classic,' says Wheen. 'I mean, that went through so many different newspapers ...The *Mirror* spent ages on it, got a lot of evidence of him being with this woman when he was a minister, and indeed when he was chairing the Culture Select Committee, taking her to events, travelling to things like the MTV awards, the BAFTAs, and they thought, well, this is a really good story. Top Tory and he's sleeping with a woman who gets paid to whip people in a basement in Earl's Court.

'Months passed, they got all the evidence, but the lawyers just went round and round in circles saying, "Well, how can we justify this?" Especially now, you know, newspapers are under more threat than ever because of Leveson. There's so many people who want to close us down and say we're being irresponsible, so how can we justify putting this? And so they really tried to think, well, is there a security risk? Not really. And so they didn't run it. And then the *Independent*, when Amol Rajan was editor, was going to run a big story about how the *Mirror* had suppressed this story about Whittingdale. But then the *Independent* suppressed it in turn, for exactly the same reason that the *Mirror* had ... The lawyer said, "Well, I don't think we can justify this." And Amol decided that it would just be more trouble than it was worth, trying to justify it.

'And so it then became a story about how the *Independent* had suppressed the story about how the *Mirror* had suppressed the story about a senior Tory MP having an affair with a spanking prostitute. And I then did a thing about it in the *Eye*.'

The story was then followed up by everyone else, and became about the relationship between the media and politicians, and what counts as a story; two things which journalists tend to resent having to write about. This was a particular coup for the *Eye*, but was hardly out of the ordinary. As a magazine, it does pride itself on not adhering to the media ethos of *lupus non mordet lupum* ('the wolf does not bite a wolf'), and will merrily use its 'Street of Shame' column to write about the actions of fellow hacks. They are also not in the lobby, so do not feel the need to write up a story given to them purely because of its news value, even if it means being voluntarily spun by whomever their source is.

'I don't like it when I feel I'm being used,' explains Adam Macqueen. 'I always want to be doing a story because I think it's a story. And there's that lobby thing of – there's always a pay-off – you're part of the story that someone is trying to push, and I think *Private Eye* should always be very resistant of that. A lot of the stuff I'm fond of doing is questioning why people are telling me things, and trying to work out what their motivation is. Because a lot of it is, with the sort of stories we do on "Street of Shame" particularly, people who have been passed over for a job and they want to get their own back on the person who's then got that job. That's not a terrible motivation; I wouldn't rule it out as a story for me. But it's just whether they were being fairly fucked over or not.'

Another thing to take into account is whether they will get sued or not (and whether getting sued for that story is worth it). Much like the diaries, *Private Eye* is seen as a place that enjoys drama and mischief so much that going out against them all guns blazing can almost certainly only end badly for you and not them. They are also an accepted part of the media ecosystem; if you become important enough in journalism or political circles, you are bound to get written about eventually – after all, few in this parish truly are whiter than white.

'First time I was written about in *Private Eye*, someone inexplicably sold a very boring Facebook status of mine to imply something weird about [his then-employer] BuzzFeed not being diverse enough,' says the *Guardian*'s Jim Waterson. 'I was quite upset, and then when it happened two or three years later, I was thinking, *Oh, it's quite nice to know that they're still interested really.*'

Not everyone is as calm about it as Waterson, though – from full-on legal threats to the occasional tentative shove, the magazine has to deal with an entire spectrum of responses. According to Adam Macqueen, 'Most people take it as a badge of honour, most people are quite happy about it. Some people get really, really cross, and they get cross in different ways. So the worst people that threaten to sue you are tabloid journalists – they really, really hate being written about. And normally, quite low-ranking tabloid journalists. Once they've got up to editor standard, most of them ignore us completely; you'll get the odd whingey letter.'

Former editor of the *Daily Mail* Paul Dacre, for instance, who has been written about in probably every issue of *Private Eye* for the last 23 years, never comments on anything, except for twice when it's been full-on legal threats. 'It's never actually got to legal action, but it's been that kind of tone of things. Mostly what you get is more "in sorrow than in anger" things. You get a lot of that, the blanket denial: "You just got the story completely wrong, you've made yourself look really stupid!" And then obviously you write back and ask: "What were the specific bits that we got wrong? Let's try and sort this out." At which point they kind of say, "Oh no! I don't want to make a fuss."'

This is because *Private Eye* stories do tend to be true, and their sourcing usually is reliable, and everyone knows that. Speaking of which, how exactly do they get their sources? After all, they are not physically in Westminster as much as other journalists, and their tendency not to do anyone any favours should be coming back to bite them in the arse. This is where the *Eye* lunch comes in; the one that proved to be such a disaster for our friend John Hemming. A long-standing tradition, it takes place every two weeks at a venue in Soho, and brings in about a dozen hacks, politicos, past, present and future sources, and some of the *Eye*'s journalists. Though not always raucous, they can be frankly boozy affairs, and some attendees have been known to leave well into the afternoon, and pretty well refreshed as well.*

If you are invited to a lunch, it seems only polite to try and come up with a decent story to drop into the lap of one of the in-house hacks once there – one should sing for one's supper. That being said, it will not be held against you if you don't, and *Eye* hacks are more than happy to play the long game if needed.

According to Adam Macqueen, 'It's not necessarily a direct pay-off, a lot of it is getting a kind of tone of what's going on. It's more like a sort of general editorial conference discussion; it's what people are generally getting exercised about, or what they're interested in, that is going on in the news at that point. You can take something from that. Some of it is just from stuff they assume that everyone else knows and don't realise because they're so close to the area, that it's actually quite exciting, and at that point your ears prick up. And some of it is just buttering people up to be contacts later at some point. That indefinite point where

---

* A pair of them once got along so well at the *Eye* lunch that they decided to drop by the bathroom for a quick shag before leaving, which shows impressive dedication to the epicurean lifestyle.

you think, *How can I check this story out? Hang on, that person came to lunch and they will take a call from me.'*

Francis Wheen, meanwhile, recalls inviting a baroness to a lunch roughly a decade ago, and not hearing anything for years: 'and she suddenly got in touch recently, emailed out of the blue, and said, "Oooh, this might interest you. Yeah, I think it might be a really good story for you." Ten years afterwards, she's paying for her lunch, she's finally come up with something.'

This brings us to a wider question: why do people leak information and pass on gossip to journalists they know will publish it? After all, conflicts are rarely solved by being played out in the press. There is always a reasonably high risk of getting caught, and if the fights are internal, any story that makes the opposite faction look bad will also make your entire side look bad. Still, people leave documents in photocopy machines, they whisper over pints and they take pictures of files then email them over. Westminster leaks like a sieve and most people don't really trust each other as a result. It would be easier for everyone to keep secrets secret, so why don't they?

PART 4

PROCESSES

'I suppose the image of Westminster to everyone outside
is that we're all wheeling and dealing and back-stabbing
in the corridors and yeah, that is how the majority of
business gets done.'

— Anonymous Labour MP

DRIP, DRIP, DRIP

Before getting into the thorny topic of leaking and briefing in Westminster, let us take a quick step back and look at society at large. In 2012, a team at the University of California, Berkeley, set out to study gossip, its purpose and the effect it has on people who engage in it. In a series of four experiments, they put a number of participants through several different scenarios, all of which involved watching two people playing a game, and one of them cheating without the knowledge of the other.

In the first one, participants were hooked up to heart rate monitors which showed that their heart rate went up when they realised one person was cheating. Given the opportunity to pass a 'gossip note' to the person playing honestly, most of them did it, and their heart rate decreased as a result. According to co-author of the study Robb Willer, 'Passing on the gossip note ameliorated their negative feelings and tempered their frustration. Gossiping made them feel better.'

In the second one, participants were first asked to fill in a form about their level of altruism and cooperativeness, then watch a game where one player was cheating. As lead author Matthew Feinberg then explained, 'The higher participants scored on being altruistic, the more likely they were to experience negative emotions after witnessing the selfish behavior and the more likely they were to engage in the gossip.'

The third experiment was similar, but with an added twist: the game between one cheater and one honest player remained, but this time participants were told that they would lose the money they were due to make from the study if they passed a gossip note, and that even if they passed the gossip note, it would not alter the overall score of the cheater. Still, a large majority of them actively decided to lose money in order to (righteously) gossip.

The fourth one kept the setting, but turned the dynamic on its head. This time, participants were playing the game and using raffle tickets to do so, which would later be entered in a draw for a prize of $50. Some of the players were told beforehand that there would be a break during the game, and that observers would be able to pass gossip notes to other players at that point if they'd noticed anyone cheating. As a result, virtually all participants acted more generously during the game, especially those who had received a low score on altruism in their questionnaire.

According to Willer, the conclusion of these four experiments was that 'when we observe someone behave in an immoral way, we get frustrated, but being able to communicate this information to others who could be helped makes us feel better.'

So there you have it: gossip is positive, both internally and at a societal level, when it is explicitly about witnessing something bad happening and wanting to tell others in order to either warn them or try to ensure that the person who did the bad thing will not be getting away with it. This is fairly uncontroversial, and the reason why we celebrate (most) whistle-blowers as people who saw something that was wrong and decided to do what was right.

The only thing is that, well, there are two kinds of wrong: sometimes, something is factually, unarguably wrong and everyone will happily agree that the thing in question could not be anything but bad. They are the minority. In most cases, 'wrong' is subjective, and its status will depend on, among others, a person's morals, beliefs, connection to the thing, and which side of the argument they are on. One man's wrong can be another's grey area, or a justifiable and necessary evil, and so on.

And this is all before getting into the fact that this study only looked at one subset of gossiping, and there are plenty of other reasons why people might want to spread confidential information around. Some of them will be unequivocally bad – say, it will make your opponent look worse in the eyes of the public if a certain something were to get printed – while others will seem selfish at first but be done for the greater good, and a whole lot of it will just be neutral, and done for the pure (and noble) purpose of entertainment.

On top of this, there can be external reasons why someone might decide to gossip about something, even if they don't necessarily want to do it. The whisper network mentioned earlier is probably the starker example of this: if there are no formal structures in place to efficiently get rid of creepy parliamentarians, warning potential future victims over a drink might well be the best course of action, even if it feels like a devious one. This logic can also work in murkier contexts: if, say, you're a junior person working for a political party and you are certain that a policy will go down badly but you aren't important enough to be listened to, what do you do? Pre-emptively leaking it to the papers while it is still only a potential policy can be one way of doing it. Your superiors won't appreciate it, though, so you must be clever about how you do it.

Now the editor of *The Times* diary, Patrick Kidd used to work at the HQ of the Conservative Party while they were in opposition. Here, he recalls one of his less-proud career moves as a young researcher: 'Oh God, this will reflect so badly on me, but on one occasion there was a policy that was under consideration that was in my area which I thought was going to be vetoed by the Shadow Treasury, so I wanted to get it out. And so I went for a drink with our press officer and a journalist to the

Marquis of Granby, and our press officer got completely pissed, so much so that she fell over. And so when there was an inquiry about how the story appeared in the papers, I'm afraid I did sort of say it wasn't me but well, she was completely drunk, she may have inadvertently passed it to them. And I'd printed it out and given it to them. So there we are, she was pissed so that gave me my alibi.'

If this sounds bad to you, it is worth mentioning that Kidd hardly is an exception here; though the subtle blaming of the sloshed colleague perhaps wasn't ideal, secretly passing on documents to journalists for more-or-less righteous reasons is often the rule and not the exception in SW1.

Leaking a bad idea before it can be formally briefed to journalists is also a well-known tactic, as it both allows you to put your own spin on why the idea is a bad one, and it can ensure that the idea is nipped in the bud. The way it normally goes is: a party, or group within a party, starts talking about something, said thing gets leaked to the press while still an idea, the party or group is forced to deny it as it is technically not something that is definitely happening at that point in time, and once that is done, it becomes very difficult for them to eventually announce the idea without it sounding like a big U-turn. The idea is dead, and everyone can move on. The opposite can work too, with an idea a person of a group thinks is good, but is obviously about to get shut down; if you can get it to a paper before that happens, it might not guarantee that the idea will not get killed, but it will certainly make it a bit less likely as once it's out, you can start getting your people defending it on the record. It might not immediately change the minds of the powers that be, but you will have turned something that was dead on arrival into an idea publicly debated by your party.

All of this applies to people as well, obviously, as Westminster is largely dominated by MPs with various ambitions and people with power forever attempting to retain it. The science of talking someone up or ensuring someone remains down deserves its own chapter (and we will get it later) but before then, it is worth mentioning something crucial: just because a story looks positive, it does not mean that its intended effect wasn't negative.

Take Lisa Nandy, for example. She has been the Labour MP for Wigan since 2010, and has been tipped for her party's leadership more times than you could count. It started in around 2014 under Ed Miliband then came back up every other month, and she was eventually known as one of those people who would definitely jump at the opportunity, should there be a vacancy. The only issue is that two leadership contests have since passed, and she stood for neither. In fact, she insists that she has never seriously considered running, and that the rumours were circulated to ensure that she wouldn't be trusted by her party leadership and colleagues:

'One of the things about leadership ambition rumours is that they are often set in train in order to prevent that sense of team developing. It can set you up to threaten some of the people in here, and make it much harder to get things done. It can be really disruptive and undermining,' she explains.

'Rumours about me standing for leader sort of reached a peak in 2015, and then again in 2016, and I can honestly say that although I was approached by some people in 2014, it was never something that I treated as a serious prospect. I wasn't planning to do it at the time, and in 2016, I denied it straight away, but it didn't stop the rumour mill from going. In fact, if anything with those sorts of rumours, the more that you deny them, the more they spread. It can be a bit disconcerting, because you don't often know why people are doing it, and deniability can be really difficult.'

This last point is crucial. There is an argument in saying that Westminster simply is a workplace, and gossip happens in any workplace, so it isn't special in its reliance on rumours. One major difference between, say, an accounting firm in Swindon and the Palace of Westminster is that Sally from HR's tryst with Bob from Accounts or Sarah's plotting to take over the biggest account in the company are unlikely to get laid bare in a national newspaper. Rumours in politics can be just that, but once they get printed and become a story, they are suddenly a tangible piece of news to which people are expected to react.

Like the tale of Birt and his toenail clippings, a lot of stories are particularly potent because there is no real way to deny them beyond reasonable doubt. As Lisa Nandy inferred, simply saying 'I don't want to be leader' to a journalist does not mean that they will take your statement at face value and conclude that you simply do not want to run for leader. Unless a story is based on a cache of documents, a recording of a conversation or something similar, it is hard to categorically deny it and be believed – once it's out, it's out.

There is also a slight issue of politicos often playing with fire when it comes to denials; while you cannot straightforwardly lie to a journalist who comes to you to check that a story they heard is correct, you do have plenty of room to try and make them less likely to publish anything. It is, in fact, the job of a good spinner to manage to deny a (true) story enough that it isn't publishable without having technically lied to the reporter. There are a number of ways in which you can do this, and here is former Lib Dem spinner James McGrory with one of his favourite ones:

'I used to say, "There's a couple of things you've got wrong in there." And they'd say, "Well, what do you mean?" And you'd reply, "Well, look. In its entirety what you've said is not right. I'm not going to help you do any more on this." Could be the day of the week that they've put to you, could be something as fundamental as a person involved. Generally, if I'm using that though, they've probably got the central thing and you're picking about, for example, "I've heard this was on Thursday" – it was actually midnight on Wednesday.'

In this context, it is easy to see why journalists won't take anything but a factual, tangible denial as proof that something definitely didn't happen. Or, in the words of a former Labour spad: 'One of the funny things about politics is that unlike in other walks of life, because people can be asked about a rumour; once a rumour's in print, it becomes something you either have to agree with or deny. Or rather if you can't deny it then it becomes accepted. Sometimes if you do deny it, it still becomes accepted.'

These aren't the only dynamics to keep in mind when dealing with a rogue rumour flying around. A lot of the time, a piece of gossip can live and die within Westminster, simply passed around until everyone gets bored, and might make an appearance in a diary column but not much else. This is the best possible scenario, apart from the one in which gossip isn't shared at all. The one issue is that it is not obvious which pieces of gossip will disappear quietly of their own accord, and which ones will eventually turn into big embarrassing stories. This is even more of a concern when the said piece of information is either totally false or has a kernel of truth to it but has been blown out of all proportion. If this happens, what should you do? If you let it thrive, people might assume that it has to be true, otherwise you would have denied it already; if you put your foot down and loudly deny it, you might make it considerably bigger than it was ever going to be.

Ask a spinner what they make of this conundrum and they will tell you that while neither is ideal, a version of the former tends to be preferable. 'I've had conversations with MPs where I've had to say to them no, you can't,' says Lib Dem Ben Rathe. 'Where they've said, "I want to respond to this." And you say, "No, you can't respond to this. We'll respond to this, but you need to stay out of this because if you respond to it then it's a bigger story, because you're then on the record and you're giving it more credence than it's worth." And that's quite a difficult conversation to have, because when you're dealing with allegations that can be difficult for people. If you're talking about sexual relationships, or if you're talking about things that would be embarrassing to those people in terms of their personal life, it's quite difficult to say to them, "No, I need you to not talk about this." Or more accurately, I need you to trust us to do our job and not be involved with it, because they feel personally invested. It's really difficult for them to say, "Oh yeah, okay, I'll let you, 20-something press officer, deal with this thing that could potentially alter my career." But if you were to rebut every rumour or thing that you heard you'd spend your entire life chasing shadows.'

Conveniently, you do not have to take Ben's word for it: history has provided us with a perfect example of how trying to make things better will often just make them worse. In fact, have you heard the story of Peter Mandelson and the guacamole? It has been more or less everywhere, and everyone with a keen interest in politics will probably have heard it at one point or another. In case you haven't, it goes like this:

When Peter Mandelson was out campaigning in the north of England one time, he decided to stop by a chip shop. As a middle-class man who had spent his formative years in north London, he was keen to prove his effortless man-of-the-people credentials. Anyway, he goes into the chippy, orders some fish and chips and glances at the mushy peas before adding, 'And could I get some of that guacamole as well?' That's it, that's the story – it might not have been roaringly funny, but it is amusing and symptomatic of an era when New Labour would just ship out poncey posh boys to working-class northern seats and that was that. The anecdote has been doing the rounds for over two decades, and is just part of the canon of Westminster gossip.

There is one small problem with it, though: it's not true. Or at least, it is true but Peter Mandelson was not the mushy peas offender. In fact, the anecdote is in writing in a book published in 1997, Andy McSmith's *Faces of Labour*. This is what it says, in a chapter about the Knowsley North by-election of 1986:

'Working from a disused office in what had been the industrial quarter of Kirby before recession had reduced it to a brick-strewn wasteland, their only source of food was a chippy nearby in a small row of shops where the shutters stayed up all day as a precaution against vandals. It was so very different from the home life of Shelley Keeling, daughter of a wealthy East Coast American businessman, who was completing her studies by spending a year working in the parliamentary office of Jack Straw, who was in Knowsley North as the candidate's political adviser. One day, a party researcher named Julian Eccles invited her to the chippy to taste the local fare. Sunk into the counter was a large metal dish containing something green and viscous. "That looks delicious; is it avocado?" she enquired. It was mushy peas.'

Suddenly, the story loses some of its charm: it is no longer about an enigmatic and divisive senior figure in the Labour Party, and Americans can be forgiven for not having heard of the

British delicacy that is mushy peas. So what happened? If you ask Westminster denizens who have been around for a while, some of them will say that the (false) story came from Neil Kinnock himself, the former Labour leader. When he gave a speech at Mandelson's leaving do in 1990, he told the story but replacing Shelley with Peter. There is another layer to this, however – why would Kinnock have voluntarily told a random false story at the alleged protagonist's bash? Maybe it's because he'd recently read it in the paper.

To be more precise, maybe he had read it in a political column in *The People* roughly a month earlier; a column that mentioned mushy peas and Mandelson in the same breath. A column written by Peter Mandelson, trying to explain that the story was false. Neil Kinnock did not reply to interview requests for this book so we will never know why he decided to make that joke in his speech, but we can probably guess that he was trying to rib the man he had by then known and worked with for years. So there you go – Peter Mandelson, the Prince of Darkness himself, presumably thought that publicly denying a silly anecdote that had been doing the rounds would put it to bed, thus making sure that it would live on for years to come instead. You win some, you lose some.

After all, the bet he made was quite a risky one: of all the bits of rumours and interesting stories that do the rounds in Westminster, few of them ever do make it to the papers and into the public consciousness. It can sometimes feel like everything that happens in politics eventually gets found out and if not leaked, at least discussed in newsrooms, but that really isn't the case. Asking people whose job it is to prevent secrets from going out produces a range of answers, but they all agree that some confidential stuff does manage to remain just that.

'In terms of the "gossip", I would say less than 10% of it actually gets out there,' says Conservative MP Greg Hands. 'I'm not trying to encourage you, but there's a whole goldmine out there you've barely mined. Also in government, everybody's terribly excited about leaked documents – the government produces an enormous number of documents on a day-to-day basis, and the number of documents that is actually leaked is minuscule. Only a small part of it leaks, but because there's now so much product out there, it creates the impression that the place leaks like a sieve.'

According to James McGrory, 'No more than about 25%. I remember someone in the lobby saying to me after I'd been doing it for about two years and I was pushing some shit story as sometimes you are, "You must see ten fucking splashes a day." And I said, "Come on, that's ridiculous, we haven't got that, there's not that many things going on." And he came back, "You know, if you just sat and thought about it." Because who's shagging who is the best stuff, but if you think of all the disagreements that you've been witness to in meetings, via email … There are people being quite catty with each other, vehemently disagreeing. That would walk onto a splash. "Huge row blows …" So there's two categories of gossip that don't make it in, I think, and that bit that I've just described of internal disagreement, it's probably less than 2%. And I know that sounds ridiculous given the papers are always full of internal rows, but actually it's how politics is. It's people having genuinely quite big debates about stuff. Clever, informed, passionate people, at the top of their profession, having genuine disagreements about important stuff. Politics is not a vicar's tea party, there are robust discussions. I've seen candidates swear at each other, lose their temper, get really upset about stuff, because they care. And in a good operation, almost none of that makes it to the papers.'

Meanwhile, one No 10 aide had this to say: 'I would suggest that although 10% gets out, around 30 or 40% is known by the media, but you have to stack it up,' which rings true. Finally, Miranda Green might just be the one who put it best: 'I was a journalist and then I worked for the Lib Dems and then I came back to journalism, and it is slightly spooky, once you've been on the other side, behind the curtain: it's quite spooky how much nobody ever knows.'

This was true of her time in politics in the '90s and is certainly true of politics now, but it wouldn't be possible to get a rounded view of the leaks of Westminster (both managed and accidental) without looking at the one thing that has revolutionised the way secrets travel around SW1: technology.

ONLINE AND UPWARDS

All the interviews with MPs conducted for this book were done in person, over lunch, drinks or coffee, and most of them were interrupted every other minute by the interviewee's phone lighting up. The notification occasionally turned out to be an email, but the overwhelming majority of them were from WhatsApp. The response was generally a glance at the screen, a resigned or annoyed sigh, and a return to the conversation. 'I don't know how many WhatsApp groups I am in, but it is more than is necessary,' said MP Paul Masterton after receiving one such notification. 'Most of them are muted, they're so annoying.' Other MPs, meanwhile, estimated that they were in around a dozen WhatsApp groups, sometimes even more.

As a matter of fact, it would be hard to overstate just how important the messaging app has become to MPs and the people around them. There are WhatsApp groups of intakes, WhatsApp groups for female MPs of certain parties, WhatsApp groups for plotting, WhatsApp groups for discussing certain TV shows (yes, really), WhatsApp groups to coordinate around a policy, and so on. MPs talk to each other and to journalists on WhatsApp, the latter who in turn talk to each other on WhatsApp, ad nauseam.

This isn't surprising: the app allows you to easily have private conversations with one or several people, groups are easy to set up even for people who don't spend their days online, and the encryption on both sides can ensure that chats have a certain level of privacy. Westminster is also a place where most of what happens comes from people talking to each other, preferably in a place where others can't overhear what is being said, so real-time online chats were always going to be a revolutionising force in politics.

'MPs are all on WhatsApp,' says journalist John Rentoul. 'It mechanises it; it makes it completely instant. In the old days you had to phone MPs on landlines, try and find out where they were, it just took forever, whereas now it's all instantaneous. And a lot of MPs would rather give you a comment on a DM or WhatsApp than actually speak to you, because they can actually fashion the words and control it much more.'

After all, with everyone being so busy and constantly running around, being able to properly talk without having to physically meet works for everyone. Journalists can watch a speech in the Commons then send the same message to a dozen MPs to see what they made of it, MPs can message a group of their colleagues to see what they make of a new policy that will affect their constituencies, and no one has to be in the same place at the same time for it to happen. Naturally, it has also made plotting and factional infighting easier to organise as well.

According to one adviser who has worked for Labour since long before the WhatsApp age, 'These groups are fascinating. I don't think that kind of conversation could have existed pre-that. If you think about some of the people who are on the WhatsApp groups, in the old days most people just sat in Portcullis House and chatted, and that would've instantly looked like a plot – you couldn't possibly do that now, you couldn't get those people together. So that is a really interesting development.'

There is a reason why this matters: in politics, it is just as important to know who is plotting with whom than it is to know what they are plotting about. A lot of the whips' work, for example, involves the ability to map out the informal networks among their benches. Alliances aren't always about policy agreements, intakes or any other obvious link; MPs might get along because they were at university together, have mutual friends outside Parliament, got raucously drunk after an APPG meeting and took it from there, and more. Knowing who these groupings are is vital if you want to understand what is going on, and not be taken by surprise if a rebellion pops up out of nowhere. These networks can also help if, say, you want to run to be the chair of a select committee, or the Speaker of the House of Commons; in order to efficiently canvass votes, you need to know where to go.

It used to be possible to get an idea of who liked whom and who didn't by observing what happened in the tea rooms, bars and Portcullis House, and it still is to an extent, but a lot of social interactions have now gone underground, making it hard to know what is really going on. There is also the issue of known unknowns and unknown unknowns. Sometimes, you will be aware that there is a social group that exists, and is crystallised by the presence of a WhatsApp chat, even if you are not part of it and do not know what they discuss. It all gets a bit more complicated when it comes to social groups you're not even aware exist, if they do exist. It is, after all, impossible to snoop around a conversation you're not meant to be included in if you don't even know that the conversation is happening.

On top of this, there is a bit of a chicken and egg situation with a number of groups: was a WhatsApp group started because of pre-existing friendships, did friendship become the logical conclusion after a WhatsApp group was created, or was it something in between? In politics and journalism as in life, temporary groups can be created to deal with one specific issue then snowball into a more generalised chat, which can then bring people together. 'I'm on a WhatsApp group which is mostly devoted to slagging off one journalist in particular,' says one reporter. 'It's called Dickwatch, and it is about one journalist we've all worked with. It's become a very eclectic group.'

There is also a group dedicated to American Football, which has now brought together a group of MPs, journalists, special advisers and others, a group of various hacks which started because they were trying to organise drinks and subsequently kept on chatting, and probably many more (though, well, who knows?).

One direct consequence of this is that information now travels *fast*; it always did, but it now does so even quicker, and through unexpected ways. This is a problem for political journalists. 'Gossip spreads below the radar now, so you can have everyone knowing that you've slept with that person, but no fact-checking at any point,' explains Jim Waterson. 'Previously it was limited to what went round the bars, but fundamentally the sleepiest MPs would only find out when the gossip column wrote it up a week later. Now if there's a good bit of gossip, every researcher in Parliament is going to see it within hours, if that. And stuff can be established as fact on an enormous scale without any checking at all.'

It also harms journalists' ability to check said gossip. The way reporting usually works is that a piece of information should be double-sourced, so if for example you hear something from one MP, you need to find another MP from a different party or faction who also has knowledge of that piece of information, and your story is then stood up. With WhatsApp, rumours travel so fast that information can be shared third or fourth hand quicker than ever, and it might travel in unexpected ways.

One MP explained this well: 'If Joe Bloggs MP says, "All right, there's going to be a new centrist party, I'm going to mention it to a sensible group of MPs," he can then put it in a WhatsApp group. Then if you as a journalist ring someone on Joe Bloggs' WhatsApp list and ask, "Have you heard that there might be …?" We have to say, "Oh yeah, I have heard that!" because no one's going to say, "Oh yeah, Joe Bloggs has just sent it round the WhatsApp group" – they don't want to compromise Joe Bloggs, so they say, "Yeah, I've heard that too!" And then you ring another MP who's on the same WhatsApp list, "Yeah, I've heard that too!" And we've all heard it from the same person. I think it is much harder now for journalists to try and distinguish between fact and speculation, and to try and cut through the crap, and we really rely on them to do it.'

What this means in practice is that a story can often seem iron-clad due to having been double- or triple-sourced, but is in fact partly or fully bollocks and based on one person hell-bent on telling everyone about that one rumour they heard. WhatsApp isn't the only culprit for this either: Twitter took over the Westminster bubble some years ago, and has also changed the way in which many things operate.

'The number of times I go to someone who ought to be a primary source, a minister or an MP, and they're telling me something interesting, and then I realise they've just read it on Twitter like everyone else,' complains the *FT*'s Jim Pickard. He is right; with its snappy addictive format, Twitter has become the ideal platform for people who enjoy reading gossip and sharing it. It can be anything from a furtive picture of an MP taken somewhere embarrassing to an overheard conversation or a wild theory about what really is happening that day in Westminster; if it's eye-catching, it will be spread around quicker than you can say, "But is that really true?" With the vast majority of MPs, advisers, journalists and assorted SW1 inhabitants partially living on Twitter, the platform has become the place where careers, factions and policies can rise and fall in the space of a few hours.

As Lord Livermore puts it, 'There's no publication hurdle – so in the old days an editor would decide, "Do I want to publish this? Is it well sourced enough?" and now there can be an anonymous account spreading pure rumour, completely unsubstantiated. No proof required, could be totally made up. And yet it can be around Westminster in seconds.'

Given that a lot of people do not feel the need to fact-check or double-source claims before they tweet them, the pace at which news (and fake news) happens now is incredible – and an issue. 'To give you an example of how much things have sped up in the way gossip's changed, in 2010 I remember being at university refreshing the Andrew Sparrow *Guardian* live blog while Gillian Duffy, the "bigoted woman", played out in real time,' says Jim Waterson. 'And it was extraordinary, because it was the first properly online election, and I'm sitting there in the library, and every five minutes there was an update! And he even put the odd funny reaction in. There was the odd tweet coming in, and he was saying, "And Sky News have got this …" and it felt extraordinary, it felt like you were following the story in real time, it felt so new and fresh. If that moment happened now, you'd have the memes within about three minutes and it would burn out within about an hour. Everyone would have gone through her Facebook within about ten minutes and the whole gossip cycle of what used to be played out over several days would happen in about an instant.'

'Nowadays, let's say a story breaks, someone says something equivalent to Gillian Duffy. It takes realistically half an hour to an hour for a newspaper website to get an initial take live. Just to check a few facts, make sure that their transcript is correct, all the rest. By that point someone will have tweeted it out, lots of people will watch the clip direct, the public will be making the jokes, and often in many cases digging on the woman them-selves. Essentially the gossip has happened; it's happening as the main story and often before the main story's put out there. Half the time you learn what the news story is from the meme or the gossip, rather than from reading the original take.'

This often ends up blurring the line between news and gossip. Sometimes, what is (rightfully) seen as a piece of gossip gets shared around so much on social media that journalists feel the need to write about it, either to debunk it or simply to try and get some clicks. On the other hand, there might be a bona fide news story that becomes gossipy because the Twitterati decides to focus on one detail of the story, usually a colourful, salacious or personal one. It is also possible for anyone with reasonable access and no fear of getting sued to start their own account and spread whatever they want for whatever reason; some of UK politics Twitter's most famous accounts are, like 'General Boles', entirely anonymous.

This makes journalists' jobs harder: on the one hand, Twitter is a handy way to see exactly what people are talking about, what they care about and what they may want to read about; on the other, a lot of what happens on Twitter stays there, and cannot be translated into online traffic for their publication. Still, this is not to say that hacks have had no part to play in the corrosive effect Twitter has had on the political discourse. If everyone else can gossip, then so can they.

Lord Wood, the Labour peer and former special adviser, explains: 'There's a classic journalist device which is to say, "Rumours about X, there's growing talk of X, hearing whispers that X," and with Twitter, well …The other day I had a good journalist message me and say, "I've got a theory about this Labour thing and what's going on there – have you got some evidence that this thing might be true?" And I said, "Not really, no," and he replied, "Well, can you categorically rule out that it's untrue, because if you can't, I might think that's enough to float it on Twitter and then get the trail going?" It's an entrepreneurial approach to a story. Eventually, he did put it on Twitter and it was along the lines of "hearing that …".'

As discussed earlier in the book, the technique of trying to float something because you suspect it to be true but can't quite stand it up isn't a new one, but it takes on new proportions if it happens on Twitter where everyone can see it instantly, as opposed to halfway down a column not everyone might read. Tweets can be retweeted, or forwarded privately to someone else in order to be secretly discussed. A rumour can start out one morning with one journalist trying to see if a flimsy bit of information might by any chance be true and end that evening with most people in Westminster broadly assuming that it must be true.

This usually happens because of a combination of WhatsApp and Twitter; someone might post a piece of gossip on a WhatsApp group, one of the MPs in it will screengrab it and pass it on to a journalist, the journalist will tweet that they've heard of something happening regarding that piece of information, the tweet will be copied and pasted into WhatsApp groups by people wanting to ask their friends and contacts if it is correct, and on goes the merry-go-round.

Unsurprisingly, some MPs have been known to abuse this system. Say you're an MP who is somewhat influential but not a government minister or a party grandee, and you want to make your voice heard on the issue of the day. What do you do? Email or message a journalist directly? They might include one line of your quote deep down in a story if you're lucky, but you are likely to get roundly ignored; you're not that important, so what you think isn't exactly headline news. Instead, then, how about posting a few paragraphs outlining your views in a WhatsApp group of, say, Conservative MPs? And after that, wouldn't it be dreadful if you or one of your mates were to screengrab your comments and leak them to a journalist? That way, the story is no longer 'MP thinks X', but 'Leaked messages from confidential MPs group reveal that MP thinks X', and we all know which one sounds like the more exciting story. The secret, once again, is to make boring news sound like gossip; the important element here is not the opinion of the backbencher per se, but the fact that information that was (apparently) meant to be private was made public.

Still, times are changing fast and even at the time of writing, this practice has already become a bit outdated; the frisson has gone from this kind of story as it is reasonably easy to tell the difference between a managed leak and a truly unplanned one. Smarter MPs and advisers have also quickly learnt not to post anything too newsworthy in WhatsApp groups they know to be sieve-like, so we might be heading towards a new culture that is more like the old one; leaks still happen, but manufactured ones are frowned upon.

According to Labour MP Chris Leslie, 'There are some very, very large WhatsApp groups, and as long as they've been administered and curated carefully, they should have completely leaked out, but they haven't. And so my faith in humanity's ability to keep gossip under wraps isn't totally dead. But obviously, I'm not a gossip in the least, so I wouldn't understand.' (Debatable.)

Still, one journalist was more – somewhat cynically – positive about the rise of technology: 'It's made it a lot easier to leak things, because you no longer have to steal a document from your office and pass it in a brown paper envelope to a journalist or leave it in a photocopier somewhere, you can just take a picture of it and whack it over. From my point of view, it's been a great thing; whether the good governance of the nation has been advanced by it is a slightly different question.'

Another thing social media platforms have been instrumental in is making the set pieces of Westminster even more momentous than they already were. Take, for example, an event that happens every other year, involves a whole lot of power changing hands, shadowy figures in a locked room deciding where the power needs to go, and everyone else trying to guess what is about to happen to show just how in the loop they really are ...

IN & OUT

'Colleagues walking around Westminster staring at phones. Not sure if they're waiting for "the call" or trying to catch Pokémon,' tweeted MP James Cleverly in July 2016, at the height of the Pokémon Go craze. The context for the quip was that Theresa May had just become the new prime minister and had to do what everyone does once they get into No 10: a ministerial reshuffle. These both happen when a new PM comes in and when a PM has been in power for long enough to need some fresh faces to join their government. The principle is straightforward enough – promote the good people, demote the bad ones, sack the *very* bad ones – but the reality of it is far more complex.

In fact, if you look at it from the outside, the reasoning behind most reshuffles is unclear at best. MPs rarely get to head departments where they have prior experience either from their life before Parliament or their backbench careers, and it is entirely possible for someone to be expected to know everything about culture then suddenly to know everything about health instead. Some MPs are seemingly plucked out of nowhere and their appointments lead to journalists having to sneakily run to Wikipedia before offering any wisdom, and others have to remain 'rising stars' for years before finally making it onto the front bench.

This is because there are many things to take into account in a reshuffle. There is the current position of the Prime Minister (or Leader of the Opposition) and why they're having a reshuffle in the first place. So, are they in full control of their backbenches or do they need to quell potential rebellions? Which groups have been causing them trouble recently? How long have they been prime minister for? Is there new blood getting restless on the backbenches? How are they doing in the polls? Do they need to show that they've listened to the public and decided to change course, or do they want to solidify their existing agenda? What policy area have they been doing well in and which ones do they need to do more in?

Then there are the MPs themselves. Is a junior minister doing well enough that they should be promoted? What sort of 'well' are we talking about here – have they been modernising mavericks or a safe pair of hands, and which one does that department and government need right now? Have they been involved in ministerial infighting with their colleagues? If so, was it on the side of the PM or on the other side? If not, what do they really think of the PM? Do they have leadership ambitions? Are they close to someone with leadership ambitions who might have promised them a better job in their administration? If so, would promoting them quench that thirst for a more important job or would it give more power to someone determined to get their own candidate in the top spot? What is their relationship like with the back-benches, and what do the backbenches make of them? Are they popular with party members? What are their personal politics? Are they driven by a sense of duty, devotion to an ideological agenda, a bit of both? Once they are in a department, will they be a big ideas person or a wonkish technocrat? Are they a good media performer? Can they be relied on to defend the government line on *Newsnight* or the *Today* programme if needed?

And you cannot forget about the personal stuff, of course. So, how do they treat their civil servants if they are already a minister? Do they play well with other departments when it comes to policy? What is their relationship like with political journalists? Are they trusted to not leak at all or strategically leak or are they a sieve? Do journalists like them or will they be waiting for them to trip? Do they have an alcohol problem? A drugs problem? A sex problem? A bullying problem? Are they currently doing anything that could turn into bad headlines for the government? Have they ever done anything bad enough that they could now turn into bad headlines for the government? And on and on and on.

Deciding who goes up and who goes down is the job of the leader of a party, a few of their most trusted advisers, perhaps an MP or two, and the whips. They are all tremendously busy people who have a number of other things to be doing at any given time, so it is fair to say that they might not be able to take every single one of those questions into consideration when working on a reshuffle, especially given that there can be dozens of positions to fill or tinker with. There is also the undeniable fact that most politicians are unhealthily obsessed with the press and what the press makes of what they do, and that journalists themselves are also too busy to consider all those aspects when deciding whether to approve or disapprove a promotion or demotion.

Here, a former senior Labour aide explains how this works in practice: 'When leaders are doing reshuffles, they're often thinking not about how the team's going to work over two years, they're thinking about how it'll be perceived by the media. And their only gauge for how it's going to be received by the media are the rumours that are knocking around beforehand. If it becomes a thing that Gordon Brown appointing James Purnell as welfare secretary would send a big message on youth and vibrancy on reforms, then suddenly that can become self-fulfilling. Everybody starts talking about someone getting a job before a reshuffle, and everyone suddenly expects it so much that if it doesn't happen it becomes a statement in and of itself.'

There is one slight problem with this way of doing things.*

Where do journalists get their information from again? They get it from MPs and advisers, and occasionally from other journalists, who probably get their bits of information from other MPs and advisers. In short, when it comes to reshuffles, Westminster becomes one giant feedback loop. This could be moderately helpful if the information passed around was about, say, people's policy agendas and whether they are or would be any good at running a department, but that is rarely the case. For

---

* Well, there are a number of problems with this way of doing things, but this book isn't pretending to try and solve every issue with policy-making in the United Kingdom, so let's stick to what we know.

MPs briefing journalists, their reasons normally relate to whether they're friends with that MP and get along with them personally, are in the same faction as them, or share the same sort of ideological outputs. For journalists, it is usually a case of whether that MP is a good and useful lunch companion, if they promptly reply to texts and if they prove to be a good source when needed. As a result, what happens is that journalists might start dropping on Twitter and in columns that X is a bright, young rising star who could do with a government job, egged on by the MPs in whose interest it would be for that person to get a job, and when it comes to the actual reshuffles, the powers that be might look at X and think, *Well, everyone seems to think X would do a great job, and we would look good giving them that job, so why not?*

To be clear, this isn't the process through which every single minister is appointed, but it certainly plays its part, to the extent that very sharp minds might end up lingering on the backbenches as they aren't necessarily clubbable, and more vacuous parliamentarians can quickly find their way to the Cabinet.

'Whenever a journalist writes who's going to go up and who's going to go down, the ones they always want to go up are just basically the ones they like. Like they're not actually any good at being ministers,' says former Lib Dem spinner Sean Kemp. 'There was a Lib Dem reshuffle where we got rid of Jeremy Brown and everyone said, "What in God's name have you done now?" But the reason was because Jeremy was a terrible minister. He didn't get anything done, he just spent all his time pontificating to journalists, and because he spent all his time pontificating to journalists he was a good source, and therefore he was tagged for promotion. And it happens where you get all these people and you don't know how they continue going up, because in terms of being ministers and doing jobs and clearing out their box and stopping bad policies and pushing good policies, they might be rubbish. But because they're good at this other bit, which is just being affable and turning up at the right think tank dinner ...'

This isn't ideal. Still, the Westminster rumour mill can be good for one thing when it comes to reshuffles, and it is ensuring that even if someone got away with having done something reprehensible, they become significantly less likely to have a glittering career. There are exceptions, of course, and this wasn't necessarily the case a few decades ago (more on that soon), but if you have a number of skeletons in your closet, people will know. The young staffer you bullied maybe didn't go to the press, and the woman you sexually harassed might not have gone to the police, but this doesn't mean that the incident disappeared without a trace.

'There would be MPs that we would have to talk to No 10 about sometimes, if we were hearing stuff that maybe wasn't the subject of a formal complaint but had the potential to be so, or you'd hear the stuff that people were saying locally about the MPs on their patch,' explains one adviser who used to work for Labour HQ. 'And that information was definitely used by No 10 when they were doing reshuffles and promotions. There would be MPs with big question marks who would not get a promotion they might otherwise get, because they were considered a risk.'

This is usually where the whips can make themselves useful as well; they might not have as much power as they want people to think they do, but they certainly can warn their leadership team that a certain someone definitely should not be getting promoted. If there are rumours floating around a certain MP, it is their job to know about it and at least try to ascertain whether they are true or not, and with tangible enough proof that they could be turned into an embarrassing story for the government. This doesn't always work, of course, as whips are only human and cannot possibly know about every single thing their MPs are up to, but it helps.

The one thing that is better for whips than reshuffles, however, is whispers about one happening imminently. A party's MPs are never as well behaved as in the week before a reshuffle is rumoured to be happening, which they are acutely aware of. It is not a trick that can be used repeatedly, so it must be deployed wisely, but whips have definitely been known to get the word out that the Prime Minister has started looking at their front bench and decided that some change is in order, even if it isn't strictly speaking the case. Naughty whips.

Rumours of an impending reshuffle are also vital for the civil service; after all, they are the ones who have to work with the ministers, and a political change at the top of their department can change everything. This is especially the case when they have teams they dislike, do not agree with or do not get along with. 'Reshuffles is the thing they're obsessed with,' says journalist Chris Cook. 'In the Department of Education, everything they did under Gove was wrapped up in Gove, and lots of it they thought was crackers. They pursued policies for years the department thought were completely nuts, and they thought it'd never work, and they're still pretty open about this fact. I would get reams of text messages from the civil servants before every reshuffle. "Is it finally time? Are we going to get rid of him?" So in that case there were things that they were consciously trying to kick down the line, because they thought they might not have to do them completely if they could out-wait Gove. And Gove sort of knew this, so it became like a self-fulfilling problem.'

This happens frequently, and is not entirely unreasonable from civil servants. If they spend a lot of time gossiping about who's up, who's down, who's got the ear of No 10 and who's pissed off the Treasury, it is partly because it is entertaining but also because it can have a direct influence on their job. After all, they are here to work on policies but can do little about the political aspect of them – whether they can go through Parliament, if they are a priority for Downing Street or will be put on the back burner – and that political side often defines just how far they can go. If, for example, a department's Secretary of State is someone known for being close to No 10 and popular with the backbenches (a rare feat), the civil servants know that they can work on an ambitious policy agenda as it will almost certainly become a reality. If, on the other hand, a minister is getting increasingly known for their drunken antics and has been boneheaded in their conversations with the PM's special advisers, and is therefore headed for the chop, civil servants know that that minister's pet policy won't see the light of the day anytime soon, so can dedicate as little time as possible to working on it.

One former civil servant recalls: 'I remember being asked at the MoJ years ago … There was a minister who basically wanted a particular policy and was pushing hard for it, and we just discounted what he said because it was clear that he was on the outs with No 10, because he'd screwed up, and so we weren't really going to prioritise it. You don't give a shit about them because if you did, you wouldn't really be able to do your job, because you have to be aware of things colliding above your head.'

Most of this has to be found out via informal means because not all of it will be in the public domain, and more junior civil servants tend to not have much access to the upper echelons of their department. There is a lot more to be said on the topic of policy-making, so much so that it deserves its own chapter, which will come later. In the meantime, let's temporarily leave Westminster and go on a bit of an adventure. Where do you fancy going – Brighton? Manchester? Liverpool? Birmingham? Blackpool? Bournemouth?

LADS ON TOUR

If politics is odd at the best of times, conference season has to be one of the oddest bits of it. Every year, each party goes away somewhere for around three days and locks itself in a fancy hotel, along with a varying number of activists, lobbyists, staffers and journalists, and ... well, predictable chaos ensues. While everyone will be there for different reasons, your typical conference day is usually: wake up early, work normal office hours, start drinking whenever it is officially socially acceptable to start drinking, keep on drinking until around 4:00am, go to bed, wake up three or four hours later, and repeat. This would be a recipe for wired neurosis and pointless drama for everyone, but given how weird most Westminster people are, conference season is often a time when everyone – to use the technical term – loses their mind.

Before we get on to this, let's go through the basics. Conference means different things for different parties: for the Liberal Democrats, it involves shaping most of their policy agenda; Labour also dedicate a lot of theirs to voting on what policies the party should adopt; the Conservatives, meanwhile, use more of an American format, where members are there but cannot vote on anything. Things also vary for small parties. What all conferences have is an absurd amount of speeches, from their main MPs, frontbenchers, mayors, councillors and so on. These take place every day in the main hall, and as a rule, the speeches are mostly as dull as dishwater. Then there are the fringe events: dozens and dozens of them, in rooms that can hold anything from 20 to over 100 people, and with debates on anything and everything, usually with panels including a selection of MPs, journalists, policy experts and campaigners. These run from 7:30am* to about 11:00pm. The ones organised around lunchtime tend to include gloriously free and offensively beige food (fish goujons somehow always feature), and any fringe event that starts after 5:30pm is expected to involve some free (cheap, warm, grim) wine. After 6:00pm, the drinks receptions start: some are strictly invitation only, others are only slightly selective, and a number of them are open to all pass-holders in the secure zone.

Most of the genuinely fun (and most exclusive) parties start at 10:00pm or later, ensuring that the night feels like it lasts forever, and from roughly mid-afternoon, it is entirely possible to just give up on events and go have a drink in the conference hotel bar, where everyone will converge eventually. So, why do people go there? It is, after all, a tremendously expensive affair, as hotel prices jump right up on the dates and every drink in a mile radius costs about £12, and apart from the occasional surprise, not much happens there.

For MPs, it depends: if you're on the front bench, you are expected to be there, either to give a speech or to generally support your leader. If you're a new MP or one with clear ambitions, it can't hurt to show your face, talk to activists, and generally be seen to engage with the party faithful. Other MPs tend to avoid the event altogether. Labour and Lib Dem members can go there if they want to help shape their party's policies, and it never hurts to be able to freely mingle with MPs you normally only ever see on telly. Lobbyists, think tank wonks and charity bods know that in order to be heard, they'd better be there, whether they want

---

* Apparently, the author has never bothered waking up that early to find out for herself.

to or not. Journalists, meanwhile, are there because where politicians go they follow, even though it can be toughest for them as they can go to up to six conferences one week after the other every September and October.

The one problem for them is that, to put it bluntly, not much happens at conference. The speeches tend to be mind-numbingly boring and unless you have an army of reporters you need your team to get lucky and happen to be at the one fringe event where a moderately well-known MP says something daft or offensive; and at the end of the day, you are stuck in a place the size of a shoebox with every other political journalist in the land, so getting a genuinely exclusive scoop isn't easy. This means that on top of being sleep-deprived and hungover, journalists tend to be a tad grumpy at conferences, and grumpy hacks are dangerous ones.

'I mean, it's just the worst way to govern a country I can imagine,' says former Lib Dem spinner Sean Kemp. 'At party conference everyone who has a speech has to announce a policy, because otherwise the journalists basically go, "We will blow up your conference." So you rush around, go shit, we need like ten policies that we can launch in this conference, most of which are going to get no coverage because we're launching another nine policies, but if we don't do it everyone throws their toys out of the pram. So many terrible policies are launched by governments at party conferences just because otherwise they won't have anything to do at the four o'clock briefing.'

Annoying as it might be for the people in charge of coming up with those useless policies, they remain the best way to try and distract journalists long enough that they don't shift their focus on to more embarrassing matters. In case the previous hint was too subtle: people get sloshed at conference. Not everyone does, but a lot of people really do get leathered, battered, trashed, hammered, whatever you want to call it. The combination of bad free food, near-unlimited free alcohol and absolutely endless awkward conversations with near strangers means that even people who usually are the type to have a half pint or two then call it a day will get merrily sozzled. This means that every year, at the very least one senior politician will be spotted being so drunk that they can barely stand, a number of MPs will walk into morning meetings very obviously looking like they've just thrown up, and so on. Luckily, hacks get just as drunk as the rest of them, so what happens at conference can often stay there. As one former lobby hack recalls, 'I remember getting a really good story from a senior MP at 4am and thinking, *Oh my God I'm so drunk, I've got to write this down because I'll forget it in the morning.*'*

Another thing that happens when you shove a lot of very drunk, tired and neurotic people together for a few days is that they tend to revert to their teenage selves a bit. What doesn't help is the fact that there is a clear hierarchy of parties and drinks receptions wherever you go, and most chats after 6:00pm are along the lines of: 'Which party are you going to tonight?' / 'Well, I got invited to X and I think I'm someone's +1 for Y and I'm NFI from Z' / 'Oh! I've got a +1 for Z so you can come with me but could you try and get me in to X?' / 'Oh, I wish but I'm already using my +1 for X for the person who's bringing me to Y, sorry!' – ad nauseam. Politics is a popularity contest for people who are desperate to be liked, and somehow these people once decided that a good way to do work and have fun was to recreate the social structures of a particularly venomous high school.

This might all seem a bit (very?) silly from the outside, but people are people and they can't help it. Westminster denizens

* It is unclear whether they did in fact write it down or if they merely remember thinking that they should.

who are on their millionth conference season can usually appear more reasonable about these things, but fear of missing out is a powerful force, especially when you've slept for seven hours in total in the past three days. After all, it's not entirely irrational to think that you absolutely must go to party Y, as it could be the one where, say, two MPs start having a fight, or that Secretary of State you've desperately been trying to talk to or establish contact with has had enough glasses of bubbles to be friendlier than usual.

If power in politics is about whom you know, it doesn't feel that unreasonable for people to tie themselves in knots when denied access to the room where it happens. Not that those parties are actually fun: a conference party always involves fairly bad booze, way too many people in one room (or worse, not quite enough people in one room), people desperately trying to go and talk to some people and those people desperately trying to avoid the people who want to talk to them. It's no wonder you have to be drunk to get through it, really.

Still, all that free alcohol has some consequences, and there is a reason why the event has been nicknamed 'Love Island for Nerds' more than once. People shag at party conferences; they have consequence-free shags, shags they regret in the morning, they cheat on the partners they've left at home, heartily snog whoever is game at 3am, then desperately try to avoid the people they snogged the day after. Not everyone shags, of course, but there is enough shagging going on to keep everyone entertained. There is the story of the woman who was handed the key to a Tory delegate's hotel room even though she'd never asked for it, and who later that night handed the key to another delegate trying to get in her pants and telling him that it was her hotel room. There is the peer who decided to have as much fun as possible at conference so spent most of it on Grindr. Then there are the countless temporary couples caught snogging in lifts because they couldn't wait to be in private to get started, the MPs very kindly making themselves available to activists after hours, and many, many others.

Everyone who has been to a few conferences will have a (first, second or third hand) story of something salacious that happened there. This is former MP Jerry Hayes' favourite: 'I won't mention the names, but I was making a film for ITN and I was with the crew, and we were all a bit pissed. But there was a very prominent MP with a very prominent lobbyist. Both pissed, both trying to have a shag. And they were both sitting on the wall but they were both so pissed that they kept falling off. And we took some photos but we never did anything about it. I thought it was right to film it for posterity ...'*

None of this is specific to political conferences, of course; novelist Colm Tóibín was once commissioned to write about a literature conference and remarked that 'there was much coming and a certain amount of going'. If you put like-minded people in a closed environment for a few days and ply them with alcohol, don't be surprised if they pop in and out of each other's hotel rooms. What is different here is that the matters at hand are somewhat more serious – with all due respect to people who work in literature, their personal relationships might not have that great an influence on the way the country is run.

Conference might be a time for a party leader to try and show what their vision of the country is and for an opposition front bench to announce the policies they want to enact should

---

* For reference, one of the author's favourite conference shag stories is that of a married Conservative MP sleeping with an activist and asking that she calls him 'Daddy' during the act. She was happy with it and asked him to call her a whore. Flummoxed, he replied: 'Ooh, erm, that's really rather rude!'

they get into government, but it is about much more. Informal relationships matter in Westminster, and they can be created, mended and broken in those few days every year. This is why everyone still goes, despite not much ever really happening there; unless you are senior in your field, it will take a ton of effort and a fair bit of luck to establish a network of important people you can rely on. If you're then given a space where you can merrily bump into a minister at a drinks reception and get their mobile number and the promise of a coffee, why would you miss it?

Still, this annual Westminster-on-Sea retreat does reinforce the uncomfortable closeness that defines the bubble. The line between professional and personal already is blurry, but when you're shagging one another, whispering about who's snogged whom and happily getting sloshed until the early hours together, it feels non-existent. It doesn't matter that not everyone does it; most people will have calmed down by the time they reach their fourth or fifth conference season, but those links have already been established by then. What matters too is the general environment and that heightened feeling of all being in the same boat. We've already seen how this impacts the way politics is covered in the press, but there is still one missing piece in this boozy, messy jigsaw: lobbyists.

INTERESTED PARTIES

Could you, with a reasonable level of certainty, explain what a lobbyist does? There are a number of definitions online, all of which say broadly the same thing: the UK Public Affairs Council once defined it as 'in a professional capacity, attempting to influence, or advising those who wish to influence, the UK Government, Parliament, the devolved legislatures or administrations, regional or local government or other public bodies on any matter within their competence'. This is fair enough, but does that tell us anything about what they wake up in the morning to do, what they do every day? *How* does one attempt to influence or advise those who wish to influence the government, Parliament, etc.? Like spinners, lobbyists have a reputation for being shadowy, powerful and lacking a moral compass, but that doesn't clear up the minor matter of what it is they actually get paid to do, in concrete terms.

If you don't have an answer to this, don't worry, you're not the only one. At least you can comfort yourself by realising that you're not the former senior political operative who snapped up a head of public affairs job at a very respectable company, then had to text friends the week before they started to ask what their shiny new job actually entailed. But let's take a step back for a second.

Say you're someone like that person – you've been hired to be a lobbyist. Who hired you? It was either a company who wants you to be the in-house lobbyist of the firm, or an agency that specialises in public affairs which has a number of clients expecting them to do their lobbying for them (and paying them handsomely for the service). Though they share ways of working, the former isn't as interesting, as it usually means that the person in question comes from a certain policy area background and doesn't have as many plates to juggle. They also tend to have got involved because they care about that area of policy, as opposed to agency lobbyists who clearly enjoy the job itself and are more worth a closer look.*

So, what does an agency lobbyist do with their time? They talk. They talk to their clients, they talk to MPs, they talk to

---

* You might disagree with this assessment, and there is nothing wrong with that, but this is sadly not your book so there is nothing you can do about it.

advisers, to civil servants, to journalists, sometimes, to policy wonks, to everyone who might be relevant. According to one of them, it involves 'a lot of breakfasts with MPs, and sometimes a little quick coffee at Portcullis House, where you're trying to do two or three in an afternoon. You pop in and you try to see how long you can secretly stay there for. Most of it is WhatsApp. Then going to events in the evening can have a massive impact – in the week I will have three or four in my diary. I think that's half of it, who you see in the evening.'

What do they talk about? It depends. If one of their clients is someone who, say, makes sugary foods, they might employ a small army of lobbyists to find out if a sugar tax really is coming, and if so, to be made aware of exactly what it will be before it formally comes out, so the company has time to get ready; they will also expect their lobbyists to speak to all levels of policy-makers and try to convince them to shelve the plans, or if not to at least delay and/or tweak it. While this might some-times be done for nefarious reasons, lobbyists' conversations are normally quite technical and dull, and about explaining why a policy might harm a certain industry in an unexpected way, or why another policy should be brought in as it would help the businesses in question without harming anyone else.

Upcoming bills tend to be set pieces, but this doesn't mean that lobbyists have nothing to do the rest of the time; most people in charge of big companies need (or feel that they need) to be aware of what is going on behind the scenes in Westminster at any given point. Because they are busy running their businesses, they rely on their public affairs team to not only keep track of what is going more generally, but also have a good understanding of who's up, who's down, which relationships are important and which groupings of MPs are worth keeping an eye on. After all,

British politics works in weird and mysterious ways, and unless you're constantly knee-deep in it, a lot of it will seem opaque to you. This last part is crucial for agencies, and what they rely on to stay in business.

According to Gareth Morgan, the director of lobbying firm Cavendish Communications, 'You need to project a type of image to stop people nicking your clients, to put it bluntly. So you're always trying to win a client, you're always trying to keep hold of a client, there's always someone else trying to nick your client. And one of the things that you use can be gossip, in the sense that I'm paying x thousand a month for this advice; what we're all doing, pretty much all what we do, boils down to the same stuff. There's no one out there in public affairs who's doing something no one else has ever thought of or ever done. Meetings, dinners, events, whatever. So how you make yourself distinct is the key, and gossip is definitely part of that. So I would say that at the core of agency that's kind of a massive deal, and I think what lots of people don't realise when they're not in it, is how much you're constantly fighting to stay in business.'

Another senior lobbyist agreed: 'It actually differentiates us from our competitors, if we can get a heads-up about something which counts as gossip from someone who shouldn't be telling you something. Or, "Just so you know ..." So if you can pre-empt something and get in before the others, it shows your worth, and it shows that kind of side to your contacts. We go, "Well, actually, I've just seen here ..." and half the time, clients love it; they find it the most interesting stuff. You'll sit there and you'll update them on policies and things. It never gets as far as who's shagging whom, but it's definitely which bit's fallen out with which bit, and who's fallen out with so-and-so, or why are they in trouble? And that's a thing that clients like. They feel that kind of salacious stuff which they get on the side is what they really enjoy. They love it if you took a quick note saying, "By the way, just so you know, I heard this today." It adds that colour – otherwise we'd just talk about policy, and it's really boring.'

In this respect, lobbyists are quite similar to both journalists and civil servants, as they use gossip to make otherwise dull conversations more interesting, and to be as good at their job as possible. Like Whitehall and its obsession with knowing which minister is heading for the Cabinet and which one is about to receive a one-way ticket to the backbenches, having that level of informal understanding of Parliament is crucial for them.*

An example of this could be, say, being hired to lobby for a tax cut for businesses in a certain industry; not a huge one, but one that those businesses could do with. If you've been employed to make it happen by the next Budget, how do you do it? Trying to make the backbenches of the governing party all rise up and grumble at once would be ideal, but hard to do. Instead, what you might do is target a few MPs, go talk to them, and explain properly to them how that tax cut would be good for your industry, and either good or neutral for their constituents, yadda, yadda. How do you pick those MPs? You need to make sure that even if they agree with that tax cut, they won't have a door slammed in their face if they try to go and talk to the Treasury themselves. As a result, what you need to know is: whether those MPs are liked by their colleagues, so they can then do your work for you and talk to their fellow MPs, whether they're seen as influential or on the way up, for similar reasons, what faction they're in and what relationship that faction has to

---

* 'Why Do So Many People Who Decided To Work In Politics Seemingly Have Little Interest In Policy', and other questions this book is not long enough to address.

the Chancellor, so whether the Chancellor would be amenable to the requests of someone from their own faction or from a faction they're trying to appease, and what their personal relationship is with the Chancellor, so whether it is good, bad, or non-existent.

How do you find out all this? It probably won't come as a surprise to you by now: 'The substantial stuff of who's well regarded and all that, you can get that type of stuff after a little while from profiles journalists write,' says Gareth Morgan. 'You can definitely Google intel and, say, put it altogether and then to a client who doesn't read those sources you can say, "Look at this amazing insight." Whereas true gossip of having sat down with the spads for lunch and found something out that probably they let you know for a reason but most other people have no clue about it ... gossip that will put you ahead of columnists sometimes; that's when you know you're on to a really rich seam. So I think when you're at the stage where you're reading stuff by whomever, and you're thinking no, I knew that, I knew that, I knew that, then you know you're in the right kind of place.'

After all, public affairs agencies are paid more than enough by their clients, and if they just wanted someone to read the week's columns and diaries and take some notes, they could just hire a few interns. Instead, what they buy is mostly contacts; as we've seen ad nauseam, people are considerably more likely to only share their best gossip with those they see as friends, or at least good acquaintances. At least when it comes to journalists, MPs and advisers can have a good reason to want to talk to you even if you're not personally close, but with lobbyists, it is harder. As Morgan pointed out, you might get the occasional morsel if someone really wants something to find its way into the public domain, but without those informal relationships, you won't go very far.

When well-meaning souls argue about the dangers of the revolving doors of Westminster, they do have a point: it can be concerning to watch so many people work in politics, learn every which way it works behind the scenes, then go sell that knowledge to private companies. On the other hand, a lot of people leaving their political jobs don't really have a lot of choices, career-wise: if you were born and bred on Whitehall and suddenly find yourself out of work in your thirties or forties, there aren't many areas your expertise is useful in. Most jobs in SW1 are nebulous at best, and though there will always be transferable skills, chances are that you aren't great at managing people, have no idea how a normal office is meant to function and have a near-physical need to stay close to the action. Luckily, there are agencies who will welcome you with open arms, if your contact book is good enough, and will let you keep floating around your old stomping grounds for a reasonable amount of money.

'The revolving door between public affairs and government is insane,' says lobbyist Andy Williams. 'Mainly government then public affairs, but occasionally the other way around. So the narrative historically has been that you go into government, and it's a dutiful thing and it's because you care, and then you want to go and sell your soul, but it's really not as straightforward as that at all. Public affairs is not that well paid; don't get me wrong, it's good money, but it's not amazing. It's not as if I'm prepared to sacrifice all of my life and principles for this incredible salary. I think there are a lot of people who go into public affairs because actually they're interested in politics and they realise that if you end up with the right client, you can make quite a significant difference to certain policy areas.'

This is very much a lobbyist's view of lobbying so must be taken with a pinch of salt, but there is some truth to it; some of the shadier companies and agencies will pay their public affairs teams very handsomely for the services they provide, but others won't, and there's not much these people can do anyway. After all, most of those who end up taking a lobbying gig were working or at least campaigning for a political party in their Westminster life, which means that any job that would require them to be completely neutral is pretty much out of bounds. In public affairs, however, being a party member is seen as a definite positive: after all, where better to make friends than in a place where (more or less) everyone is fighting for the same cause, or at least fighting each other over which faction is best placed to advance the said cause?

'My best contacts are people I met when I was young and on the piss,' says Morgan. 'I think the best PA people are current political people as well. So, for instance, my politics is Labour, and I will have people who will give me intel because they trust me as we're trying to chuff someone else in the Labour Party together, so that kind of internecine factional stuff is sometimes the best route to get in that trust. So I can get stuff from that person they would never ever give me by taking them out for lunch, meeting them at a think tank event. In the industry you're always saying to your people, "I need you to be a political member and I need you to be campaigning, and I need you to get in that office during the election period." You know, the trenches with the guys, and afterwards they'll say, "Okay, I'll take the call off this guy."'

In short, a good lobbyist needs to be one who is entirely part of the Westminster ecosystem; ideally a member of a party, but at the very least going to the drinks receptions, occasionally popping by the terrace and the Red Lion and so on. Most of these interactions will be purely informal and involve general chats about whatever people are whispering about at that point in time, as opposed to straightforward discussions about what that lobbyist is working on. One good example of this is conference season. While it might feel obvious that everyone there is attending in order to do their jobs, trying to collar MPs and going in dry with a chat about policy will rarely work.

As one lobbyist explains: 'Some of my clients are really shit. They won't understand the subtlety of it, will go in aggressively to MPs at conference and say, "Why haven't you changed this bit of regulation?" And they'll say, "What do you mean, why haven't I changed it? It's not much to do with me, and I would try but <moaning noise>." And then that MP says, "I fucking hated meeting that person. They're awful, every time I meet them." And then they just don't take a meeting.'

Instead, a savvy public affairs operation at conference involves one thing: alcohol. All lobbyists might not be as well paid as they'd like you to think, but what most of them have in common is a rather generous expenses account. Their bosses know that good chats don't come cheaply, and nowhere is this truer than in a conference bar where the cheapest pint will cost you about £7. Some lobbyists have been known to swan from one conversation to another, politely buying rounds for whoever needs them; others just stand by the bar and merrily offer to pay for punters' drinks. These expense accounts are a known part of the scenery, and it is not infrequent to see other Westminster denizens actively seek the nearest lobbyist when their drink is starting to look dangerously empty. This might sound a tad unethical but in most cases, these free drinks won't ever lead to any effective lobbying on behalf of someone's client. If anything, some cynical young lobbyists have been known to provide drinks to their friends all night, expense the lot, then explain to their boss that they were busy making very important work contacts, which is only really true if you squint.

Oh, and at least things have changed in the past few decades. Here, former MP Jerry Hayes recalls one particular instance of rather brazen lobbying: 'I remember the good, or the bad days, whichever way you look at it, of public affairs. Ian Greer was a very, very old friend, and he once pulled off the most amazing coup. Couldn't do it today because it would be regarded as vaguely corrupt, which I suppose it was. Tories had promised that we'd privatise British Airways. Nothing happened. Sir John King, who was the chairman of British Airways, did not get it. So Ian Greer bussed 132 Tory MPs to the Savoy for the most delightful, expensive, drunken lunch you could possibly imagine. John King gets up and says, "I'm glad you enjoyed your lunch, blah blah blah. Don't forget your manifesto commitment." Within three weeks, a bill was presented before Parliament for the privatisation of British Airways.'

We can probably all agree that while successful, this was perhaps a bit much, and it is good that such practices would be frowned upon today, though who knows? Perhaps today's occasional conference rounds will look equally questionable in decades to come.

In the meantime, let's come back to something that was mentioned earlier in this chapter, and a few other times before that: the whole 'who's up, who's down' business. After all, most MPs are in Westminster for a reason, and it isn't just to represent their constituents.

NEW SHERIFF IN TOWN

The majority of MPs would like to be prime minister. They might know that it realistically will never happen, or only happen in 15 years and with a whole lot of luck; they probably wouldn't admit it to anyone else, and they may well have come into Parliament thinking that they never wanted to be PM, but there they are. As a result, most things that happen in Westminster should be looked at through the prism of knowing that a lot of MPs probably think that they could do a better job than their leader. It's not that they're all spending their time plotting, just that they aren't *not* plotting most of the time.

A lot of it isn't active; sure, the occasional 'wide-ranging interview' (always a good sign) or impressive speech at a think tank can help, but most of it is about creating a network of people you like, who like you, and whom you can trust. How do you do this? It depends on the person – some will become a permanent fixture on the terrace, others will find themselves turning into an extremely helpful colleague, always willing to lend a hand to other MPs, and some will always make sure to have their lunch in Portcullis House, where anyone can join them for a chat. There is no one way to go about making friends in general, and preparing to run for the leadership of a party is similar. Still, you usually do have to be seen and heard as much as possible, and WhatsApp alone won't cut it; friendships (and convenient partnerships) need a certain level of physicality to them.

'The most surprising people would be very good friends with one another,' says one former senior Labour staffer. 'And those alliances, they're important in leadership contests. I don't think people actually vote according to their politics first. A lot of the time people vote on the basis of relationships.'

According to academic Tim Bale, 'If you look at the leadership contests, you can see very, very clearly on a number of occasions that people have either won or failed to win the leaderships of our major political parties because they are not seen as good "people" people. In other words, they're not seen to be people who could work a room, chat to anybody. And the obvious illustration is that Major won in 1990 because he was precisely that, he was sort of "Hail fellow, well met!" Very good with people. Very tactile. But it's not just physical, it's the ability to just talk about almost anything with people on a day-to-day basis and no doubt occasionally that does involve gossiping.'

Running for leader is, after all, a popularity contest of sorts: first, with your own MPs, then with your party's members. Had this book been written a few years ago, it probably would have argued that an MP who rarely schmoozes in the tea rooms almost certainly does not stand a chance to ever lead their party, but both Theresa May and Jeremy Corbyn proved to be amusingly timed exceptions. The former never showed any interest in social-ising in Parliament, and the latter was part of such a fringe of his party that he rarely interacted with the mainstream. Though they are very different politicians, both their leadership campaigns were quite unique: May won by standing still as everyone else fell apart, and Corbyn benefited from a Labour Party in tatters and new voting rules which welcomed outsiders. At the time of writing, it would be impossible to say whether these were both one-time occurrences or turning points.

MP James Cleverly thinks it's the former: 'At some point in the future, there will be leadership campaigns for both major parties. And it will be very interesting to see whether we will revert to the more traditional method of personal contacts, whom do you know, whom have you spoken to, had a drink with, chatted with over the years, or whether the non-gossip is the new normal.

'I suspect that we'll revert to the normal, which is having a leadership team of people who have worked together – you see a side of people when they're working, and that's import-ant. You need to know that. But also you get the measure of someone when a colleague's going through a difficult time. It's quite interesting to see which colleagues rally round, and which colleagues revel in it. And for a lot of people they would regard that as being just as important as seeing how good they are at making speeches, or what they do at the despatch box. And so I think that in the future we will revert to the more normal way of having a cloud of people who know you well.'

Given the sheer unpredictability of the past few years, this book is reluctant to unanimously make a prediction one way or the other, but Cleverly is probably right. In any case, something that still hasn't changed is briefing and counter-briefing. If you are an MP who wants to run for leader and might well have a shot at it, it is not enough to tell your mates about it and bide your time; rumours about your suitability for the position need to become part of the background noise of Westminster as early as possible. Oh, and you should try and rubbish anyone else you know is planning to run too, but in a way that means it's impossible to pin it back on you or make you look bad, obviously.

You can also kill your opponent with kindness: the politician that is touted as the next leader for the longest usually never ends up winning, and being seen as the frontrunner has traditionally been a poisoned chalice.

One former Labour adviser explains how this works: 'Gordon's people, when he wanted to run for the leadership, used to have this tactic that they didn't talk down his opponents, they talked them up, which is quite an interesting strategy. Their view was that they had a problem, that it was Gordon who was the obvious person, but then other interesting people would knock around as the challenger, and all Gordon had to do was lose. And therefore what they would do is, when someone started to look like they might be in a position to be an outsider, they talked them up, because you have to go up before you have a fall. And they talked them right up, and then [found] some moment of crisis. And so, John Reid it happened to, Andy Burnham it happened to, Alan Milburn it happened to. I could go on.'

Another one is the classic tactic of smearing your opponent, usually with a story about their personal life that makes them look questionable. If the story is true, then hand it to an unscrupulous journalist, sit back and enjoy the show. If it isn't, or only might be, that's not the end of the world – get your people (and it really must be your people and not you) to spread the rumour around, and it might well stick. After all, something doesn't need to be known by the public at large to have an influence within SW1. Once someone's image is tainted, things will never be the same for them: even if people aren't certain that what they've heard is true, they often won't risk hitching their wagon to the wrong person.

If you are hell-bent on destroying someone, there is also no limit to how low you can go; as an adviser who understandably did not want to be named explains: 'If you say so-and-so is a sex pest, that may be true or that may be not, but it's very difficult for the person affected to respond by saying: "I understand where that came from but it's not true" – once you're explaining you're losing.'

Still, the grapevine can sometimes be benevolent, and if a rumour is put out about you, someone will eventually come to warn you that people are whispering behind your back. 'If I heard that someone who would be running for leader had been involved in things with people underage, or something, my golden rule has always been to go to the person or someone I know close to them, and say something like, "You're about to fly close to the light. I've heard this. If it is true, then maybe you should consider what you're doing. If it's not true, you should consider why this is being said about you,'" says one former Conservative adviser.

As we've seen before, there is no simple solution to dispel myths floating around about you, regardless of whether they are true or not. A simple denial will make cynics think that, well, obviously you would say that if you'd done *that* and then tried to run for leader, and talking to the press to rebut a rumour rarely ends well. What you need is for people to trust you more than they trust whoever started or propagated the rumour. It isn't an easy feat, but it is doable: after all, trust is one of the most important things in politics. If that fails, you can always attempt to find out who is trying to do you down and go to war with them, and hope that you come out on top. Briefing battles aren't always edifying, but they can help you gain power you otherwise wouldn't have.

'A lot of MPs are quite malleable and quite like being told what to do, or like to make sure that they are in the herd,' says one MP. 'So I think there's a lot of MPs that feed off gossip to make sure that they place themselves appropriately. So if there's a big briefing war going on between two, and it's clear that one is going to come out on top of this, people like to know that so they can move over to what they perceive is the right side.'

This is why a lot of defining moments in leadership contests or the days that lead up to them involve people moving very suddenly in one direction. The obvious example of this is the days that followed the death of Labour leader John Smith in the '90s. Of Blair and Brown, it had until that point been broadly assumed that the latter would be the obvious leader, yet it took about 24 hours for the winds to change after his passing, and for the former to be accepted as the natural follow-up. This doesn't mean that (all) MPs are sheep simply waiting for someone to point them in a direction and blindly follow them, it is simply not a good thing to be left out in the cold as an ambitious parliamentarian. If there is a leadership contest and you campaigned for the person who ended up losing, there is probably no point in you waiting by the phone around the time of the next reshuffle.

It can also not be enough to only vaguely support someone. If you want to get the right job, you must do your best to be as publicly and enthusiastically behind your preferred candidate, though be careful: push it too far and you'll just come across as sycophantic. Still, the worst thing you can possibly be is duplicitous: in a world based on trust, turncoats are not looked upon kindly.

According to former MP Jerry Hayes, 'One of the things that Tony Benn and Jim Callaghan did in the leadership election, which obviously Callaghan won, was to actually swap lists of people who said they supported them. And all those people, who pretended to Callaghan and vice versa, they never got jobs.'

This is because a party leader, more than perhaps anyone else in Westminster, needs to be able to truly trust their inner circle. The more power someone has in politics, the more secrets they have, need to know about, and have swirling around them, so it is not surprising that they need to have complete faith in those close to them. On which note: let's pop our head around the door of 10 Downing Street and see what actually goes on there.

PART 5

POWER

'Look at him — last year he took two women up to his hotel room for a threesome; this year he'd be lucky to get a handjob — but I guess that's politics.'

— Overheard at the Labour conference

IN THE EYE OF THE STORM

By the time you walk into No 10, either as the Prime Minister or someone who works for them, you probably do have an idea of what you're doing. Well, maybe you do. After all, you've either been an MP for years and years or an adviser or civil servant who has been knocking around Whitehall for a while, so you are broadly aware of how politics really works. Downing Street is a different beast, though, especially if you arrive there as a party just leaving opposition. Running a general election is life-consuming, you're never truly sure you're going to win, and you are so busy in the last few weeks before the big day that you won't really have the time to pop by No 10 to measure the curtains. There is also no buffer between the results and the beginning of your term, as is the case in some other countries; if you're in, you have to hit the ground running.

This leads to everything being, well, a bit of a mess. Take Peter Hyman, for example: he made his mark on Westminster as Tony Blair's head of strategic communication between 2001 and 2003, having originally started as a parliamentary researcher in the mid-90s, and was never technically told he had a job in Downing Street in 1997. Speaking to Ben Yong and Robert Hazell for their book on special advisers, he explained: 'I was not formally offered a job in No 10. As polling day got closer, I started to think about the future, but like others in the office never dared raise the issue with Tony in case it looked presumptuous. Now I assumed I had a job because I was told there would be an introduction to No 10 first thing in the morning.' And that was that: someone told him to turn up one day, and he left six years later.

Hyman's case was by no means an exception; even today, a lot of people walk into senior Westminster jobs without a proper process. 'Politics is a distinctly unmodernised institution; lots of things in politics haven't really changed for hundreds or tens of years,' says Will Tanner, who used to be a Home Office special adviser then was the deputy head of the PM's policy unit in No 10 under Theresa May. 'It's not a particularly professionalised industry – in politics I never really had a formal interview. […] Politics is fundamentally about trust. It doesn't matter whether you're good in politics; if you're trustworthy, you are far better.'

This is not limited to No 10. While in the rest of the world, people at least vaguely attempt to look like job offers must be in some way linked to the quality of a job application or the competency of someone at an interview, politics has little time for such pretences. An amusing example of this comes from Damian McBride's memoirs, where he recalls the day when he interviewed to become the head of communications of the Treasury after spending several years as a floating civil servant.

'Gordon looked down my CV silently, occasionally muttering a word from it, as if trying to work up some enthusiasm either for me or the process: "Customs"; "V-A-T" (each letter spat out with contempt); "Riots?"; and then finally, as he read my "personal interests", he came alive: "Celtic? You support Celtic? How can you support Celtic?" He seemed genuinely affronted. "Where were you in '94, eh? I bet you didn't do any singing that day," alluding to Raith Rovers' famous League Cup final victory over my dad's team. "Yeah," I said, "but it was at Ibrox," the home ground of Glasgow Rangers, "and they did deliberately flood the pitch so we couldn't play our football."

'"That's a bloody lie!" he yelled at me, then – turning to the sofa of rather confused Englishmen – "These bloody Celtic fans, they can't take losing. Always the same. You got beaten fair and square. Fair and square!" My CV was now scrunched in his hand. At this point, I was more worried about escaping alive than getting the job, but we ended up going back and forth for half an hour, swapping stories and jokes about Scottish football. "When can you start?" he concluded, with a beaming smile.'

Would he have got the post if his CV hadn't been good enough? Probably not. Would he have got the post, then risen to become one of Brown's closest aides if he'd not had that Scottish football connection? Probably not.

This lack of formality isn't inherently problematic; each Downing Street administration is unique, and there would be little point in issuing one-size-fits-all guidelines. How No 10 operates depends on the Prime Minister, their party, the size of that party's majority, how united or divided that party is, and so on. It is also an odd place. On the one hand, it is at the centre of everything: 10 Downing Street has tentacles reaching across Whitehall and into the Palace of Westminster, and needs to be aware of as much as possible in order to function well. On the other, it can feel cut off from the rest of the world.

'Most departments are about policy, but No 10 is about politics,' says Will Tanner. 'No 10 is basically managing different individuals in different places to get them to do the things that you want them to do. So when I was in the Home Office I spent basically 95% of my time dealing with problems in the immigration system; things that affect real people's lives. In No 10 it's the other way around: 95% of the time is managing Westminster and not dealing with things that affect people's lives.'

Still, he argues that 'in No 10 you just generally know much, much more about what's going on. Departments are naturally siloed and you have a very fragmented picture about what other bits of government are doing and when they might be doing them.'

One former senior civil servant who worked there for a few years disagrees. 'In No 10, in one sense you have loads of information, you're obviously dead in the centre of things, but sometimes people will be trying to withhold information from you, both the civil service and spads. It's a mix of both having loads of information but then being distant as well. I mean, it's a surreal place: the gossip just comes to you because you're there, you'll see stuff. You will see people, cabinet ministers chatting to one another, looking pissed off. All that stuff, it's just there, you just have to look around. But then in other ways you're in this weird bubble.'

This is largely because of three things. The first is obvious and linked to the odd geographical constraints of Westminster. As former No-10-adviser-turned-peer Lord Wood explains, 'If you work in Downing Street, you're just cut off from the gossip that happens in Westminster; we heard about stuff from journalists. Once you're away from Westminster, even just over the road, you don't really have a sense of what's going on.'

The second is that in Westminster, information is power; knowing something makes you powerful, passing on that something can make you more powerful if it is the right person and the right time, and strategically withholding information can make you more powerful. The third is about accountability, the press, and the very nature of party politics. Here is Lord Wood again: 'I used to work for the Leader of the Opposition and the Prime Minister and you find yourself responding to gossip much more than you should, partly because it's such an incestuous world and everyone's always gossiping about each other, and partly because it's such a pressure cooker world and everyone is spending way too much time at work. If you're a prime minister or a leader of the opposition, there's an asymmetry which is that if someone does something stupid, or is accused of doing something stupid in government and you don't react to it, you'll be accused of negligence if you don't take action.'

Part of your job as a leader is being responsible for the actions and conduct of your MPs, which either means making sure questionable things do not happen or, more realistically, responding in the right way if questionable things do happen on your watch. In order to do this, you must be aware of as much as possible, and as early on as possible. As former No 10 spinner Sean Kemp puts it: 'You're just ringing people up, going, "Can you please tell us what you're doing?" and then "Why on earth didn't you tell us what you were doing?"'

A good example of how this has become embedded in the fabric of British politics is Prime Minister's Questions. Now happening every Wednesday at noon, the weekly set piece involves the PM going to the chamber to be questioned on one or several topics by the Leader of the Opposition, then by a selection of backbenchers picked from a ballot. It is famous for representing what some call the worst side of Westminster, and is often accused of trivialising important issues facing the country by turning them into a Punch & Judy show. Scratch the surface, however, and you'll notice that PMQs is about a lot more than that.

Take a step back for a second, and imagine you are the Prime Minister. It is Wednesday morning and you are about to be asked six questions by someone desperate to do your job. You do not know what the questions will be about, but you know you need to answer them well, as otherwise that person might get one step closer to getting your job. What is the most important thing you need? Information. What you need is to know everything that has happened on your watch in the past seven days, so you can know what to say if it is brought up. Sometimes, departments will merrily get in touch and own up to having screwed up at some point in the last week; most of the time they don't. This is where the Research & Information Unit of Downing Street steps in. As Theo Bertram once explained in a piece, it was he and his team's job to find out exactly what had happened, track down who was behind the blunder, and make them explain just how they were going to fix it before the Prime Minister stood at the despatch box at noon. Most weeks, some would try to pretend everything was fine, and sometimes they did trick the R&I team, but most of the time the culprits were caught.

How? Because 'information flows to us, like water to the sea. Even if you don't give it to us, it will find its way to us. It always comes here. It belongs to us. [...] We do not think any less of them for making a mistake. We admire them more for telling us what we need to know so quickly. Just tell us. But if you don't, if you choose to dawdle, deceive or shift blame, then we will remember. We will add it to our repository of information. Because we are the people who own information. We collect it. We distribute it. When the right time comes, then we will be unfailingly polite, remarkably helpful, and we will share whatever information is requested about you, just in the right way, at just the right moment. You may never even know we did it, but we will fuck you up. Because this is what we do. We know what information is, how it flows towards power. We know when to collect it and when to give it out.'*

Still, the point is, you might not see it when you groan at MPs shouting 'Hear, hear' in the chamber once a week, but PMQs mostly is a wide information-gathering exercise, aimed at centralising information in No 10.

---

* People who work in politics sure have a flair for the dramatic, huh?

The other side of this is that because No 10 is at the centre of everything, an incredible amount of mostly useless information finds its way to the building. Some of it will be the fun but generally irrelevant shagging rumour, others will be nasty but low-level infighting between groups of MPs no one really cares about, and so on. While those are the sort of stories junior staffers and journalists are desperate to hear about in order to feel like they are in the thick of it, those with actual power usually have more important things to do than deal with the vast majority of gossip. There is also a bit of a motherly (or fatherly) feeling to it all, with people wanting to tell on their enemies to the grown-ups in charge so they can get them in trouble, and/or to look like the exemplary sibling. Oh, and there will always be people who simply adore gossip, and assume that everyone else loves it as much as they do so consider it their duty to tell everyone everything.

This happened to Bertram when he worked in Labour's No 10, and he was pursued by endless stories about a certain eccentric Liberal Democrat MP. 'Lembit Opik was the subject of lots of pieces of gossip which were of no value to anyone,' he says. 'It was remarkable just how often the gossip that would come in from different corners would be about Lembit Opik, and we didn't need more information, or any information, about Lembit Opik. I was at a reception in Downing Street when someone came up to me, who had nothing to do with politics, and said, "Oh yes, someone said I should talk to you about Lembit Opik." I don't want to, I don't need to hear any of this.'

Wood agrees with the (implied) point of the anecdote: 'Good people around a senior politician filter a lot and don't pass things on; a lot of the job is to not pass on the tittle-tattle because it could be wrong, it could be vindictive. There are all sorts of reasons why gossip gets passed around.'

Another former Downing Street adviser concludes: 'The senior politician will set the tone in terms of whether they're interested in gossip loosely. I mean, both senior politicians I've worked with were very interested in gossip, and therefore people knew to collect it and share it in that environment. Every politician I've ever known is desperate to know exactly what's going on, with whom, where, when and why.'

This is also valid within No 10: just because there can be an us versus them mentality in 10 Downing Street does not mean that there aren't power struggles, infighting and near-comical bouts of miscommunication in the building itself. After all, there are between 150 and 200 people working there at any given point, and a number of them will have differing agendas. Special advisers will occasionally try to get one over the civil servants (and vice versa), special advisers themselves usually have their internal cliques, people truly loyal to the PM and people there out of convenience or biding their time won't always see eye to eye, etc. There is also a reasonably clear hierarchy within No 10: just because you can brag to people outside of it that you're impossibly important due to where you work, everyone in the building will know it if you really are just the tea boy. And on top of everything else, most workplaces in Westminster are chaotic and dysfunctional, and there is no reason why Downing Street wouldn't be the same.

'In No 10, though, you're right in the centre of things and everything's on a need-to-know basis. There's not some meeting that everyone goes to where they say, "This is all the stuff that's going on …," and you can find out quite big shit randomly,' says Greg Beales, who used to work for Gordon Brown. Though a senior adviser to the PM, he found out the hard way that being important does not always mean that people will tell you things. 'After the 2010 election, I didn't even know that we were considering negotiating a deal with the Lib Dems, until day two when I got phoned and asked if I could go into No 10 to work on a possible coalition. I was up at my mum and dad's, just for a few days off, see what happens on the news, and then I get a phone call saying, "Oh yeah, we're all in." "I thought we were voted out?" "But no, we're all in, we're working on this thing, so can you come and have a look at this agreement?" So I drove back into No 10. And it was pretty much dead by the time I got there.'

Still, if you are the Prime Minister, the Deputy Prime Minister in a coalition or the Leader of the Opposition, you are usually aware of decisions this big. As mentioned earlier, the smaller stuff is what becomes interesting. Say you're a political adviser who is close to their leader, how do you decide what to pass on? If you're good at your job, there are problems you and your colleagues can deal with without having to trouble your boss, who probably has bigger things on their mind. Equally, and even if it is something that can be dealt with without them, at what point do you decide that they need to be aware of it in case they're asked? All of this depends on the leader you have, and on everything else. Some party leaders just love a good gossip (Ed Miliband's name came up more than once in that context during interviews for this book), others do not, and most are in between. What they do all have in common is that they are people: immensely busy and stressed people, but people nonetheless.

The hours they work are too long; they can't just go to their local pub at the end of a long day to unwind, and a lot of what they might want to whinge about are things that categorically cannot be whinged about publicly or to friends they do not fully trust, and those are few and far between. What this means is that sometimes, a PM, DPM or LOTO (Leader of the Opposition)* will just want to have a normal chat. It doesn't need to be about rumours they must absolutely know about, plots they should be aware of, or anything that would truly influence the way they run the country and/or their party. Most people enjoy having a bit of a gossip once in a while, and senior politicians aren't any different. James McGrory had a lot to say on this:

'Part of my job as Nick Clegg's spokesman was to be with him a lot. You got a lot of long car journeys, train journeys, boring meetings. Partly what makes you good at your job is that you know what he thinks, because you've spent so much time with him. There's very little Nick Clegg ever said where I thought, "I've not heard this before." We'd speak at six in the morning, speaking until midnight, I'd be with him 14 hours, 16 hours a day.

'You've got to understand, they're human. People forget. I mean, people really do forget. These people are human beings, they're normal people, they've got a family and a wife and a job, and other interests outside of politics, and so sometimes he'll want to be properly, "What are we doing, what are we saying, what are we doing on this?" Sometimes he'll want you to be fucking honest with him. That was shit, this is shit, no, we're not saying that, no. Be critical, give him a bollocking, have an argument. Sometimes he'll want you to shut the fuck up. That is also what you should know. You might have two and a half hours in front of you in the car. He's knackered, or he's got stuff on his mind, or he's doing other shit. Shut the fuck up. Your input is not needed there.

---

* What an acronym soup.

'But do you know what, sometimes he'll want to talk about his kids. He'll want to say they were playing football yesterday, or they did this, or Miriam and I went to a really nice restaurant, or we're thinking of going on holiday. Like any normal person would say, "You know, we're thinking of going on holiday to Asturias this year. We're really excited because we think we've found this ..." Just like a fucking normal person would if you were having a drink with them. They spend so much of their time wrestling with really big issues, having really intense conversations. Sometimes taking really big decisions about whether you're going to commit troops to a war. There's so much of their lives absorbed with really quite heavy stuff that will weigh on you, and some of it will really weigh on you. And then sometimes, they just want to have a bit of a chat with you as another human being about stuff. As well as being then my boss, and certainly my political hero, and the greatest man I've ever met, he was also my friend, and sometimes you wanted to say, "I heard so-and-so was sleeping with so-and-so in the office," or you know, "I heard that so-and-so got really drunk at the X party," or "So-and-so lost his temper with ..." It's going to affect them zero politically, this is not intel. This is pure gossip. Whether two of the team are having a fling in the office, it's not going to affect his political decision in any way, shape or form. Nor how he deals with them. But we all do it, we all need a bit of entertainment.'

In a nutshell: gossip is a vital part of life in politics because it informs a lot of decisions, changes the behaviour of those in power and can alter the course of history, but it is also something that people who are overwhelmed with stress and responsibilities can use to remember that they're human. Politicians aren't machines, and politicians on the verge of a nervous breakdown aren't going to govern to the best of their abilities, so allowing them to have this release valve is crucial. That being said, we're here to show that gossip is more than just that in Westminster, even when it comes to lawmaking. Let's leave Downing Street for now, through the door and past the barriers, and go back down to Whitehall.

WHY ARE WE HERE?

We've talked about parties and factions in Parliament, whips tasked with getting votes through the Commons and MPs rebelling for reasons ranging from the genuine to the petty. We know that bills can live and die in the Palace of Westminster for reasons not always linked to the effect they will have on the real world, but what happens before that? There can be an assumption that civil servants in their government departments are the grown-ups in the room, less likely to let personal reasons influence their work, but that's not really the case.

For a start, a lot of their job relies on how they work with the ministerial team and special advisers, who can come and go unexpectedly. A productive working relationship in other areas of life tends to rely on at least a degree of stability, but that is not a luxury government departments have. Ministers get reshuffled and usually take their advisers with them, and restless civil servants aren't expected to spend decades on end in the same building. What is also required to make things go as smoothly as possible is good communication which (try not to collapse in shock) is not exactly an area Westminster is good at. Private offices can be fiercely protective of their ministers, which is an issue when other civil servants are meant to have an in-depth understanding of what that minister wants to get done during their time in that department. Mix those two together and you will find that trust becomes hard to come by, which complicates matters further.

'Knowing how much juice the given minister has is very helpful in knowing what kind of agenda you can work on, but you do see senior civil servants who take that to the next level, and try and use the perception of gossip about ministers to try and influence what ministers do,' says a former permanent secretary. 'So if you were a director or a director-general, a somewhat high-ranking but not absolute top-ranking civil servant, it's very difficult for you to say, "This is a bad idea, Minister, I disagree with what you're doing." But I have seen fascinating examples where I'll have a civil servant come to me and say, "I think you should know, I'm hearing rumblings that people are unhappy with this that the minister is doing." And you know, sometimes frankly, it's total bullshit, and is it maybe because you don't want to do it? And you don't have the guts to tell the minister that. It's a bit like a medieval court in that respect.'

Elsewhere in departments, more junior civil servants have been known to be so confused about what ministers want them to do that they carefully read every interview their political boss gives to the national and trade press, then attempt to reverse-engineer the policies they assume they want. As with every space where important information is lacking, that gap then tends to be filled with received wisdom, whispers and half-certainties, with predictable results.

'The grapevine would create weird impressions about what politicians wanted,' explains one former Labour adviser. 'I did loads of work on healthcare infections, and trying to get hospitals clean, and early on in that work you would get all these weird rumours about what the Secretary of State, who was Patricia Hewitt initially, and what the Prime Minister wanted to do and not do and what they were looking for. So you'd be trying to build up your 'what works' approach, but you'd do it within these weird parameters of what the politicians thought about stuff. And what they thought about stuff was totally hearsay, because nobody ever got this written down. It was hearsay, and then over time what we found was that a lot of these rumours about what the politicians would or wouldn't accept turned out to be completely half-baked rumour mill-type stuff.

'For example, I remember there was a really strong thing that Blair and Patricia Hewitt wouldn't accept any cleaning contracts being moved back into hospitals' control after they'd been moved out under PFI, so the policy thing was, we can do all this, but you can't touch these cleaning contracts because that's not their personal agenda. So for about six to nine months no one went anywhere near these contracts for that reason, and in the end there was some meeting and we just brought it up and said of course we can do more here, but we'd have to do something about these PFI contracts. And Blair was saying, "Yeah. Yeah yeah." And we responded, "Right. Okay. We haven't really done anything on this," to which he replied, "Why aren't we doing something?" So I had to say that we would do something.'

This is a bit of an extreme example, but also the reason why it is good for civil servants to develop a good network of contacts beyond Whitehall. If a lot of your job is going to rely on informal pieces of information you get from your personal contacts, then it does seem judicious to have as large a network as possible. According to a former permanent secretary, 'There are some networks which I find useful for gossip purposes, for the informal information. One is the private office network as all the ministers' private secretaries across Whitehall have quite a strong network and clique. The other is parliamentary clerks, and sometimes it's quite smart for civil servants to form a relationship with a government whip. It's a bit unusual because they don't generally do a government brief, but if you're really trying to make the department aligned to what ministers are trying to do, you need to rope in the special advisers, need to rope in the whips, and you can't be too fussy about whose side of the line you're on. You've got to form these quasi-political relationships, and it's quite a grown-up thing to do and requires a bit of judgement.'

This is because politics is about, well, politics: a policy can be as good as it gets in the technocrat world but if the optics of it are uncomfortable to the party leadership, or it is for whatever reason unpalatable to the backbenches, it won't be going far. It might not be the job of civil servants to come up with policies that satisfy all the internal politics of the main party in the House of Commons, but policies that do not are likely to turn into one gigantic waste of time, which is useful to precisely no one. That logic also works for keeping an eye on who gets along with whom in the government, and how much they can be made to work together. A lot of policy work needs pitching from several areas of Whitehall, but the formal structures aren't always there to ensure that this can always happen without a hitch. As a result, the personal relationships of ministers can have a tremendous influence on civil servants' abilities to get on with their jobs.

'So much of it is based on how those ministers worked together,' says Nicole Valentinuzzi from the Institute for Government. 'When I worked at the Ministry of Justice, Jack Straw worked really well with the Home Secretary, Jacqui Smith, and there were a lot of cross-departmental policies. When they had meetings together, they could come out with something and both private offices would be saying, "Okay, this is all pretty good, we can send this to write-round." Whereas after a meeting with two Secretaries of State who didn't get along as easily, the private secretaries would come out after and be saying, "Well, actually, that's not my interpretation of what was agreed." So much is based on the relationship between these people, rather than any kind of rationality.'

On top of all of this, the civil service itself is not one gigantic blob with everyone peacefully agreeing with everyone else all the time. It has internal strife, power battles, personality clashes and needs effort to remain as functional as possible.

Cross-departmental plotting and cooperation happens at a number of levels: there are the informal drinks and gossip networks we mapped out at the beginning and the private offices network, but coordination also happens at a higher level. The Wednesday morning meeting, where departments' permanent secretaries and the Cabinet Secretary gather, is the stuff of legends. Because nothing ever really leaks from it, it has become the obsession of various political operatives throughout the years, who end up convincing themselves that it is the 'real Cabinet meeting', and the place the country really is run from. Even ministers have fallen into that paranoia, with David Cameron sending one of his secretaries of state to spy on the civil servants during the coalition.

A former permanent secretary recalls: 'Michael Gove, when he was Chief Whip during Francis Maude's reign of terror, inserted himself in the Wednesday morning meetings. So he would come every other week and we couldn't exactly exclude him, because he got permission from the Prime Minister, but it was deeply, deeply awkward. He would sit there next to Jeremy Heywood, writing a longhand note, and he wouldn't say a word in the meeting, but occasionally he would say, "Very interesting." And I would say afterwards, "How did you find it, Michael?" "Very interesting. Very interesting." God knows what he was doing with his notes but he was clearly writing it like he was the Cabinet … "Thank you very much. Very nice."'

That still does not answer our question: What really happens there? Here is what two people who used to attend them had to say: 'There's usually a slightly fumbling, not very good presentation from someone on something, which is their time to shine in the sun. Sometimes they're good, sometimes they're not so good. Sometimes we get a really good lively conversation, sometimes there's a feeling that the real action's happening outside the room. The Cabinet Secretary generally constructs an agenda, it's pretty informal, it's usually constructed two days before. There are two or three items of business, but we do have some pretty frank conversations about security, for example, or how the Prime Minister is feeling at the moment in case you get something from No 10.

'Then we get a sense of how the civil service is doing corporally, so rotation, whether it's trusted, whether some things have happened which have undermined us or supported us or professionally reflected well on us or otherwise. Do we still have significance and presence? Are we still in the room? Are we still players? It's a bit of self-help. Civil servants don't have many defenders so we defend each other quite a lot.'

The other puts it more succinctly: 'There is a lot of gossip around the Wednesday morning meeting, just as I imagine there is; in the margins of Cabinet. Do you know why so few things leak from it? Because it's so boring. During my years, very rarely was there a very interesting discussion in the Wednesday morning meeting.'

There is no doubt that they're being somewhat facetious, but there is an interesting dynamic at play here. Cabinet meetings usually leak a bit or like a sieve depending on the administration and its current state, but Wednesday morning meetings rarely do; 1922 Committee meetings often leak, but meetings of the 1922 Committee's executive (almost) never do. There are things in Westminster which will always come out, and others which won't. As with everything else, these rules aren't set formally, but they do exist. At a more personal level too, there are things it is socially acceptable to gossip about and others that will reflect badly on you. We've now spent a lot of time discussing what people talk about; let's take a look at what they don't.

WHAT WE DON'T TALK ABOUT

Gossip spreads in Westminster and elsewhere because people are told about something, then decide to tell other people about it, who will then tell others, ad nauseam. There has been academic work on why people decide to pass on information, but not about the situations in which they decide not to. This must have happened to you too; someone once told you something and you decided that, on balance, you probably shouldn't tell anyone else. Why was that? Let's assume that it wasn't because the something in question was simply very dull, because that would make your decision pretty self-explanatory.

Maybe you didn't say anything because the person made you swear not to tell anyone else, and you didn't want to betray their trust. This is a straightforward reason, and an honourable one. It is, by definition, impossible to know how much of it exists in politics, but there is one example of someone just keeping their mouth shut because he felt he had to: Tony Newton. 'One of the massive pieces of gossip of our time was John Major shagging Edwina Currie, which was a genuinely clandestine secret,' says *The Times* diary editor Patrick Kidd. 'The only person who was confided in was Tony Newton, who was the MP for Braintree.

He'd been in the same social security ministerial teams as both Major and Currie, and was trusted by them as a confidant, and he didn't blag. After it came out, he just said, "Well, they told me not to say anything about it, so I didn't." Didn't even gossip about it.'*

Though it is possible that you really are the sort of person to take trust so seriously that you would keep shtum about something if asked to, there are other reasons why you might decide not to repeat a piece of gossip. Say, for example, that your boss confided in you about something one of your colleagues did, and which none of the people at your level could have known about. The temptation to share that piece of information with your office friends will be there, but it has to be counterbalanced with the fact that it might then spread and eventually get back to your boss, which would guarantee that said boss would never confide in you again. On the one hand, you can enhance your status with your peers by handing them information that they do not have access to; on the other, doing this might mean shutting off your supply of privileged information, as well as wider consequences. Which one would you choose? Risky short-term gain or potential long-term gain?

Unless you're decidedly Manichean, chances are that your answer will be: 'It depends.' This comes back to our journalists explaining that there are no definitive rules on what should and shouldn't be published. If, for example, an MP who is an excellent, high-level source does one slightly silly thing once, it might not be worth publishing a hit job on them and losing

---

* This is another topic for another time, but it is worth pointing out that had Newton blabbed before Major got to No 10, it seems almost certain that he never would have made it to Downing Street as a result. Just because you aren't saying anything doesn't mean that your actions don't have consequences. Then again, maybe Newton knew this, and did not want to have the responsibility of a seismic political change resting on his shoulders.

that relationship. This logic works away from the media as well. Lobbyist Andy Williams explains this well: 'Most people who work in politics are narcissists to some degree, and that includes people in public affairs, because they want to feel like they're more in the game than they are, and they want to look like they're more in the thick of things than they are. There's a constant judgement call going on, which is: where does this friend of mine fit in, and are they a good enough friend that I'm prepared to keep what they said quiet? Or actually are the chances that it's never going to come back to me, so I don't mind telling someone? If it gets into the public domain they probably won't find out. But there's also something about power relationships. When it comes to gossip, often someone really well known or senior or in the know might tell someone more junior something, and they just don't expect you ever to say anything. Because they think, well, why would you sell me out? Because I'm more useful to you than you are to me.'

This makes sense: if gossip is used as currency in Westminster, then people must be careful about whom they use it with and how much of it they use, especially if they want to go far in their given field. As Catherine Haddon from the Institute for Government puts it: 'One of the things to prove you are important and have influence is whether or not you're in the know. So being in the know, being in the room, being in the email chain, all of that kind of stuff, is part of your domain, your power. But the interesting thing is gossip, like other forms of information, is one of those things where you have its power as long as you know it and somebody else doesn't. So, as soon as you tell them about it, you're showing off your power, but you're also losing it, because then more and more people know.'

The other point made by Williams is also interesting: whom you're telling something to matters just as much as who told you the something and what the something is. Relationships in Westminster are fundamentally transactional, so there is little point in just sharing a piece of explosive gossip with someone if you know that they will never be able to reciprocate or return the favour in some other way.*

There are also more concrete reasons why you might want to keep your mouth shut when you learn of something juicy that would piss people off if it were to get around. Sure, you can decide not to spread the rumour because you fear it may come back to bite you in the arse at some point in the future, or because you've decided that your relationship of trust with the person who told you in the first place is too important to be broken, but it might also be about the future of your career. As we saw a few chapters ago, the role of spinners is not only to make sure that good stories end up in the papers, but also that bad stories never see the light of day. To do this, they can 'not quite lie but slightly mislead' journalists, make sure they know where the bodies are buried in advance, but they can also just threaten the journalists. It's a risky tactic, and it can only work if you have the clout to pull it off, but it is a tactic nonetheless.

As the former press secretary to Lib Dem leader Paddy Ashdown during the New Labour years, Miranda Green has opinions on the topic: 'At the time I was doing that job, Alastair Campbell was my opposite number,' she says. 'Can you imagine? It was absolutely hilarious. I was 28 years old and all of the tricks that he could use to just shut people up … I mean, I had no power. I mean, what political editor would have wept if I had threatened to throw them into the deep freeze and cut them

* This is why starting out in SW1 can be especially hard when you're a journalist; more than sharing gossip, people would much rather trade it, but in order to receive information, you must have information to offer yourself – it's tricky.

out from Lib Dem briefings? It's laughable, right? Whereas he could exert control by excluding people. And that's what they did, Alastair Campbell and Peter Mandelson; their system was not just favoured journalists to give the stories to, but also, you know, you piss us off, we won't give you the info for a while until you're really scared that it's drying up. I couldn't do any of that. So what you can do to control rumour and gossip depends on your pecking order in the Westminster hierarchy.'

This is a way in which politics differs from the real world: though it would be generally ill-advised to spread gossip about one of your superiors at work, there generally will not be formal ways in which that superior will be able to strike back and make your working life worse. They might try to make sure you don't get a promotion, or remain stuck with dull projects, but anything genuinely serious could end up with HR on your side. If, on the other hand, the head of comms of a political party suddenly decides that you won't get access to off-the-record briefings for a few weeks because you printed something they wanted to remain secret, there's not much you can do about it. The threat is also quantified in a way that it might not be in a workplace outside of SW1: while there's no guessing how a manager might react if you tell everyone in the office that you saw them drunkenly kiss a woman who was not their wife, it's a pretty safe bet to assume that, say, you'll suddenly have a hard time booking ministers on your current affairs TV show if you pissed off the No 10 broadcast team with a story about how dysfunctional it is.

That being said, there is other reason why you might decide to keep a rumour to yourself which is altogether more universal: you like the person that rumour is about. This works on two levels: the first one is that it is not in your interest to, for example, tell several of your colleagues that your office best friend cheated on her boyfriend at the Christmas party. She is, after all, your office best friend, and unless you're a sociopath, you probably do not want everyone to find out about the mistake she made. The second one is that you are more likely to take a kinder view of the problematic things those close to you have done. Take that cheating example: if the drunk cheater is someone you dislike already, you will probably take the sloshed snogging as extra evidence that that person is untrustworthy and/or a mess, depending on why you dislike her. If, however, she happens to be a close friend of yours, you will be more likely to find extenuating circumstances; she really was very drunk, he leapt on her, her boyfriend is awful anyway, etc. Seen from that angle, the story immediately becomes less juicy, and there is less urgency to share it with everyone you know.

This happens in Westminster as well. Here is how a senior political journalist puts it: 'The relationship with a source can definitely be corrupting. We like someone, therefore we are reluctant to believe bad things about them. I mean clearly, interestingly, no one seems to like Andrew Griffiths very much, that's what you learnt when that sexting story came out. But I think that if it turned out a popular MP was having an affair, you'd find everyone was much more understanding. Because we wouldn't want to believe it, we're all fond of him, we don't want to believe wicked things about him, even in the face of obvious evidence of it. And that's hugely problematic in a way.'

Finally, there is one other reason why something might not spread: it is too bleak, too personal, or a mix of both. There is one story that illustrates this perfectly, and relates to something tragic that happened to someone who is very close to a person who was a very senior politician at the time. That event definitely was news, as it was something big which would have deeply touched the politician, who in turn was running the country. The whole lobby knew about it; most political journalists who weren't around at the time now know about it. Still, it never made any of the papers. This is how it went down, according to one lobby hack who was there: 'That happened more or less the week I joined the lobby, and I found myself in this weird situation where I didn't even have a parliamentary pass, so I couldn't get into the building. And this was a major moment, and what the hell are we supposed to do? And I only had it as gossip. And I basically just sat there and I said, "Well, okay, we'll see if it's in the Sunday papers." We won't be first with it, but we had to have it, because the feeling was that this might prompt [that politician] to resign. And this very strange thing happened, and I felt it was absolutely right not to run it. At every level it was right not to run it, and the most amazing thing is that that held. And that was still an internet age. So you could find things out about it, and if you Google the right words, you'll probably find it.'

This book is not the right place to reveal what happened; the judgement of political journalists is not always the correct one, but they were right on this. It is also not the only occurrence of this kind; sometimes, the graveness of a story is more important than the story itself, and though it could be shared around the bubble and with the public outside of it, it isn't.

What is interesting about these stories, besides the fact that they reveal that some people in Westminster actually do have some principles, is that the line between what is and isn't acceptable to gossip about changes with the times. What is considered good gossip is intrinsically linked to the values of the people sharing it. Something seemingly irrelevant a few decades ago could now be huge, and vice versa. To look at this in a bit more depth, let's take a detour via the good old days.

CHANGING MORALS,
CHANGING TIMES

There are many reasons why someone might decide not to spread a rumour about something, and there is one we did not get into in the last chapter. What happens if a piece of information you were given simply isn't interesting, or relevant? Like journalism and its 'man bites dog' rule, a bit of gossip only becomes that if it is about something out of the ordinary, or surprising. You wouldn't run to your colleague if you saw your boss buying his lunch from Tesco, for example. Still, it's worth trying to unpack this: why isn't a piece of information interesting? That Tesco lunch image was purposely mundane to the extreme, but it does get a bit more complicated when we start straying from one's meal deal options.

For a start, who gets to decide what is and isn't out of the ordinary? Societal values evolve with time, so what counts as peculiar enough to pique people's interest isn't set in stone. What you think of as an explosive story would perhaps not have mattered at all to your grandparents, and vice versa. The obvious example of this is people's sexual orientation. Asked about the things that have changed the most since their early years in politics 30 years ago, one Conservative adviser-turned-peer said: 'At the time, one of the common topics would be whether somebody was gay or not; that was more widely talked about than most things actually, who was gay.' Former New Labour spad Lord Livermore brought it up as well, saying: 'Back in the early days of the Labour government, quite a lot of politicians were outed by the media, and there was a big *Sun* headline, "Is Britain being run by a gay mafia?" because there were three Labour politicians outed.'

Meanwhile, this is what a House of Commons member of staff had to add: 'I don't think any colleague joining now, a gay colleague, would think twice about that just being a thing that everyone knew about. I was very cautious in the nineties, and I think I was right to be in some respects, because in the division lobbies late at night, you'd hear references to "the buggers", and sort of public school, 1955-type chat. And it was by no means only on one party.'

This is all pretty bleak, but let's come back to the example brought up by Lord Livermore. It all started in late 1998, when Welsh Secretary Ron Davies was robbed on Clapham Common one night. Clapham Common was then known as a cruising spot for men, and though no specific details came out about the alleged robbery at the time, the fact that it happened where and when it did and that Davies resigned from the Cabinet on the spot was enough for rumours to start swirling. A day later, former Conservative MP and out gay man Matthew Parris was interviewed by Jeremy Paxman on *Newsnight*, and said that Trade Secretary Peter Mandelson was 'certainly' gay. Paxman quickly moved on, and two days later, the BBC issued an internal memo telling its employees that 'under no circumstances whatsoever should the allegation about the private life of Peter Mandelson be repeated or referred to in any broadcast'. This was a valiant effort by the BBC to put an end to the story, but it did not work.

Under a week later, Agriculture Minister Nick Brown came out. Though it appeared spontaneous, his hand was forced by the *News of the World*, who were getting ready to out him whether he wanted it or not. The *Sun* then decided to pour some more petrol on the fire by publishing a splash entitled 'TELL US THE TRUTH TONY – Are we being run by a gay mafia?' Choice quotes from the editorial that followed include 'the public has a right to know how many homosexuals occupy positions of high power' and 'there are widespread fears that MPs, even ministers, are beholden to others for reasons other than politics'. They even decided to kindly open a phone hotline for 'ministers and MPs who are secretly homosexual' and wished to come out with the help of the *Sun*.*

Though the tabloids' actions feel unquestionably outrageous today, the late nineties were a point where the wind was still just about turning on the question of homosexuality. Section 28 was still in place, and when the *Guardian* commissioned a poll to try and shut the *Sun* up, it found that 52% of people thought being openly gay was compatible with holding a Cabinet position; though 52% is a majority, it can hardly be called a landslide. The *Graun*'s conclusion was that 'the days when it was assumed that the British public was overwhelmingly intolerant of homosexuals are over'. This was perhaps optimistic, as only two years earlier the British Social Attitudes survey had found that 55% of people thought that sexual relations between two adults of the same sex were 'always wrong', but change was in the air. A day after that *Guardian* poll, the *Sun* did a screeching U-turn and announced that it would no longer out gay politicians unless there was an overwhelming public interest reason to do so, and columnist Matthew Parris was sacked from the paper.

These momentous few weeks didn't put an end to rumours about people's sexual orientation, but they do represent a turning point. Section 28 was eventually repealed in 2003, and attitudes towards gay and bisexual people have been slowly but steadily becoming more liberal with time. 'I'm told that there are several MPs on Grindr now and nobody writes that story,' says gay

---

* You will be surprised to hear that not much came out of that.

Labour MP Chris Bryant. 'Attitudes around homosexuality have completely changed; since I was first involved in politics when I first stood for council in 1993, every element of the law has changed. I remember Chris Smith being out, being the only one, and now I don't even know who's gay. I had to ask somebody recently, who I'd been on three trips with, I had to say, "Are you gay?" I'm completely incompetent at being able to spot gays any more, which is really quite shocking. Maybe I'm just too old, but that's good, it doesn't matter. He's just another MP, who happens to be a sponsor of LGBT Labour. Does that mean he's gay? Maybe it means he's gay.'

As Bryant points out, behaviour and expectations in the bubble have changed because the world that surrounds it has changed as well. In fact, a study conducted by Gabriele Magni and Andrew Reynolds shows that in the general election of 2015, a candidate being gay had no impact whatsoever on how they fared compared to their straight counterparts – well, zero percentage points plus or minus half a percentage point. This changes the dynamics of political coverage entirely. If tabloids could once justify their outing of gay politicians by saying that the public deserved to know and act in consequence, the fact is that nowadays, when the public knows, its behaviour no longer changes. When there was once a (morally dubious but nonetheless existing) public interest angle to the outing of MPs, there is no longer one. At a personal level too, the currency of knowing that someone is gay and not out is no longer as valuable as it used to be; it is not something that will destroy the career of an MP, they will not feel pressured to resign if it comes out, and the only person left looking bad will be the person who shared the story in the first place.

This is the best example of something no longer being a story worth sharing because people's attitudes have changed, but there are also cases where a change in social attitudes turn previously dull stories into ones people avidly share, or amusing stories into dark ones. Booze is the obvious one: one of the biggest changes in the House of Commons over the past few decades has been the amount of alcohol consumed by the people working in it. According to a long-term Commons employee, 'When I joined over 20 years ago, I mean it was fun, don't get me wrong. I'd be a lying, hypocritical toad if I said it wasn't fun. But you'd see people absolutely pissed; if you went in Strangers' at four o'clock you'd see them absolutely pissed, and the suspicion was that one or two had had a good breakfast as well. It's not like that now; we can probably both reel off half a dozen names of members who at any given moment of the day probably won't be sober, but had this been the nineties, you probably could have done that with 60.'

This is not an exaggeration; any book written from or about Westminster in the 20th century practically reeks of old port and ale. In *Order, Order!*, Ben Wright tells one eyebrow-raising story about Horace King, who was Speaker from 1965 to 1971: 'Horace came in at 9:25pm, and he had two goes at getting up into his chair and the second time he fell to the right across the Clerks' Table with his wig 45 degrees to the left and Bob Mellish (the Government Chief Whip) called out, "You're a disgrace, Horace, and I'll have you out of that chair within three months." Horace turned round so abruptly that his wig was then 45 degrees out the other way, and he gave a brilliant riposte: "How can you get me out of the chair, Bob, when I can't get myself into it?"'

In the MPs' defence, they weren't a sozzled oasis surrounded by dry land, the journalists drank just as much as they did, and did so until quite recently. Now more responsible when it comes to alcohol, senior hack Rob Hutton recalls his first days on Fleet

Street: 'I came into journalism in the late nineties; I was quite interested in production, so I went and did a shift at the *Herald*, and the night editor said I could come and sit behind him. This was 1998, and his thing was he would lay out a story and go to the pub. Have a half, come back, lay out another story. Go to the pub, have another half. Because I was young and arrogant, I refused to drink halves, so I was having a pint each time, and they more or less had to pour me into a taxi at the end of the night. The next day, talking to one of my lecturers about it, whose husband worked at the paper, she said, "How was it?" and I said, "Well, it was really interesting, but to be honest, I don't think I can drink that much every night."'

There are enough stories of inebriety in the Palace of Westminster to fill a whole other book, but for the sake of brevity, we can end it here, as the point has probably been well proven already. In any case, things have changed and you are now more likely to be asked to pick between still and sparkling than red or white if sitting down for a lunch. What this means in practice is that excessive drinking is now a story in itself. Back in the days when most people would drink too much and do silly things too often, the bar was very high when it came to properly good boozy gossip. With less drinking, more responsibility and sterner social attitudes towards casual drinking in the world at large, the nature of those stories has now changed. Firstly, it is a lot rarer for someone to do something properly hilarious or shocking in public while inebriated, so news of mistakes like these tend to travel around faster. Secondly, the tone has changed; everyone is allowed the occasional drunken antics, but if you're seen to have one pint too many one night a week too many, the whispers will probably be about concerns for your mental health and your suitability for a career in high office.

While the most hedonistic among us might argue that this is a loss of fun, it probably is good that having a serious alcohol problem while running this country (or covering the people who do) now makes you a rare exception, thus worthy of people talking behind your back. This change in dynamics has also been observed elsewhere, in an area often connected to excessive drinking: sexual harassment. Once again, personal shifts in the bubble have been mirroring wider changes in society at large; after all, #MeToo originally started in Hollywood and took a number of weeks to make its way to Westminster. Though the whisper network has always existed to an extent, the arrival of many more women in SW1 and the growing feminist movement has meant that handsy men are no longer talked about in the same way.

'It was treated a bit too flippantly, even by the women,' says one female former Labour adviser. 'I'm sure it could upset people, but generally people didn't go, "That guy's always trying to shag researchers," and the like. That would be said as a light-hearted thing rather than in a massive condemnatory way.'

Gossip about male MPs being handsy was still being shared around, but it was treated as salacious or vaguely interesting as opposed to straightforwardly damning. This has, in a way, gone in the opposite direction of stories about gay politicians; while an MP putting his hand on the arse of a young aide would not have made the front pages even a few years ago, it can now be front-page news, which in turns makes that piece of information more valuable. Knowing something embarrassing about someone is one thing, knowing something that you know could end their career is another.

Moral values have also evolved on the topic: at the time of writing, an international conversation is still ongoing about what behaviours are supposedly 'just banter' and what are unforgivable. As a result, the way people whisper about these things is bound to keep evolving. Take MPs cheating on their spouses and shagging younger women, for example. Until not that long ago, a lot of the judgement would fall on the latter, who were assumed to have tempted the older politician/thrown themselves at them/pretended to be older/delete as appropriate. Even in supposedly consensual relationships, there is now a growing understanding that different situations can give different meanings to the notion of consent. If a woman said yes to an encounter because she felt that she was not in a position to say no without potentially risking the rest of her career, did she really say yes at all? Shades of grey are being looked at in a different way, and lines between what is acceptable, questionable and wrong are being renegotiated. The natural conclusion of this is that the way these instances are talked about is changing as well, and as it is still changing, it seems futile to try and predict where it might end up.

Still, if we are going to talk about what people don't talk about and how that may evolve with time, there is one person we now need to bring in. Given that this is a book about gossip and politics, his absence has probably been noticeable already; if anything, talking about gossip and politics in Britain without mentioning him would be futile. Given that the elephant really has been in the room this entire time, let's turn to him now.

THE BONFIRE OF VANITIES

Paul Staines is Guido Fawkes, and Paul Staines fundamentally isn't that interesting. He is Irish, middle-aged, right-wing, and he hates all politicians so he decided to start a political gossip blog in 2004. It was, and is, about 'tittle-tattle, gossip and rumours about Westminster's Mother of Parliaments.* Written from the perspective of the only man to enter Parliament with honest intentions. The intention being to blow it up with gunpowder.' Many profiles have been written about Paul Staines, the enigmatic libertarian figure who drips cynicism and longs to unleash chaos on SW1, and they are easy to find online if you would like to know more about him as a person. If you don't, we can just move on and talk about what really matters: Guido Fawkes.

Guido Fawkes is petty, vindictive, mean, sexist, biased and shameless. Over the past 15 years, it has been the home of gutter stories that no one else would have published, the lowest of blows, hints at rumours the writers knew not to be true, and items so far from the public interest that calling them 'journalism' would be an offence to all journalists, alive or dead.

It has also been impeccably briefed, terrifyingly well informed and, more importantly, intoxicatingly fun. Its continued existence and power in Westminster is incredibly telling and reveals the fundamental hypocrisy at the heart of British politics. Over 80 people were interviewed for this book, most were asked to talk about Guido, and nearly every single one of them either refused to talk about it on the record, or at all. Part of it was fear, as Guido relishes a feud and has been known to hit back harder if hit first. Mostly, though, this refusal to engage with the topic seemed to come from a place of uneasiness. It is all fine and good for the majority of people in Westminster to decry the effect the website has had on the bubble – the phrase 'the Guidoisation of politics' was used more than once – but it is undeniable that it never would have become what it is today if it hadn't had a helping hand from everyone else.

---

* As a side note, "Mother of Parliaments" means England, so the tagline makes no sense, but each to their own.

Paul Staines fundamentally isn't that interesting because he is just one man, and the string of mischief-makers he has hired throughout the years to help him in his quest (mostly) haven't been remarkable either. Just as it takes a village to raise a child, Westminster as a whole is responsible for the rise of Guido Fawkes. After all, you can only report on things people tell you; without sources, there is nothing to be written about. Instead, what Staines did was to provide a space where people could go as low as they wanted. Had they collectively decided that undignified mud-slinging was below them all, Guido Fawkes would have come and gone. It hasn't.

According to one person who used to work there, 'All sides speak to Guido, all sides brief Guido. Remainers brief Guido. People in Labour brief Guido.' According to another, 'It would be fair to say that at times Guido has been briefed by MPs from almost every party, including the SNP – when it suits them.' Though they could perfectly be saying that to make themselves sound more important than they were, it is undeniable that Guido carries stories about every corner of Westminster, which wouldn't be possible if the people at those meetings and in those rooms and WhatsApp groups weren't up for leaking what they know. The website might have a more natural home on the right of the Conservative Party, but its tentacles reach everywhere else as well.

This is partly because it was the first of its kind: a publication from the bubble, for the bubble. *Private Eye*, Popbitch and the diary columns might enjoy stirring up drama for the sake of it, but they do need to remain aware of the fact that their readers are what matters; if people outside the postcode couldn't care less about a niche but amusing piece of gossip, then there is usually no point in them publishing it. Guido, on the other hand, prides itself on being the insider's insider; it doesn't matter if only a few hundred people care about a story, as long as it's the right few hundred people.

'I never thought that Guido and us were doing the same thing at all,' says Adam Macqueen of *Private Eye*. 'Because Guido stuff is entirely bubble stuff. I mean, it's genuinely like, what spad has been appointed? And you read it and you think, so what? I don't know this person. Unless you're telling me what the significance of this is. It's deliberately written for insiders. If you know these people it's really, really fascinating.'

Another thing is that it arrived at precisely the right time; by the early and mid noughties, the internet was revolutionising the way the media functioned, but newspapers were slow on the uptake. Some thought digital media would only be a fad, or that physical newspapers would always be the way to go, and others didn't want to dedicate proper resources to something they didn't really understand, and which was in a constant state of flux. Still, technology soon meant that stories no longer had to be printed on paper or included in news bulletins to reach readers, and that news frenzy promptly reached Westminster.

Guido got there early, and aimed to be publishing a steady stream of pieces of gossip throughout the day, every weekday. There was no Twitter at the time, so people in the bubble couldn't just sit at their desk and endlessly scroll whenever they wanted to avoid working. Instead, they would be refreshing the Guido website every few hours, both hoping and fearing that a new morsel had come out. This created a paranoid atmosphere among those who could plausibly be written about by the website, which was pretty much everyone. Because it was so unashamedly insidery, Guido could get away with publishing stories about minor aides or junior journalists as long as they were fun or damaging enough. There is no straight answer to this, but it is worth wondering what effect this had on the behaviour of people in SW1, and whether it turned out to be accidentally positive.

If you knew that there was a new outlet in town who would gleefully report on any questionable actions from anyone in your world, would that make you think twice before doing something you probably shouldn't? Its continued existence shows that it clearly could never make everyone in Westminster suddenly start behaving impeccably, and there is no real way to measure a potential shift anyway, but some signs are there.

For a start, one former Guido employee points out that they used to love running stories about MPs claiming very small expenses, with classics including Stephen Hammond's £4.50 for mileage when going to Remembrance services and Jim Murphy's two cans of IRN-BRU for £1.30. Over the past few years, however, this stream of stories has stopped, because MPs no longer send in ridiculously small expenses claims for things they really should pay for themselves. 'The thing about Guido is, no story is too small for Guido,' says someone who used to work there. 'If it's the tiniest, tiniest little hypocrisy, we will run it. As a funny sort of, just pointing out this double standard, in a way that no other news organisation would. That's the thing that some politicians don't like, because they'll say, "Oh, for goodness' sake, is this really a story? You're just saying everyone's awful, you're just corroding the public view." Well, I take the view that there is no story too small. If a politician has done something that is two-faced, even if it's on the most minor issue that doesn't affect anyone, it shows something about their character that voters should know about.'

This is all fair, but does paint Guido in a rather flattering light; a lot of the time, this explanation stands, but the website will also happily publish small, petty stories just because it wants to. Its view, after all, is that politicians are all out for themselves, few of them have any redeeming qualities, and the ones who are seemingly squeaky clean only appear so because they've not been caught yet. 'I have colleagues of whom I am enormously fond, and some of the best lobby correspondents out there, and one of the things a lot of them have in common is they always believe the worst about everyone,' says Rob Hutton. 'So there's the Guido view, which is that everyone is always absolutely awful and everyone gives into their worst instincts at all times. So there is no possibility of a man and a woman going on an overnight trip without shagging, that's the Guido view; there is just no way in which that happens.'

Lord Livermore goes even further: 'It's the descent into a view of the world where every politician is on the take, automatically; that you can't trust a single politician. Obviously trust in politicians is at a historic low, but you know, "They're all cheats, they're all liars, they're all on the make and our job is to try and prove that." That I think is so corrosive of democracy. I've been lucky with the type of people I've worked with in politics, I'm sure, but the people I've worked with genuinely come into politics for the right reasons, genuinely want to make Britain better, want to do their very best, believe things deeply and passionately and want to put those beliefs into practice. I'm sure there are some politicians who come in for less noble reasons, because in any walk of life you get good people and bad people, but that sort of cynical agenda, that they're all bastards, is, I think, really unhealthy, and really worrying.'

If you see the world through that lens and your goal is to prove that the entirety of Westminster is rotten at its core, then publishing any negative thing, minor or major and about someone senior or junior, becomes a no-brainer. What remains surprising is that everyone else played along for so long. After all, it is not in most political people's interest to consistently make politics look even worse than it is, but short-term personal gains are easy to put above long-term structural pains. The partial dysfunctionality of Westminster is also to blame. As we have seen throughout this book, SW1 is a messy place full of incomprehensible conventions, informal networks filling in for the lack of formal processes, and chains of events linked more to the personality of the people involved than anything else.

In this context, it is not hard to see why people might feel the need to leak, even to a website they find distasteful. As spinner Malcolm Tucker puts it in one of the later episodes of *The Thick of It*, 'If a government can't leak, do you know what happens? Dark shit builds up, and it bursts.' And yes, sure, people could just go to newspapers instead but it isn't quite the same; most papers will put their own slant on a certain story, but lobby journalists are more likely to – shock, horror – seek a proper response from each side involved before publishing anything. It is not hard to find out which hacks are friendly with which factions, thus potentially outing you, and they might just decide that your story is too toxic or transparently vindictive to be printed. For the most part, Guido Fawkes doesn't have such qualms.

According to a former Guido employee, 'The birth of the brand and becoming the brand was all to do with that, kind of, dish the dirt on everyone, anarchic, freewheeling approach, and obviously that does put people off you. It's always the trade-off, isn't it? Who are you serving? Are you serving your readers or are you serving your sources? That is the classic dilemma. And I think that on some days, to be frank, you could look at certain bits of the output and think, that serves sources more than it serves readers.' Given the primary readership of the website, this isn't always a bad thing; more than what a story is, what matters as well is the fact that a certain story was given to Guido at all, so even the most pointless and vicious of briefings can be of interest.

Still, what is so interesting about Guido Fawkes isn't just its rise, its fall can tell us a lot about the way Westminster works. How do we define its 'fall'? It isn't easy, but one metric is the fear it inspires, or doesn't. Ask people in Westminster how scary they find the idea of getting Guidoed and you will come across a certain generational divide. While most of those who were around before roughly 2014 or 2015 have first- or second-hand experience of either having their career ruined or dented by them, or seeing one of their friends go through it, more recent additions to SW1 are less likely to experience that clawing fear of being named by the website. They are also less likely to viscerally hate it. Talk to MPs and aides who were around in the first five or so years of Guido and you will see a fair few of them snarl. 'I was working for the Party when blogs first came on the scene, and particularly Guido, and that became a real thing,' says a former Labour staffer. 'Everyone started reading Guido, because they would print stuff that the newspapers wouldn't, and everybody became a bit obsessed with who was going to be in Guido next. And in a way I don't think they are any more, it seems to have moved on a bit.'

There are several reasons for this. The first is timing; Guido could only be the one fast-paced Westminster-based outlet for so long, and it eventually found some hefty competition in other blogs and, more importantly, Twitter. This is what the *Guardian*'s Jim Waterson had to say on the topic: 'When we started BuzzFeed Politics in late 2013, we were at that point largely focused on doing elevated gossip, so it was all, you know, 11 weirdest tweets from MPs, or this Tory MP just put a picture of him hugging a dog on Facebook. And it was almost like we were taking short diary column stuff and doing it in-depth, and it was funny because we were treating it with reverence and all that.

'For about a year or so that did enormous traffic and people thought it was really fun, because the thing that they previously struggled to get in as a diary piece somewhere was suddenly a thousand words with loads of pictures told in a fun way on BuzzFeed. And then in about 18 months we noticed traffic dropping, because basically it had all transferred to Twitter. The cute picture of the dog wasn't waiting to go in a publication, it was just being tweeted about by some intern who realised they could get a bit of a following. And then it becomes competitive because the weird picture of Michael Gove doing something strange becomes bigger than you think, and everything becomes a meme within seconds.'

BuzzFeed and Guido Fawkes might not be very similar publications at first glance, but this analysis works for the two outlets. They built an editorial strategy out of publishing things no one else would publish (both because they were too small or niche, the former because they were too weird, and the latter because they were too controversial), then Twitter came in and ruined it all. In order for Guido to remain an ever-present threat, it needed all the space it could have; as soon as people found something else to anxiously refresh all day long, it instantly lost some of its power. The other explanation behind its decline has to do with Westminster, and what it does to people. It never could have been enough for Guido to sit back and wait for the tips to pour in; otherwise, Paul Staines never would have needed to have any staff working for him. Like any other kind of political reporter, Guido had to become a part of Westminster in order to cover it as well as it wanted to, and that slowly destroyed it. The famous example given by those seeking to show that the once-rebel organisation had become a part of the establishment is that when Guido organised a party for its tenth anniversary, the bash was attended by many senior politicians, and David Cameron himself recorded a birthday message. Another one could be that when Harry Cole left for the *Sun*, the advert to replace him involved a line about the potential new reporter having the opportunity to wake up sloshed on the sofa of a minister's office if they played their cards right.

'I don't think Guido would pretend not to be part of the mainstream media,' says one person who used to work there. 'Paul very much still has a view that pretty much all politicians are bad, but Guido has been part of the mainstream for a very long time now, I don't think it is an outsider. Our office is near Westminster, we go to the pubs of Westminster every night, and it wouldn't work if we didn't do that.'

This is fair enough, but if there is one thing about Westminster it is that you cannot be in it and not of it. You can hate politicians all you want, but if you spend enough time around SW1, you will end up making friends and enemies like everyone else. Once that starts happening, it will be obvious to those who know where to look; stories will suddenly start coming from some quarters more than others, or will be spun in a way that slowly becomes predictable. Another thing that happens when you go mainstream is that you will start being seen as not just a conduit for mischief, but a good place to get something out if you want it seen by everyone in the bubble.

Like indie bands deciding to sign to a major label and losing their edge along the way, this can have its downsides. The dynamics of everyone dishing dirt on everyone else is different from party structures getting involved, and once that starts happening, there is no going back. After all, Guido Fawkes has lost some of its gratuitous viciousness over the years, but it fundamentally remains a gossipy political blog. It being used strategically by parties to attack others has made some uneasy. 'What I don't think is legit is a big press operation using Guido as one of their main story outlets,' says one person who used to work at the Conservative Party headquarters. 'You've got a team of people writing up stories, digging on people, getting good stuff that ends up on a blog, and you get a half-arsed write-up that then disappears when the next story comes on. It gets put down the list. You should be reserving this; putting it in a war book, ready for the next election, or putting it in real papers and getting real hits out of it. It's losing its impact, and stories are losing their impact. There hasn't actually been a juicy cock-up story recently that's got a lot of traction that's come out of Guido. This should come out of the actual papers.'

Once the line starts to get blurry between the lobby and the blogs around it, both can suffer. On the one hand, Guido getting involved in the big, serious news stories of the day instead of keeping it short and salacious makes it lose some of its purpose. After all, no one goes to Guido Fawkes to get a run down of that day's news agenda. On the other, the bar for what is and isn't a story can shift, and suddenly the political discourse starts to get that bit more lowbrow. Paul Staines might not have been responsible for the human nature of people working in Westminster, but by providing a space where people could be their pettiest, nosiest selves, he opened Pandora's box. 'I do think there's a Guidoisation of politics,' says one Labour peer. 'To take a really topical example, I read *The Times* Red Box email every morning, and this morning it started with – it actually shocked me and maybe this is ridiculously naive – "MPs are on holiday, the House has risen, anyone who spots an MP on holiday, please take a photo, please email it in. Please let us know if anyone's been upgraded to business class on their flight, let us know what hotels they're staying in." And I just think it's terrible, it's so wrong, and yet that is *The Times*, in an email that I respect, a newspaper I respect. It so fundamentally crosses a line.'

This comes back to our earlier conundrum of what is news and what isn't, but also asks another question: how much personal life should politicians be allowed? Journalists, especially on tabloids, have always pushed that line a bit too far, but always at least pretended to care only because the personal lives of MPs had an influence on their professional ones. One magnificent example of this comes from *The People* who, in 1992, bugged the house of the mistress of minister David Mellor to catch them in the act. In order to justify that invasion of privacy, then-editor Bill Hagerty explained: 'Mellor has complained he's been unable to write speeches because he's too tired. Now we know why; Mr Mellor's love life has interfered with his effectiveness as a cabinet minister – and that's a matter of legitimate public interest.'

This justification is about as shameless as it gets, but at least it felt necessary; affairs have stopped being the scandal of choice for the political press, but other personal matters can now be covered with fewer qualms. According to one former Guido hack, 'Politicians do make a large amount of their private lives public by default, when they become politicians. They are volunteers; nobody makes them do this. They get a lot of power and influence from doing so, relative to the average person.' As a result, a lot of what they do and say is fair game, even if it was not said or done in the public eye.*

Still, Guido's success became its downfall. Like diary columns before it, its influence meant that what made it special

---

* Hold that thought – we'll come back to it shortly.

could suddenly be found nearly everywhere else. As one Guido alumnus puts it, 'I don't think there is actually that much difference between Guido-style reporting and lobby reporting. You will see a lot of political news stories in newspapers that are single-sourced, or worse than that, that are untrue and are just run with the denial at the end. So for example you will see lots of political news stories where an assertion is made in the top line of the story, "X is happening". There'll be three paragraphs of filler. And then at the bottom a spokesman for the politician will say, "This is completely untrue." The threshold for what is a story, and how much evidence or proof of how true the story needs to be, there's not much difference between lobby and Guido.'

On top of this, one thing happened which meant that Guido's position was always going to be unsustainable: Brexit. While the website always managed to broadly remain open to all sorts of factional infighting despite liking the Conservatives more than it liked the Labour Party, the referendum made it pick a side, and pick it for good. Once that happened, Guido's mischievous lightness disappeared and became pointed gossip with a purpose, which automatically is less fun. Like Popbitch, people sent information to Guido Fawkes because they knew that the blog would gleefully tarnish the reputation of anyone in Westminster. Lose that, and you lose the impetus people had to go to Guido with their rumours, as opposed to other outlets.

It is impossible to say whether Guido will pick up again once the wounds from the referendum start healing in Westminster and the country, or if this state of affairs is permanent; at the time of writing, things do not look good for the website that once dreamt of blowing everything up. Maybe it was always meant to be ephemeral; stuck forever in those few years after the internet started to democratise gossip, but before everyone realised what else the internet could do to secrets hidden in a bubble.

BURSTING BUBBLES AND THE DEATH OF CONTEXT

We roughly know what the differences are between gossip and news, but how about what separates a piece of gossip from a conspiracy theory? If you really think about it, they are quite similar. Let's reuse that example of MPs from different parties who are all on the more centrist end of their sides' politics having a very visible lunch together in Portcullis House. Say you're a parliamentary aide who walked past that lunch, and decided to text a journalist you know about it. That journalist then writes a column mentioning it, and their conclusion is that the centrist party is one step closer to happening. They don't necessarily have any extra information, they just know that these MPs are centrists, have been distancing themselves from their respective leaders recently, and they met socially in a place where they knew they would be seen. Concluding that they were plotting involved taking a bit of a leap, but it remains believable. If filed quickly, that column can definitely be good gossip.

What would be needed for it to turn into a conspiracy theory instead? Let's take that story and add on to it then see what sticks. Say that there had been a story attacking the Labour Leader a few days before that lunch, clearly briefed out by some MPs. If someone were to tweet that the lunch proves that the story had been leaked by MPs who are about to jump ship anyway, some eyebrows would surely be raised. Or let's say that the lunch wasn't a group of MPs, but rather one centrist Labour MP and one centrist Conservative

MP. If someone were to write a blog post about how that two-person lunch definitely proves that a new centrist party is about to be launched, they would not be taken very seriously. Now, let's mix those two together; if someone were to claim that one lunch between a centrist Conservative MP and a centrist Labour MP is clear proof that the Labour MP was behind the media leak as that MP is about to launch a new centrist party, you would almost certainly be teased about the effectiveness of your tinfoil hat.

So what's the difference between the two? Both gossip and conspiracy theories can involve noticing dots and creating a pattern with them. 'Woman A and Man B were seen having drinks last night' + 'Man B arrived at work today wearing yesterday's clothes' = 'Woman A and Man B are probably sleeping together'. There was a series of events and it is possible to draw a conclusion from them. That's gossip. If Woman A happens to be an MP and Man B is a journalist, it is political gossip. If Man B then writes a glowing profile of Woman A without disclosing anything about the nature of their relationship, that's news. If Man B's publication once ran a piece attacking an MP who happens to be an opponent of Woman A's and you conclude that the two events simply must be linked, it's a conspiracy.

The line here is about the distance between the dots; if you've decided to create a narrative out of a few events, you need to make sure that it is not too far-fetched. Concluding that two people are sleeping together because they spent an evening cosied up to each other then jumped in the same cab is reasonable; taking those same facts and concluding that months before that night, the journalist personally influenced the editorial line of his newspaper to align itself with the ambitions of an MP isn't. That does not mean that it definitely isn't true; maybe that journalist really had been fancying that MP for a long time; maybe he really is influential in his organisation and maybe he isn't one for media ethics, but that is a whole lot of maybes. There is no hard and fast rule on when assumptions become inherently problematic, but you can usually spot it when you see it.

Another dynamic can be previous knowledge of context. If you don't know the whole story, it is easy to see something and get carried away, and if there is one place in this world with endless layers of informal context, it is Westminster. It can be that you know that the two MPs who had lunch happen to have a train line which starts in one of their constituencies and ends in the other's, and they need to discuss future plans for it; and maybe our Man A and Woman B have known each other for years so were enjoying a catch-up drink, then took a taxi together because they're neighbours. If you don't have access to that background information, everything can quickly start to look suspicious. As a result (and once again), the nature of the information isn't the only thing at play here; the person sharing that information is just as relevant.

This brings us to what might actually be the most important distinction between idle gossip and corrosive conspiracy theories: intent. Most conspiracy theorists have an inherent lack of trust in the establishment, and their attempts at joining dots come from a belief that things are being concealed from the public and are just hiding in plain sight, waiting to be uncovered. If you look at Westminster through that lens, anything can become suspicious; any friendship, any dinner, any group of people pictured talking together at a drinks reception. It is also a view that both assigns the personal, human side of politics too much credit and too little. On the one hand, a special adviser and a civil servant can never be just friends, and must be plotting something together if they are found to be friends on Facebook.

On the other, simple proof of acquaintance can be used to imply wrongdoing: is it really a coincidence that a journalist went a bit easy on a minister during an interview given that his wife's cousin is the politician's partner? And so on.

Beyond the simple mindset, this way of thinking normally comes from having an interest in the political bubble but not being part of it. For a start, it would be near impossible for anyone to have access to all that informal knowledge if they aren't physically in Westminster, and if there is something they want to double-check, they can't quickly take a fellow bubble dweller out for coffee to confirm or shoot down their theory. Secondly, it is a lot easier to be given gossip and to turn it into factual evidence of sinister forces being at play when you're not confronted with real, live humans who work in politics on a day-to-day basis. In the words of one No 10 civil servant (and many others): it's always a cock-up, never a conspiracy. While it is perfectly possible for clever people to scheme and plot in SW1, most of them are not very good at it or, to be perfectly honest, very clever to start with.

'I think there's no middle-ground with MPs,' says academic Phil Cowley. 'I'm sure this is wrong, I'm sure they are normally distributed, but it doesn't feel like that. It feels like they're either really clever, or you sit there and they've got this theory about this and you find yourself thinking, how did anybody ever select you? How did any selection committee think, that's the one for us! That man or that woman is really going to put us on the map. Absolutely thick as pig shit, some of them.'

This combination of remarkably bright people and ones who were lucky to get an expensive education can certainly make for some interesting chains of events, but most aren't inherently nefarious. After all, every workplace will have its own drama, and every workplace will probably look worse than it is if you only hear the worst or most intriguing bits of information about what goes on there. There is no reason why you would hear about them unless you worked there or had friends who did, though, which is why scandals in, say, the accounting world rarely make the headlines. It is also why political journalism is so important, and deciding what is a story and what isn't is crucial; the job of reporters is to contextualise and explain everything that happens in a closed-up and confusing world. Stripped of those layers of context, loose bits of information can be spun in a million and one ways, most of them bad, and basically, all of them incorrect. Seen from the outside, it can feel unfair that some pieces of gossip simply stay within the bubble, but it probably is for the better. Of course, this has all become easier said than done.

The internet has democratised many things and information is one of them, especially when it is information that is scandalous or titillating. It doesn't always matter if it is true or not; if it's entertaining enough, or damaging enough and aimed at someone disliked by some online communities, it will get shared and shared and shared, and there is not much anyone can do to stop it. This is especially true when politics is particularly partisan and the country is divided, which is very much the case at the time of writing and, unless something dramatic and completely unforeseen happens in 2019, will remain so until further notice. Just like Blairites and Brownites used to leak the slightest bits of information to make the other camp look bad, supporters of the main parties or the main Brexit tribes will gleefully hold on to a seemingly frivolous piece of information and weaponise it. The problem is, of course, that a lot of this information will be bollocks, or have its meaning stretched so thin that it might as well be bollocks.

There can also be concerns about people's privacy and their security; the Eye Spy MP Twitter account is a good example.

Set up years ago (almost certainly by Paul Staines but he won't formally confirm it), it aimed to tweet out overheard snippets of conversations between Westminster denizens, or note interesting-looking meetings and drinks. A lot of it was confined to the bubble, and revolved around sightings of puzzling combinations of people drinking at the Red Lion, or chatting in a corner of Portcullis House. Then technology evolved and suddenly people were able to take good-quality pictures on their smartphones and send them to the account in a second.

Nowadays, Eye Spy MP features pictures of MPs asleep on trains, having drinks in bars away from Westminster, or attending gigs. Some of it can be eyebrow-raising – why is a prominent frontbencher at the theatre instead of the chamber on the night of a big debate? – but most simply feel invasive. There has been some pushback recently, especially from female MPs – Lisa Nandy is one of them, and argues that, 'Eye Spy MP feels problematic, because you do need spaces in here where people can have private conversations with each other without being afraid that it's going to get out into the public domain. And I think there's a question about public interest, and there's also quite a serious question about people's safety at the moment.'

After all, Labour MP Jo Cox was murdered in the street in broad daylight in 2016, countless MPs have been receiving dozens of death threats over the past few years, and fake news on social media remains a problem no one really knows how to solve. If you want to release private information about public figures for the sake of mischief, you also have a responsibility to make sure that information doesn't end up harming those people. Your argument might be that if someone does something, then they are ultimately responsible for it if it does come out, but that doesn't absolve you from much. There are reasons why some things remain secret; if you take it upon yourself to decide that they shouldn't be, you become a character in that chain of events.

Once again, it is hard to predict where this might all be heading. The Westminster gossip ecosystem is a fragile one, and though it can live through changes in morals, personal conduct and ways of communicating, it is unclear what happens when the bubble starts disintegrating. Though the internet aimed to try and democratise SW1 and open it up to the rest of the country, it might well make it even more closed-up as a result.

'I think people are much more scared of engaging personally with others in the 2015 and 2017 parliaments,' says one former Conservative adviser. 'The people who came in the 2010 parliament, we all came in and it was like a party. It was a great time. You were able to go out on the terrace and have drinks, and they were saying, "Oh yes, of course!" The later series of MPs who've come in are much more scared about their personal lives, and that's partly because of the "WhatsApp-ification" of politics, and it's also partly the "fake news-ification". Guido was really scrappy pre-2010, it was sweet, and now there's a litany of correspondents and then there's all the contenders to the throne. Very few people put stuff into WhatsApp any more; they're more reluctant to do anything.'

THE POLITICAL
AND THE PERSONAL

What would happen if gossip disappeared from politics? It is unlikely to ever happen, and this isn't a sci-fi book, but it is worth thinking about it for a second. What would happen? There would be no bars in the Palace of Westminster and the pubs of SW1 would be full of American tourists realising they don't actually enjoy ale. MPs would work on constituency matters and legislation then occasionally have good-natured, internal debates about policies. Journalists would watch the House of Commons and the House of Lords and receive press releases and have the occasional phone call with someone to double-check something. Parliamentary aides and special advisers would be hired based on the relevance of their CV and the quality of their job interviews. Everyone would come into Westminster to work in the morning and leave in the evening to spend time with their non-political loved ones.

That still would not be enough, would it? Whips' offices would either have to not exist or do their jobs by politely trying to convince their MPs of the merit of their leadership's policies. Civil servants would be able to have meetings with their ministers at short notice about any aspect of their work. Anyone who went to university with anyone else would have to be told not to bring their friendship into SW1, and only discuss work-related issues if they are to meet in SW1. It would not be allowed for anyone to become romantically or sexually linked to others they might work with at some point. Most of Parliament would probably be open to the public. Every discussion between, say, a journalist and an MP or a civil servant and a special adviser should be logged. Ad nauseam.

With all of this in place, it seems reasonable to assume that gossip would no longer play a part in Westminster. Still, two questions arise. The first one is: would the country be run better that way? There have always been arguments in favour of professionalising politics further, and as the past chapters have hopefully shown, the informal tends to gain importance when formal structures aren't working well enough, or at all. It would also be fair to say that gossip, rumours and idle chats aren't a reliable science, and it is surprising just how often things do *not* fall apart in corners of the political scene. But can it really change? The dozen hypothetical rules above are drastic and unrealistic, but more importantly, why would anyone want to work in a place like that one? There will always be bright wonks and big minds with large hearts who think they can change the world, but they aren't a majority. Even they might not want to hang around for long if all the personal is stripped clean from their professional lives. After all, politics isn't like any other area of work; the hours are painfully long, the jobs can be frustrating, most of the public hates you, there is no stability and you can get spat out of it at any moment, and none of this would change with the aforementioned rules. If you would still want to work in politics in these conditions, you are either lying to yourself or so intent on having power that you probably shouldn't be working in politics.

On top of this, people working in Westminster need to spend a lot of time around each other. Good Parliamentary assistants pretty much spend all their time with their MPs, and so do special advisers with their ministers. MPs sit most of their working days in the chamber together and whatever happens, a competent reporter is one who spends their days doing just that: reporting. If the nature of the people you spend so much time with matters so little to you that you won't ever take it into account, you are in a small minority. Though everyone can technically work with everyone else, being able to develop good relationships with people will usually mean that the pair of you will become more efficient. This is not controversial, and is true of the country at large. Removing any possibility of this will alienate people from their jobs, which is not something we want if that job involves being in charge of the country. Still, where there are friendships, there are feuds, there are unrequited and mutual crushes, drinking, sex, drama, enemies – the whole, messy spectrum of human relationships – and where there is all of that, there will be gossip and that gossip will become important at one point or another.

This brings us to our second question: what does it tell us that the only way to surgically extract the influence of gossip on politics would be to change it in a way that would be so thorough and so revolutionary that it will never happen? Informal conversations and relationships gain weight in policy-making and everything around it when and where formal processes fail, but maybe that's not a bad thing. Maybe formal processes could never take care of everything anyway, and if they could, it is far from certain that they would do a better job than what we have now. In fact, Lord Norton thinks that the way of working we have now has distinct upsides: 'You find something out by being in the chamber, by being in committee, but it's complemented by what you hear talking to colleagues. What happens in the chamber at committee could be a culmination of what you've already heard, or at least what you've heard feeds into it and shapes your views, so it'd be difficult to isolate official behaviour from the rest of what goes on in the Palace. And you can argue that we'd be much worse off if we didn't have that informal form of exchange. In a way it would strengthen the executive, because it'd have more of a monopoly of information that's provided to members.'

Lord Norton is right: if information is only ever shared formally, that means that whoever is in charge of releasing that information gains an immense amount of power. Britain is a parliamentary democracy and its Parliament is thus sovereign, and it exercises its status by democratising its information away from the government.

This is not to say that the current system is perfect and unquestionable; it isn't. Relying heavily on the personal means creating endless concentric and converging circles which are hard to penetrate for those who might not be of a certain world or of certain political persuasions. It also means that who you are, how you talk and whom you talk to can become more important than what you actually say and want to achieve, and the right ideas might only win if they are backed up by the right networks of people. If this isn't ideal, it's because human nature isn't. Perhaps you think it isn't universal behaviour and it can be altered, but this book will have to disagree with you, or at least watch you try to change it before changing its conclusion.

In the meantime, bottoms up! Let's head to Strangers'. My round ...

BIBLIOGRAPHY

Adkins, K. (2017). *Gossip, Epistemology, and Power*. Palgrave Macmillan.

Anwar, Y., Keltner, D. and Stellar, J. (2012). *When Gossip is Good*. UC Berkeley.

Banks, A. (2017). The Bad Boys of Brexit: Tales of Mischief, Mayhem and Guerilla Warfare in the EU Referendum Campaign. Biteback Publishing.

Barnett, S. and Gaber, I. (2001). *Westminster Tales: The Twenty-first-Century Crisis in Political Journalism*. Continuum.

Brandreth, G. (2014). *Breaking the Code: Westminster Diaries*. Biteback Publishing.

Clark, A. (2011). *Alan Clark: A Life in his Own Words: The Complete Diaries*. Weidenfeld & Nicolson.

De Bois, N. (2017). *Confessions of a Recovering MP*. Biteback Publishing.

Dunbar, R. (1998). *Grooming, Gossip, and the Evolution of Language*. Harvard University Press.

Ellwardt, L., Steglich, C., & Wittek, R. (2012). *The Co-evolution of Gossip and Friendship in Workplace Social Networks*. Cambridge University Press.

Epstein, J. (2012). *Gossip: The Untrivial Pursuit*. Mariner Books.

Flinders, M., Cotter, L.-M., Kelso, A. and Meakin, A. (2017). *The Politics of Parliamentary Restoration and Renewal: Decisions, Discretion, Democracy*. Oxford University Press.

Gunn, S. (2011). *So You Want to be a Political Journalist*. Biteback Publishing.

Hamilton, T. and Hazarika, A. (2018). *Punch and Judy Politics: An Insiders' Guide to Prime Minister's Questions*. Biteback Publishing.

Hardman, I. (2018). *Why We Get the Wrong Politicians*. Atlantic Publishing.

Hayes, J. (2014). *An Unexpected MP: Confessions of a Political Gossip*. Biteback Publishing.

Hazell, R. and Yong, B. (2014). *Special Advisers: Who They Are, What They Do and Why They Matter*. Hart Publishing.

Hickman, M. and Watson, T. (2012). *Dial M for Murdoch: News Corporation and the Corruption of Britain*. Penguin Publishing.

Jones, H. (2016). *How to Be a Government Whip*. Biteback Publishing.

Jones, N. and Pitcher, S. (2015). *Reporting Tittle-tattle: Twitter, Gossip and the Changing Nature of Journalism*. Taylor & Francis.

Laws, D. (2017). *Coalition Diaries, 2012–2015*. Biteback Publishing.

Levin, J. and Arluke, A. (1987). *Gossip: The Inside Scoop*. Springer.

Levin, J. and Kimmel, A. J. (1977). *Gossip Columns: Media Small Talk*. Oxford University Press.

Macqueen, A. (2016). *Private Eye The First 50 Years: An A–Z*. Private Eye Productions Ltd.

Maxey, C. (1948). *A Plea for the Politician*. Western Political Science Association.

McBride, D. (2014). *Power Trip: A Decade of Policy, Plots and Spin*. Biteback Publishing.

McSmith, A. (1996). *Faces of Labour: The Inside Story*. Verso.

Mitchell, A. V. and Goulds, S. (1982). *Westminster Man: A Tribal Anthropology of the Commons People*. University of Michigan.

Mullin, C. (2009). *A View From the Foothills: The Diaries of Chris Mullin*. Profile Books.

Norton, P. (2018). *Power Behind the Scenes: The Importance of Informal Space in Legislatures*. Oxford University Press.

Oliver, C. (2016). *Unleashing Demons: The Inside Story of Brexit*. Hodder & Stoughton.

Quinn, T. (2012). *Spin Doctors and Political News Management: A Rational-choice "Exchange" Analysis*. Springer.

Renton, T. (2005). *Chief Whip: The Role, History and Black Arts of Parliamentary Whipping*. Politico's Publishing Ltd.

Rogers, R. (2012). *Who Goes Home? A Parliamentary Miscellany*. The Robson Press.

Rogers, R. and Walters, R. (2015). *How Parliament Works*. Routledge.

Salovey, P. and Wert, S. (2004). *A Social Comparison Account of Gossip*. Yale University Press.

Shipman, T. (2016). *All Out War: The Full Story of How Brexit Sank Britain's Political Class*. HarperCollins.

Thurlbeck, N. (2015). *Tabloid Secrets: The Stories Behind the Headlines at the World's Most Famous Newspaper*. Biteback Publishing.

Willis, T. (2010). *Nigel Dempster and the Death of Discretion*. Short Books.

Wright, B. (2016). *Order, Order!: The Rise and Fall of Political Drinking*. Gerald Duckworth & Co.

CAST OF CHARACTERS

Nice try